F*CK
DIVORCE

F*CK DIVORCE

DIVORCE

A Science-Based Guide to
Piecing Yourself Back Together
after Your Life Implodes

ERICA SLOTTER, PhD,
AND PATRICK MARKEY, PhD

Skyhorse Publishing

Skyhorse Publishing books may be purchased in bulk at special discounts for sales promotion, corporate gifts, fund-raising, or educational purposes. Special editions can also be created to specifications. For details, contact the Special Sales Department, Skyhorse Publishing, 307 West 36th Street, 11th Floor, New York, NY 10018 or info@skyhorsepublishing.com.

Skyhorse® and Skyhorse Publishing® are registered trademarks of Skyhorse Publishing, Inc.®, a Delaware corporation.

Visit our website at www.skyhorsepublishing.com.

10 9 8 7 6 5 4 3 2 1

Library of Congress Cataloging-in-Publication Data is available on file.

Cover design by Erin Seaward-Hiatt
Cover photo credit: iStockphoto

Print ISBN: 978-1-5107-5160-6
Ebook ISBN: 978-1-5107-5161-3

Printed in the United States of America

To our children: Charlie, Grace & Lucas,
you are the loves of our lives.

To our parents: thank you for your unfailing love and faith in us.

And to our ex-spouses:
without whom we never would have found each other,
or written this book in the first place.

Contents

Prologue

(Or, "Why the hell did we want to write this book anyway?")

The Tuesday after Valentine's Day, I (Erica) opened a letter from my divorce attorney. Contrary to my expectations, it wasn't yet *another* bill. It was my divorce decree. I was officially a single woman. I remember feeling two things. One: thank God that's over. Two: What the fuck do I do now? I went inside, drank a large bourbon, and ate a frozen pizza all by myself. Okay, there were two bourbons . . . and perhaps two pizzas . . . but I digress.

I was glad the divorce was over. We had been married for almost exactly seven years when my then-husband came home and told me he no longer wanted to be married. I don't want to go into the reasons why my marriage ended here—they are too sad, too personal; and it really does take two people to destroy a relationship (plus, I'd like to avoid a libel suit from my ex). But there I was, finally, officially, single.

And here's the fun-filled nugget of irony: I am a research psy-chologist who has spent the last decade studying what makes romantic relationships work and what dooms them to fail. How could I have been so blind to what was going on in my own marriage? What really surprised me the most wasn't the collapse of the marriage, but how strange it felt to restart my life. Now that I was single, I needed to figure out who I was. How would my life be different? How would it be the same? And, most important, how the hell was I going to survive dating again? I promptly signed up for eHarmony.

Around the time I started dating, a colleague of mine, who had gotten divorced a year before, stopped by my office to offer his condolences. Fun-filled nugget of irony, part two: this divorced colleague (Patrick) is also a research psychologist who studies romantic relationships. His divorce story is its own uniquely warped journey—he has two wonderful children, maintains (mostly) friendly contact with his ex, and definitely did his fair share of, ahem, "mingling" after his divorce. He suggested that we hang out as divorce-buddies . . . trade dating war stories, bitch about our exes, etc. So, we did. For months we were just friends (I swear!) who got together once a month or so over a meal to commiserate, trade advice, and laugh at how ridiculous our lives had become. Then one night, we drank. A lot. And got naked. Fast-forward to today—we're madly in love, married, and have added a new tiny human to our crazy family.

Through our divorces, we were shocked to learn how little science-based information there was available for divorced folks. So, our mission became to put our research and life experience to good use and write about life after divorce (and yes, "What the Fuck Just Happened?" was proposed as an alternate title). *F*ck Divorce* is not a book about divorcing (which sucks); it is a book about being divorced (which doesn't have to). In *F*ck Divorce*, we want to help you through this bizarre journey using science and humor. Let's face it, a lot of what you're going through right now is such an absurd shit show that laughing at it is really the only option. How else do you respond when your Tinder date thinks a bondage club offers a cozy ambiance in which to get to know each other?

F*ck Divorce is about how to navigate relationships after divorce—with yourself and with other people. It is a book about how to avoid doing jail time for murdering your twat-waffle ex-spouse. (Okay, really it is a book about not murdering your ex-spouse. We're not lawyers; we'd be worse than useless at getting you out of jail time.) Most important, *F*ck Divorce* will teach you how to start over in your new (exciting, we promise!) second chance at life. It is about dating again, getting naked with someone new, finding love, and doing your best to make that love last.

Besides, what could possibly be more abso-fucking-lutely adorable than two people writing a book about love, who had previously lost at love, who study love, and who are now *in* love? Nothing. Not even puppies.

Welcome to the world of being divorced. It's good, bad, ridiculous, and sometimes your blind date smells like cabbage. Pull up a chair, pour yourself a drink (or three), and let's do this shit.

F*CK
DIVORCE

Chapter I

Eat, sleep, take your Prozac. Repeat: Self-care in the post-divorce haze

Okay, so here's where we start. You and that asshat you once called your spouse for however many years are officially going to live separate lives. The money and custody arrangements are in the process of getting figured out, and your official "I'm single now, bitches!" paperwork has been issued. In short, you are in the middle of the divorce tornado that is cutting a path of destruction through the center of your life. You are not in Kansas anymore, sweetheart.

A million questions are racing around in your mind . . . will your tinman ex ever grow a heart? Will you date a munchkin? Will your ex's next romantic partner ride a broom and have a gaggle of flying monkeys at their beck and call? You also may be feeling so rejected, dejected, and generally overwhelmed that you are contemplating whether you should just lay down in a field of poppies and sleep for a while. Let's face it, divorce royally fucks you up. And as if that weren't plenty obvious from . . . well, look at you, the scientific research resoundingly supports your experience.

As early as the 1970s, psychologists began documenting the intricacies of divorce as a stressful experience.[1] This stress comes from two different but equally obnoxious places. First, the big "D" itself is a major, often traumatic, life event. When people are asked to rank the top ten pain-in-the-ass events in their lives, divorce falls in the number two slot . . . just behind the death of a spouse (which you might be thinking would be preferable right about now).[2] Second, life events, like divorce, are not only difficult emotionally but also bring numerous logistical challenges along for the ride. Divorce can precipitate financial upheaval, major shifts in our sense of identity, parenting difficulties . . . you get the idea. These are serious life changes, and they're just really stinkin' hard.[3]

But divorce stress doesn't stop there. It's a one-two sucker punch because these large-scale changes make lots of the little things more difficult. With time, the "stressful life event" period of divorce passes—usually, when the stuff is divvied up, custody is finalized, and you're starting to think about putting on real pants again. But, the second way divorce kicks your tokus is through the never-ending minutiae that will become more challenging now that you're on your own. After you finish worrying about whether you have enough money to afford your house (the major life event part), you will find that your daily finances are tighter now that you're single (a constant, ongoing pain in the ass). When your kids are done adjusting to the new living situation (the major life event part), you will discover how emotionally taxing single parenting can be, such as when little Suzy uses a drill to curl her hair or Timmy tries to skip rope in Rollerblades (or any other daily pain-in-the-ass-kid-buffoonery).

All this stress is bad news for you. Divorcees are at a higher risk for depression and anxiety than their married and never-married-sex-and-the-city single friends.[4] The big "D" will also prematurely age you. Both of your dear authors felt like they were turning into fossils during their divorces—Erica found her first gray hair (guess where?), and Patrick started to lose so much hair that he now uses more toothpaste than shampoo. High levels of stress may even damage a part of your DNA called telomeres.[5] The short and dirty version: telomeres are protein chains on the end of your chromosomes that help protect them from damage and deterioration.[6] The shorter your telomeres are, the more prone to cellular damage you become. Think of short telomeres as the precursors to crow's feet and fiber supplements. If that wasn't bad enough, a study of over 3,500 adults found that divorcees have shorter telomeres than just about anyone else.[7] So, if you're feeling a bit like the crypt-keeper these days, it's probably because your divorce has nudged you just a little bit closer to the grave.

Speaking of graves, you are now at a higher risk of suffering from various health problems than if you had stayed married or skipped the acid trip to the altar altogether. Divorcees are at increased danger of cardiovascular disease,[8] catching a cold,[9, 10] and insomnia.[11] Disturbingly, divorced men and women are about 50 percent more likely to kick the proverbial bucket for any reason compared to married folks.[12] No wonder we have insomnia. But, before you resign yourself to feeling miserable and updating your last will and testament, there is emerging evidence that some individuals are remarkably resistant to the dangers of divorce.[13, 14] Phew! Like resilient superheroes, certain people can even use the stress of divorce as practice to become less affected by the evil stressors perpetrated by future supervillains.[15] This knowledge is so incredibly reassuring because it means that just because you got divorced, you are not automatically *dooooomed.*

The key to surviving and thriving in your post-divorce world is how you handle it. It is not so much the divorce *per se* that could be killing you; it's the stress that comes along with divorce that's doing you in.[16] This is good news. There are things you can do to cope with the stress of divorce to spare yourself oodles of heartache, wrinkles, and an early demise. The goal is to turn you into one of those resilient superhero divorcees who emerges stronger, more self-assured, and sexier than before the end of their failing, flailing marriage. But before you pick up your cape from the dry cleaners, you need to gain five fundamental superpowers to help get you there: basic care, self-efficacy, self-compassion, a redemption story, and social support.[i]

---

i   In cultivating these superpowers, you may want to grab a notebook or journal, or iPad . . . anything you can take some notes on. Throughout this chapter, and really the whole stinkin' book, we have exercises and quizzes and such designed to help you navigate your post-divorce journey, so you might find it useful to write your responses and thoughts down somewhere.

Basic care: Brush your goddamn teeth.

After your divorce, you may be feeling like you were hit by a truck. Only to have the truck reverse and slam into you a few more times just for good measure. Before we get to the psychological heavy-lifting of dealing with these feelings, we need to start with the basics. Are you wearing clean underwear today? Seriously, basic self-care and hygiene are the cornerstones of getting your shit together. We're not trying to be condescending here. It is much too easy to go around thinking, *Who cares if I wear the same sweatpants four days in a row and eat Cheetos for dinner? No one is going to see me anyhow, and even if someone did, so what?* Do not, we repeat, *do not* fall into this trap of self-pity. Four-day-old Cheetos breath is not a pleasant parfum. Each day, you must: shower (with soap); put on clean clothes (including underwear); brush your teeth (for more than two seconds); comb hair (or at least try); and eat something reasonably healthy (ramen and Kraft Mac & Cheese do not count). We are going to act like your parents on this one (and we have lots of experience here . . . our teens view hygiene as more optional than we'd prefer). Before noon, you must do all these things—or no Instagram for you.

It's easy to forget to take care of yourself in a practical sense amid the emotional and logistical mess divorce has dumped in your lap. However, by keeping yourself together (at least so you're not stinky), you will have more confidence and mental clarity than if you skip showering and pull out a questionable old T-shirt from the bottom of the dirty laundry hamper.[17] Once you've gotten basic hygiene down, add physical exercise to your daily routine—nothing is better revenge on your asshat ex than looking *fabulouuuuus.* Not to mention, exercise releases lots of endorphins and other feel-good neurochemicals that can help you combat the divorcee-doldrums.[18] Getting your sweat on also reduces your risk of maladies like heart disease, which will help you better withstand the impacts of divorce-related stress.[19]

Beyond self-care, you have practical responsibilities that you cannot shirk no matter how bummed and overwhelmed you feel. Go to work and pay your bills. Getting evicted or receiving a foreclosure notice helps no one. Get to the grocery store—for aforementioned healthy food. Don't forget to get your kids on the bus each morning. You get the gist. You need to get back into your daily routine—or establish a new one. Soon you will find that maintaining this new routine will help you make more sense of your life, plan better, improve your sleep, and feel more alert and positive.[20]

Self-efficacy: Choose vodka and Chaka Khan.

After finding her paramour and boss in flagrante delicto with another woman, Bridget Jones, the cringeworthy dating inspiration for millennial women everywhere, claimed, "I have two choices: to give up and accept the permanent state of spinsterhood and eventual eating by Alsatians (her dog), or not. And this time, I choose *not*. I will not be beaten by a bad man and an American stick insect. Instead, I choose vodka. And Chaka Khan." We firmly encourage you to take this sage advice.

Okay, maybe limit the vodka to a reasonable amount and replace the eighties dance music with something a bit more tolerable but every bit as empowering.[ii] The spirit behind this bit of Bridget Jones's wisdom is one that we resoundingly support. Empower yourself in any way that feels good to you. The science-y term for this empowerment is *self-efficacy*. Self-efficacy is your belief in your ability to work toward goals that are important to you (a happy, fulfilling, love-filled life full of puppies and kisses) and to cope with challenges (a fucking divorce) that come up along the way.[21] A strong sense of self-efficacy will enhance your well-being by making you feel optimistic about your future and more resilient in the face of disappointments. Best of all, it makes you more likely to try new things and set lofty goals for yourself because you believe, deep down in your nether-loins, that you are capable of succeeding.[22, 23] This sounds like something you want, right? So, how do you get it?

---

ii   Bucking the trend of traditional gender roles, Erica preferred drinking single malt whiskey while listening to "Hurt" by Johnny Cash during her divorce. Whereas Patrick, who is comfortable with his masculinity, turned to sipping appletinis while Gloria Gaynor bellowed "I Will Survive" into his tiny earbuds as he contemplatively stared through a rain-lashed window.

Become a badass. One way to grab some of that self-efficacious goodness is to become a badass. If you kick-ass at something, you are more likely to feel like you can kick-ass at it again, and at anything else you put your mind to. If you fail miserably at something—and let's face it, many of us view our divorces (at least initially) as epic fuck-up moments in our lives—you'll feel less equipped to deal with problems in the future. It turns out that self-efficacy is a self-fulfilling cycle.[24] The challenge is to get past this post-divorce moment as a failure,[iii] and instead capitalize on this phase as an opportunity to whoop some serious booty.

Ask yourself . . . what makes you feel good, strong, and capable? Your options here are endless, and what makes you feel like the badass version of Bridget Jones is going to be just as unique and individual as you are. Some people like riding horses, are awesome at ping-pong, enjoy cooking, love singing, or feel great after a workout. Patrick tried to feel better by updating his wardrobe after his divorce and trading his dad jeans in for skinny jeans. Granted, in hindsight, the skinny jeans were probably a mistake given his age and body type, but that is the power of self-efficacy. While Patrick was waddling around like a duck in his new leg suffocaters, he *felt* great about himself. They made him feel sexy and cool again. You need to find your skinny jean equivalent (maybe with a little more "ball room"), and do the things that you enjoy doing. If you're not sure what those are, stay tuned. Figuring out who *you* are now that you're divorced is the theme of the next chapter.

Weirdly enough, another way of increasing your self-efficacy is to find the things you feel insecure about and tackle them head on.[21] Really, what could be more badass than that? Erica found it empowering to get a handle on her post-divorce finances. Her ex had always handled everything from bills to taxes; so, meeting with a financial advisor and learning how to budget, plan for retirement, and even do something as simple as

---

iii   Seriously. During one of Patrick's darker post-divorce moments, he was on a walk moping about life and was bitten by a neighborhood dog. At the time, he thought, *Of course the dog hates me. No one loves me. I am going to die alone.* So . . . yeah, low self-efficacy at its finest.

use tax software made her feel like a million bucks. The key is to tackle the insecurities brought on by your divorce in a way that gives you a sense of control, rather than experiencing the situation as making you its bitch. It's all in your mindset. Which brings us to the next way you can increase your self-efficacy.

Roadblock or speed bump? Change how you view the situation. Anytime you're faced with a roadblock, speed bump, or detour on the highway of life, you can think about that event in one of two ways: as a challenge or as a threat.[25] Challenges are issues that you feel you have the resources to cope with—things that you feel like you can rise up to and overcome. In contrast, threats are difficulties that you feel overwhelmed by—things that you simply do not have the resources to deal with. Generally, problems are more likely to be viewed as threats if they negatively reflect on your skills/abilities (*cough,* your divorce), call your self-worth into question (*hack-hack,* your divorce), and are public, making you feel like your failures are occurring in a fishbowl for all to see (*gasping for air,* your divorce). [25] That said, people differ in their tendency to feel challenged versus threatened by life's bullshit. People who view rough patches as challenges tend to be psychologically tough—real He-Men or She-Ras of mental fortitude. The short quiz below can provide some insight into your psychological toughness and how you tend to view the shit sandwiches you have been served at the picnic of life. Just answer

Indicate how accurately you believe each statement below describes how you tend to respond to stressful life events.		
Not at all how I would usually respond 0	About as likely to act this way as to not act this way 1	Pretty close to how I would behave 2
1. ____ Remain calm under pressure.	6. ____ Know how to cope.	
2. ____ Like to be in control.	7. ____ Don't lose my head.	
3. ____ Quickly recognize possibilities.	8. ____ Am relaxed in tense situations.	
4. ____ Am not embarrassed easily.	9. ____ Can stand criticism.	
5. ____ Automatically take charge.		

the questions as honestly as possible. Don't worry, no one is looking over your shoulder, and you aren't getting graded on this quiz.

Before we tell you what your score means, we want to caution you about these types of quizzes. Although we like to think of ourselves as awesomely powerful psychologist-superheroes who can "get into your head" and solve all your problems, the truth is much less glamorous. Even the best questionnaire typically reflects what you already know or at least suspect. The quiz you just took, which contains items created by the Oregon Research Institute, is not magical.[26] So if you disagree with the results of this test—you're probably right! Just think of these quizzes as a way to encourage you to contemplate a given part of who you are or your life. Don't ever let a quiz tell you how you should be thinking. This goes double for quizzes you find online (we're lookin' at you, Buzzfeed) or in magazines with no scientific backing . . . like the ones that tell you which type of cheese matches your personality. One of your dear authors maintains that she is definitely a smoked gouda and *not* a brie.

Now add up your score on the quiz and see how you compare to other adults below.

Score		Description
0–10	Stuff is scary! Run awaaaay!	Your score puts you in the bottom 25 percent of people's mental toughness scores. You often view stressful events as threats which contribute to feeling overwhelmed, powerless, and unsure of how to act. Like King Arthur's knights in Monty Python's *Search for the Holy Grail,* when faced with a challenge, such as a divorce, or a murderous rabbit, you want to *RUN AWAAAAAAY!!!*
11–14	Maybe, I got this? Eh . . . maybe not?	You are in the middle 50 percent of mental toughness. You're equally likely to view the sucky moments of life as threating as you are to see them as challenges. Be glad you aren't that poor soul who scored 2 on this test, but don't get too cocky—you still got some toughening up to do.
15–18	Challenge accepted, bitches.	You are a tough cookie . . . a coping savage. Your score puts you in the top 25 percent of mental toughness. You're inclined to view the stresses in life, from slow wi-fi to your doomed marriage, as challenges to be overcome and catalysts of personal growth.

There are some real advantages to being mentally tough and perceiving the stressors of life as challenges instead of threats.[25, 27] If you label something as a challenge, you are more likely to be successful in dealing with it. For example, research has found that when students view math tests as challenges rather than threats, they perform better on the math tests![28] Replace "math tests" with "property settlement" or "custody negotiations," and you've got a pretty frickin' powerful tool in your corner. Furthermore, consistently viewing difficulties as threatening is not great for your health. Threat perceptions cause blood pressure to increase in a way that challenge perceptions do not. If you're in constant freak-out mode for months as you cope with the process and aftermath of your marital implosion, it's going to take a toll on your heart. No bueno. Your ex has already stolen years of your life—don't let them shorten it any further, okay?

The good news is that whatever your current level of mental toughness, you can tweak your view of your divorce (and other stuff) as a challenge or threat. A challenge orientation toward your divorce can be cultivated the same way you increase your feelings of self-efficacy, by becoming a badass. In fact, the relationship between your self-efficacy and how you view your divorce is cyclical. Greater self-efficacy increases the likelihood of perceiving situations as challenges rather than threats, and viewing tough stuff as challenges increases self-efficacy.[29]

Reframing your situation in an objective light also can create just enough psychological distance between yourself and the issue at hand to be helpful, without you being in denial or avoidant. As weird as this sounds, try to think and talk about your divorce in the third person. We know, it's super creepy, but give it a shot (at least in the privacy of your own home when there's no one around to wonder if you've lost your marbles). For example, when Erica was going through her divorce, and she thought, *How is* Erica *is going to handle* the *meeting with* her *ex-husband to discuss alimony arrangements,* rather than, *How am* I *going to handle* my *meeting my ex-husband to discuss alimony arrangements,* it allowed for a giant mental step back from a scary situation.[30]

Self-compassion: The joy of cooking kindness (and chocolate cake).

When you look in the mirror these days, what do you see? *Failure. Old. Ugly.* More important, *stupid* to marry that asshole? Or to *stay* married to that asshole for as long as you did? It's easy to feel like you're a worthless mess and you will never recover. We truly understand how you feel. Which is why we hope you'll believe us when we tell you: *STOP THAT SHIT RIGHT NOW.* Seriously, enough already. If another person talked to you the way you've been talking to yourself, you'd probably kick their butt. You need to knock it off, or (said in our best Liam Neeson voice) *we'll have to find you and come kick yours.*

One of the absolute best things you can do to combat the stress and nastiness of your divorce is to cultivate compassion for yourself. Self-compassion is no different than the compassion you have for other people (excluding, perhaps, your ex); it's just directed inward instead of outward. Having compassion for your sorry ass is, hands down, one of the best gifts you can give yourself to celebrate your freedom from the chains of unhappy matrimony.[31, 32] Self-compassion predicts a looooong list of good stuff for us, including . . . (deep breath, here we go): increased happiness, optimism, gratitude, life satisfaction, curiosity, emotional intelligence, intellectual flexibility, and social connectedness, as well as less anxiety, depression, physiological stress responses, fear of failure, unhelpful perfectionism, annnnnd rumination about past mistakes (whew!).[32, 33] Furthermore, divorcees who are more compassionate toward themselves fare better than those who are not.[34] In 2012, a group of clinical psychologists at the University of Arizona interviewed over one hundred recent divorcees about their split from their partner. Folks who had more self-compassion after their divorce had more positive emotional experiences months later than folks who were rougher on themselves. As a bonus, as time moved on, these more self-compassionate people thought less, and were less upset, about their ex and the divorce.[iv]

---

iv   And this list of self-compassion benefits continues to grow. As of this writing, there were over one thousand published research articles or book chapters on self-compassion—what it is, what it buys us, and how to get it.

We all have more or less default levels of self-compassion that we walk around with, built from both our biology and our past experiences.[32] But, it would be a pretty asshole move on our part to tell you all about this delicious marvel, only to inform you that you're stuck with what you got. We wouldn't do that to you. Your ex would, but not us. We love you and think you're swell. Luckily, like a perfect flourless chocolate cake, you can whip yourself up a big ass serving of self-compassion if you have the right ingredients and know the secret recipe. Unfortunately, nowhere on the ingredient list for self-compassion will you find butter, sugar, or chocolate. Self-compassion simply has three low-calorie, life-changing ingredients: self-kindness, shared humanity, and mindfulness.[32]

Self-kindness. Western societies typically place a heavy emphasis on kindness toward others, even when they make mistakes; but when we—*ourselves*—make mistakes, we have a tendency toward self-flagellation. In contrast, self-kindness involves viewing ourselves with warmth and understanding, especially when life is not going according to plan. In order to have compassion for yourself, you need to recognize that no one (not even you) is perfect and that everyone struggles from time to time. Instead of criticizing and berating yourself, try offering yourself the same care, love, and unconditional acceptance that you would offer a loved one. You are, after all, a loved one to yourself—so treat yourself that way.

Shared humanity. All humans are flawed works-in-progress. We all mess up. We all hope for things we won't, or can't, have. We all have had things happen to us that we desperately wish hadn't. These experiences are just part of being human. In the United States, a couple gets divorced every forty seconds. By the time you are done with this chapter, if you have an average reading speed, about sixty more people will have called it quits on their marriage. Others have been and will be exactly where you are right now. This can be intensely comforting at a time when you're probably feeling cut off and alone. Recognizing your shared humanity also helps put your problems in perspective. Remember when your mother (or at least our mothers) used to guilt you about eating too many cookies with the familiar proverb "There are starving children in [pick somewhere] who don't get any cookies, so I guess you don't have it that bad"? As a kid, this was a compelling argument for why you needed to stop being a brat who complained about being denied a dozen Oreos. As an adult, this adage is a good reminder that, while getting divorced sucks monkey balls, there are people out there dealing with way bigger issues. So maybe, just maybe, the suckiness of your life at present is not *soooooo* profoundly awful in the grand scheme of things. Besides, now that you are all grown up, you can eat an entire package of Oreos whenever you want (suck on that, Mom!).

Mindfulness. Speaking of keeping things in perspective, the third ingredient of self-compassion is something called mindfulness. Mindfulness involves being present in the, well, present.[35] It encompasses being aware of whatever you may be thinking or feeling, without judgment, at any given moment. We all enjoy a good wallow from time to time, but the idea here is to allow yourself to feel all the feels—the good, the bad, and the ugly—but don't unpack and take up residence in any of them. Taking this slight step back from your feelings lets you observe and accept them while allowing you to deal with them in new (and perhaps healthier) ways because you're not trapped in a glass box of emotion (bonus points for the reference . . . .*).

The recipes. How exactly do you end up with self-compassion from a cup of self-kindness, a dollop of shared humanity, and a spoonful of mindfulness? There are many different recipes you can use to bake yourself up some, and we wish we could take credit for coming up with them. But we can't. That would be plagiarism, and that is frowned upon by, well, everybody (we should know, we came up with the word *plagiarism*). Bad

---

v   Correct, sir! It's Ron Burgundy in *Anchorman*. We are so proud of you!

jokes aside, Dr. Kristin Neff, a psychologist who conducted the pioneering research on this topic in the early 2000s, has developed short, easy, do-it-yourself, and (importantly) free exercises that you can use as recipes to boost your own self-compassion (check out www.selfcompassion.org for her original versions of these). What are you waiting for? Grab your apron, get out your best spatula, and preheat that oven because you got some self-compassion baking to do!

If you like these recipes, check out Dr. Neff's website, www.selfcompassion.org, which is like a giant cookbook full of these compassionate recipes. And the nice part is, unlike that chocolate cake, self-compassion comes guilt-free. It can even help you feel less guilty when you do decide to bake a real cake (because now we're *all* dreaming about cake) and eat the whole damn thing in one sitting. Remember, self-compassion is not self-pity, self-indulgence, or overly inflated self-esteem. These ingredients have no place in your compassion-cake. It has nothing to do with letting your problems run your life or how good you feel about yourself. It's about meeting yourself where you are with the same kindness and

---

The Jambalaya Journal

Directions

Step 1: Every day for a week (or longer if you want), set aside 10 minutes to keep a self-compassion journal. Before bed might be a good time, but whenever you can squeeze it in works, too.

Step 2: Write about the emotional events of your day—not just what you did, but how you felt. Focus on anything that caused you stress or pain. Maybe you got into a fight with your ex, maybe you weren't the parent you hoped to be that day.

Step 3: Write about the event through the lens of the self-compassion ingredients.

Ingredients

Mindfulness: Take a balanced approach to your feelings. Be accepting of them, without being overly dramatic.

Shared humanity: Write about how other people experience similar circumstances. You might feel alone, but many people have gone through this—write about what you have in common with others.

Self-kindness: Close your journal by offering yourself a few kind and loving words. They may be as simple as "I'll try again tomorrow." But end your journal by taking the opportunity to be gentle with yourself.

warmth that you would offer a close friend. Doesn't that sound positively yummy?

Redemption stories: *The Silver Linings Playbook.*

In the hit book and film *The Silver Linings Playbook*, the central character, played by a very dreamy Bradley Cooper, tries to get his life back together after his wife leaves him for another man. Unfortunately, he lands himself in a mental institution when he beats the crap out of her lover. We bet you can relate, right? In order to maintain some sense of hope during these hardships, Bradley keeps repeating the mantra, "I don't want to stay in the bad place, where no one believes in silver linings or love or happy endings." Suffice to say, after some foibles and fumbles, and a lot of Eagles football (*E-A-G-L-E-S, EAGLES!* What can we say? We live and work near Philly), Bradley finds meaning, peace, and love again—and cue credits. It's a nice story. It's also more than that; it's a story with a lesson that is supported by science. Just like Bradley, how you choose to narrate the story of your life will have an impact on how you withstand Hurricane (insert your ex's name here) after she or he blows through, taking out your trees, roof, and all the silver linings.

Humans are natural storytellers. In every culture throughout human history, from cave paintings to movies, we are obsessed with legend and fable. Perhaps it's not shocking then that we also tell the stories of ourselves, our memories, the things that happen to us, and how we feel about them.[36, 37] We are the narrators in our own lives. Erica imagines that Sandra Bullock does the voice in her life's movie; Patrick wants James Earl Jones. Like movie genres, when telling the stories about our life events, we employ basic themes. For some, these themes are more akin to a romantic comedy, like *Silver Linings Playbook*; whereas, for others, they're more similar to the horror movie *The Shining*.[vi] As you might guess, ideally, you want to narrate your life events in the most positive manner possible.[38] This is true for any crappy situation, from splitting with your spouse to being trapped in a bathroom by an ax-wielding manic (assuming you survive). The goal here is to make lemonade out of the lemons that get chucked at your head by life. Psychologists call this the *redemption story*.

Redemption stories occur when people look for the silver linings—the surprising sunny outcomes—in their terrible, awful, really bad experiences.[36] For example, if we (Patrick and Erica) hadn't gone through the suckiness of divorce with our exes, we wouldn't have had our first date. We wouldn't have fallen in love. We wouldn't currently be in the most fulfilling relationship of our lives (we know, we're disgusting, but we don't care). We wouldn't have our wonderful family, including our moody teens, smelly dogs, and new little potato-head baby. And we certainly wouldn't be sharing our sage (and questionably funny) advice with you. *Kaboom!* We just created a redemption story that makes us happy our first marriages ended.

---

vi   A fun-filled nugget of digression here: we develop our tendencies for how we tell our life-stories through the early conversations and storytelling we engage in with our parents.[28] Seems like a good reason to focus on the Disney, rather than the Brother's Grimm, versions of fairy tales, if you ask us! More happily-ever-afters and less mermaids dying and turning into seafoam and such.

You might think that when you pull off a redemption story, you are just tricking your brain into being happy. And you would be right! That is exactly what you are doing, and that is also why redemption stories predict all sorts of psychological goodness.[39] People who make tootsie rolls out of the poop in their lives tend to have better mental health overall and a greater sense of purpose. Specific to your situation, redemption stories are really helpful when you're dealing with a case of broken-heart-itis.[40] A study by Erica (what we like to call a little bit of "me-search") tracked the daily emotions of people after the implosion of their romantic relationships. Turns out, on days when people thought in terms of redemptive themes (tried to find a silver lining in the end of their relationship), they also felt less distress.

The take-home seems to be this: Yup . . . divorce is a stinky, smelly, trash-heap of suck. But, no truly happy and functional marriage ends in divorce, so now's your chance to shift your perspective on the whole refuse pile and engage in some psychological recycling. Eco-friendly and awesome. Use this as your personal silver lining's playbook: Getting divorced means that you get to start over again and make a new, even better, life for yourself. You would not be where you are now, with lessons learned and exciting places to go, without separating from your spouse. Incredibly wonderful things will happen to you post-divorce (we promise), which would not have been possible if you'd stayed married to poopy-pants magoo. So thank your ex for the part they played in your story, mark their adieu with applause and champagne, perhaps take up working out in a trash bag tracksuit and enter a dance competition with Jennifer Lawrence . . . but, most of all, seek your chance for a silver lining.

Social support: Because friends don't let friends drink alone.

All this advice on building your basic care, self-efficacy, self-compassion, and redemption story is all well and good. There's nothing like a few good ole home remedies for what ails you (reminder . . . it's your split from your slug-breath ex that ails you). But sometimes traveling this road on your own isn't enough. You need to enlist the people in your life who love you, and perhaps even some well-qualified strangers in your post-divorce arsenal if you're going to get through this in one piece.

Receiving support from others is an essential piece of your post-divorce first aid kit. Social support makes you feel loved, valued, and part of a bigger network of people who look out for one another.[41] When people feel supported, they are protected from depression and anxiety. They show more psychological resilience when dealing with both chronically stressful stuff, including a variety of serious illnesses (like serious, serious: HIV, coronary disease, kidney disease, etc.) and acute trauma.[41, 42] Heck, receiving a healthy dose of social support can even help protect you from having a heart attack or catching the common cold.[41, 43] If you're still not convinced, one study found that a lack of social support can shave two to three years off a person's life.[44] We need other people to function—or at least function well. And, at no time is social support more important than when you're dealing with stressful shit, like divorce.

Social support provides you with the extra resources you need to cope with the crap-ton-of-crazy that life shovels in your direction.[45, 46] These resources can roughly be divvied up into two different flavors: emotional support (mmm, chocolate), which includes warmth, love, and acceptance; and practical support (mmm, peanut butter), which is comprised of tangible problem-solving ideas to deal with whatever is stressing you out.[41] Now, both are tasty as fuck to be sure, but they satisfy different cravings. Emotional support feels amazeballs and helps turn that frown upside down by reminding you that you are valued and loved. Practical support is less about positive feelings and more about helping you get your act together so you can start adulting again.[45]

Finding friends who can provide you with emotional and practical support after your divorce is key. Unfortunately, your divorce is almost certainly going to cause you to lose some friends. This is especially true if you have a va-jay-jay.[47] Dunno why. Some friends will disappear like your car keys, wallet, or will to live. Mutual friends you and your ex shared are probably going to pick a side, and it might not be yours no matter how *obviously* saint-like you've been through this whole mess. Your married friends will fear that divorce is a bit like the measles, and they don't want to catch it, so they might slowly back away from you and your divorce while applying embarrassing amounts of hand-sanitizer.[48, vii]

These changes to your social network will sting more than a little, but the good news is that social support can come from a lot of different places. Many divorcees find that their friendships with their single friends become even stronger after divorce.[49] Parents and siblings are likely to offer increased emotional and practical support during this difficult period.[50] Groups that you belong to—book clubs, poker buddies, or that drinking, ahem, we mean wine appreciation, group—can also be important sources of support. After her split from stink-o-pants, Erica joined a group of ladies dedicated to all things baking, and they became a crucial lifeline for her (meetup.com for the win!). All you need to do is Google groups dedicated to the shit you enjoy doing, and you'll have a ton of new friends at your disposal. Worst case, volunteer. Do some good *and* meet people you might enjoy. Damn, we like the efficiency of that. You know who you shouldn't turn to for support? Your ex. Like the drug resistance and education (D.A.R.E) movement of the eighties and nineties taught us, just say, "No!" As we'll chit-chat about in Chapter 3, being too close with your ex-spouse is generally not the best idea you've ever had. It's fine to play nice, but their role as the primary pillar of your sanity is over and done with. It's an adjustment, for sure, but one you need to make.

If you aren't finding the support you need from friends and family, new or old, don't hesitate to contact a professional. Navigating your post-divorce life with a well-trained therapist at your side is never a bad

---

vii And it turns out they may actually be right: some sociologists have argued that divorce is a bit like the common cold—it tends to make the rounds among friends—perhaps in part because watching other people survive divorce encourages people that they, too, can get out of a less-than-perfect union and be okay afterward.

idea, and there's no shame in seeking help. Find someone you feel safe with and whom you can talk to—you'd be surprised how much therapy can help.[51] It can be well worth the time and expense (although many insurances cover mental health care nowadays . . . cuz, ya know, it's the right thing to do), save you years floundering about being a hot mess, and get you back to feeling like your old shiny-unicorn self in no time.

That said, getting back to exactly who you were pre-divorce is impossible unless you can invent a time machine and bring along a ton of wine to forget your past mistakes. Divorce changes who you are, for good, bad, and ugly. Baking up all the sunshiny self-care recipes and compassion cookies we mentioned earlier is a great start, but you still need to figure out who *you* are, now that your marriage is over, and tackle creating your new post-divorce identity. In this new version of you, you can be (just about) anything and anyone you want. Wanna be a superhero? Go for it. Flying over tall buildings in a single bound might be out, but you can definitely try to be someone who stands up for justice and the little guy. Supervillains more your style? Sure, why not. Start working on that plan for world domination. So, what kind of post-divorce comic book character best fits the new you? Spider-Man or the Green Goblin?

Chapter 2

Discovering the post-divorce you: Older, wrinklier, and more confused

*A*vengers, assemble! Today, products from the Marvel Comics Universe (MCU) are everywhere. Sure, the traditional comic books are still around, but beyond that, there's a multi-billion-dollar film franchise. As we write this, there have been twenty-three movies, grossing over $22.5 billion at the box office alone, since the newest iteration of the MCU film franchise launched with *Iron Man* in 2008. There are also toys, video games, clothes, and a myriad of other merch making this company a pretty penny. But, Marvel wasn't always the sexy, special-effects-laden, hot Hollywood institution it is today. When founder Martin Goodman first launched Marvel Comics in 1939, the company was focused solely on print comic books, and comics remained the company's core identity for decades. But then, in the early nineties, they ran into trouble. The comic book market collapsed. With the advent of things like home video gaming systems, children just weren't overly interested in spending time or money *reading* (just ask our teens; they think reading is on par with a root canal). So, to try and breathe new life into their failing corporation, the execs at Marvel reinvented themselves and branched into filmmaking. The early movies were either hit or miss. For every successful film like *X-Men,* there were some real stinkers, including the infamous *Howard the Duck.* Today, this movie is not only remembered because it lost over $20 million, but also because it proudly featured duck nipples, duck condoms, and duck masturbation (which is a pretty bold move for a movie marketed as a family film). It wasn't until Kevin Feige took over as president in the mid-2000s that things started to turn around. Finally, Marvel figured out who they were going to be—and got it right. They started making the films that have become known as the *Infinity Saga*. From *Iron Man* to *Avengers: Endgame* and beyond, this iteration of Marvel has been the most praised and profitable era the company has ever seen.

As MCU reinvented itself, it took time to shed the old, print-driven version of the company. There were some false-starts, setbacks, and missteps along the way, but through persistent tweaking of its corporate identity, Marvel emerged triumphant—bigger, better, and more badass than ever before. Think about your sense of identity in the same way. Your married identity: the outdated print version. Who you are post-marriage: confused and a bit misdirected—like *Howard the Duck*. And who you are going to be: motherfucking *Thor*.

The *who* of you.

According to the classic rock band The Who, figuring out the question "Who are you?" ("Who, who?") can be complicated and one that, apparently, can't be asked too many times. When we find ourselves contemplating who we are, we are usually struggling with our identity. This is why it isn't uncommon to find teenagers—who are transitioning from childhood to adulthood—staring blankly at their walls, trying to figure out who they are and who they want to become. For decades, psychologists have also been staring blankly at their walls (and computer screens) trying to sort out exactly what identity *is*, what it's made of. Here are four elements of identity that we, as researchers, are pretty certain of . . .

Element One. Your sense of self is made up of all of the attributes, likes and dislikes, values, beliefs, hopes and fears for the future, and even physical attributes that you would claim as "me" or "mine."[1, 2] Yes, even that mullet haircut you rocked in seventh grade was part of your identity, at least at the time. An easy way to get a sense of what comprises your identity is to complete the phrase "I am . . ." Go ahead, give it a try with whatever comes to your mind. "I am . . . blond." "I am . . . intelligent." "I am . . . someone who likes to eat Goldfish crackers in bed, crumbs be damned." You get the gist. Once you come up with one "I am . . ." phrase, keep brainstorming. The first ten things that readily came to your mind are the things that are the major defining features of who you are—your identity.[3]

Element Two. In addition to all the gobbledygook that makes up who you are, you also have holistic feelings about whether you know yourself. This is referred to as self-clarity in psycho-speak. Self-clarity is the extent to which you know who you are. You could feel that all the jagged puzzle pieces of yourself fit neatly together, revealing a stunning seascape, complete with smiling dolphins; or maybe you have a discombobulated bunch of cardboard bits for an identity that, try as you might, you just can't make sense of.[4] Confusion about who you are is related to various negative characteristics (like being a neurotic mess), unpleasant psychological experiences (like feelings of depression and anxiety), and poor relationship outcomes.[4, 5] Fun fact: your certainty about who you are increases as you age.[6] So if you feel like you have a better sense of yourself at forty than you did at fourteen, you're correct!

Element Three. Your sense of who you are is determined, at least in part, by your relationships with other people.[2] You might have noticed that some of your top ten "I am . . ." phrases above were social roles: you're a mom or a dad, a friend, a sibling, someone's child, etc. There is no doubt that other people affect your thought processes, your feelings, and even your behavior.[7, 8] What all this means is that you create a slightly different version of yourself when you're with different people in your life.[9] You're still you, but you will highlight the aspects of you that best mesh with the people you care about when you're around them.[10] When we accentuate aspects of ourselves to mesh with those around us, this is known as self-expansion. When Erica goes home to visit her family, most of whom live in the south and have accents to match, she suddenly develops one helluva twang y'all. Bless her heart.

During adulthood, romantic relationships (especially marriages) are where we self-expand most.[11, 12] In these relationships, we tend to think of ourselves as part of a "we" rather than as only a unique "I." Dating and married couples spontaneously use first-person plural pronouns (we, us, ours) more than singular ones (I, me, mine), especially to the extent that they feel committed to their partner. One person we know, Susan, has vivid memories of this happening to her when she was in college. Throughout her young life, she was never passionate about following sports. Then, while at college in Chicago, she started dating a dude who was a football fanatic. She vividly remembers going home for Thanksgiving and showing up for dinner in a Chicago Bears jersey, and she couldn't stop talking about "da Bears." While her family wasn't impressed that she knew Walter Payton amassed almost 17,000 yards rushing and 110 touchdowns in thirteen seasons, it serves as a great example of how people integrate their sense of self with their close others', leading to all sorts of shared attributes, interests, beliefs, and goals.[13]

This all means that, over the course of your marriage, your ex-spouse changed you pretty profoundly, for better and for worse.[14] And everyone reading this collectively groans, "fuuuuuuuuck." Way (waaay) back when you were happy, you developed a sense of "we" that applied to just you two. You highlighted the parts of your personality that best fit with your partner's, and you even adopted many of your spouse's preferences, values, goals, and whatnot as your own. It was all part of building your partnership.

But now you're divorced, or at least divorcing, and one social role that you no longer occupy is "spouse." So, what happens to your sense of self, the one that was so deeply touched and influenced by the person you once loved and now loathe more than any other? This question leads us to the fourth element that we researchers know about identity . . .

Element Four. Divorce fucks up all of your shit—elements one through three—royally.[15, 16, 17, 18, 19]

Divorce is an earthquake, and you are a rickety, not-up-to-code building.

Late in the evening of May 22, 1960, the most powerful earthquake ever recorded rocked southern Chile.[20] Coming in with a whopping magnitude of 9.5, the Valdivia Earthquake killed approximately 1,655 people and injured over 3,000 others. It caused (adjusted for inflation) $2 billion worth of damage in Chile, while its related 61 tsunamis triggered additional deaths and millions of dollars of destruction from Hawaii and Japan to the Philippines and the west coast of the mainland of the United States. This was the BIG one, and it messed up a lot of stuff. In terms of your identity, your divorce is the equivalent of the Valdivia Earthquake, and its tectonic activity has left behind some serious rubble.[21]

Think about it—a major social role that you occupied is just . . . gone. The person who helped develop your identity over the past however many years is no longer there. When your cataclysm of a divorce sent your world shaking, this shared sense of "we" that you'd built is one of the first structures to crumble to dust. All of those traits, preferences, values, and goals that were once shared become casualties of the divorce-quake as they fall away from your sense of identity like bricks out of a toppling building.[17, 22] Your appearance might even change. Seriously, we know a guy who tried to bleach his (brown) hair blond after one particularly painful breakup. It didn't go well. He looked like Charlie Brown's Great Pumpkin.

All this jettisoning of the stuff that people adopted from their former lovey-poo (whose name is now doo-doo) makes them feel that sense of identity has shrunk.[i, 18] The bummer for you, dear reader, is that after romantic relationships end, we tend to feel less sure of who we are, and

---

i   That is unless they didn't adopt a lot of stuff from their partner to begin with. People who didn't really expand their sense of self in the first place during their relationship report the opposite effect: instead of a shrinking self, they express feeling like their self is growing and blossoming like a flower.

this loss of self-clarity can persist for months, if not years. To make matters worse, this deficit of self-understanding dramatically increases your feelings of sadness and depression. There seems to be something about not knowing who you are that really fucks you up.[17, 19, 23]

Rebuild, reinvent, and rediscover.

You and your ex were together for a long time, and during this time, you self-expanded to take on many shared attributes, interests, and goals that now need to be replaced.[30] In short, you need to figure out how to put your Humpty Dumpty self back together again once the aftershocks of your divorce start to settle down. Experience, and weirdly morbid children's rhymes, teach us that relying on the king's horses and men may not be your best bet. So, let's first take stock of the damage . . . how cracked is your egg? Consider the statements in the table below. How many of them would you say describe you right now?

Indicate how accurately you believe each statement below describes how you feel right now		
That's a negative. Not me at all. 0	Eh, I guess, maybe? Sorta. 1	Totally. Are you reading my mind? 2
_____ 1. I don't feel like I know who I am.		
_____ 2. If someone asked me to describe myself, I'd have a difficult time.		
_____ 3. I feel like I am a mixture of lots of different characteristics that rarely make sense together.		
_____ 4. I often find myself trying to figure out who I want to be.		
_____ 5. When I think about the kind of person I am, I feel confused.		
_____ 6. I find it hard to define myself.		
_____ 7. I have trouble making decisions because I don't always know what I want.		
_____ 8. I sometimes feel like how I act isn't consistent with who I really am.		
_____ 9. I often feel like my wants conflict with each other.		
_____10. When I think about myself, I feel like the pieces don't seem to fit together into a cohesive whole.		
_____11. I feel like other people understand themselves in a way that I don't.		
_____12. How I see myself always seems to change.		

The quiz you just took measures your self-clarity and will help determine how much superglue you are going to need to put yourself back together.[24] By adding up your score, you can get a sense of how your clarity stacks up to other adults by using the table below.

Score		Description
0–10	Knowing Thyself	Your score puts you in the top 25 percent of self-clarity. You are an identity beast. Besides possessing a clear sense of who you are, you are also keenly aware of your strengths, weaknesses, and potential.
11–17	Figuring out Thyself	You score squarely in the middle 50 percent of individuals regarding self-clarity. You have a decent sense of your identity, but you still struggle to figure out where you stand on some issues.
18–24	Misunderstanding Thyself	Who are you again? Your score puts you in the bottom 25 percent of self-clarity scorers. Feeling unsure and conflicted about yourself is almost part of your daily routine.

As we talked about previously, self-clarity is the feeling that all the pieces that make up your identity fit neatly and cohesively together in a manner that allows you to "know thyself." Based on the quiz, if you are "misunderstanding thyself," you're pretty uncertain about who you are in the post-divorce haze. This is likely due to all the parts of you that changed when your marriage ended. You might feel the desire to rush out and replace the attributes you lost to your divorce with new stuff (maybe buy a loom and take up weaving), but hold on there buckaroo—it may be in your best interest to take a brief breather. When people are feeling unsteady in who they are, they are far less likely to adopt new attributes into their sense of identity in the first place. The idea is that adding more things to an unstable foundation, sort of like the end stages of the game *Jenga* may topple the whole thing over.[25, 26] If this is you, keep employing the advice we gave you in the previous chapter, and wait until you are feeling a bit more certain of yourself (and get a higher score on the self-clarity quiz) before moving ahead.

Those of you who are "knowing thyself" possess a pretty good understanding of your new identity. You can still tweak some minor elements of yourself, but you probably don't need a major identity overhaul. For the rest of you who are "figuring out thyself," get ready to start redefining who you are to be even more fabulous, shiny, sexy, and magnificent than ever before. It's doable, but first you need to figure out what parts of your identity will change and which will remain.

Creating the shinier, new and improved you.

Back when you were still doing the Darth Vader gig with your own personal Emperor Palpatine, you two shared all sorts of hobbies (Death Star construction), goals (galactic domination), and preferences (for black robes). Dropping all this baggage is a big part of what's messing you up right now. I mean, dear old Darth literally dies when he finally breaks up with his partner in crime by throwing him down an air shaft, which we don't suggest you try with your ex. Does this mean your sense of self is similarly doomed? Nope-ster . . . the force is strong with you. It turns out you can self-expand to add more goodies to your sense of self all by yourself. No partner required!

One of the best ways to create and discover your new identity is to expose yourself to new things that you haven't done before. This is your golden opportunity to try anything you fucking want! Want to learn how to play paintball? Grab some goggles and head out to an arena. Want to be more of a humanitarian? Find a place to volunteer in your free time (which you probably have more of now that you're not dealing with stinky-ex-magoo). Want to learn a language? Find a class and *Eat, Pray, Love* it out. The key here is that whatever you do, it needs to be novel for you. Doing the same old shit (aahhh, Netflix) isn't going to help you create a new identity, but exposing yourself to new things will expand your sense of who you are and fill in the holes left by your ex.[27] You don't need your ex to redefine your identity—you got this one all on your own. Just think, without the Emperor's mind voodoo, maybe Vader would have taken up a hobby that didn't require galactic fascism . . . like golf.

While you are exposing yourself to all these new adventures and interests, consider who you've always *wanted* to be. In addition to the current version of you, there's an ideal version of you–someone who you could possibly be, who embodies all of the qualities you want to have.[28] When people reflect on how the current version of themselves is different from their ideal, it triggers feelings of discomfort and dejection. So, drawing closer to the person you've always wanted to be is a great thing for you. It reduces your emotional discomfort and increases your feelings of happiness and life satisfaction.[29] This means you don't want to redefine yourself with qualities and goals you could never achieve; doing so will just breed disappointment. Patrick knows this feeling firsthand as he is still upset about not achieving his ideal vision of himself as a Jedi. Like Patrick, you need to redefine your new identity to be awesome, maybe just not Luke Skywalker–awesome.

As you're recreating the new and improved version of you, the question will inevitably arise of what to do with the old you? The you that overlapped so heavily with your ex. Like when you two were dividing up your shared books and DVDs and muffin pans, you'll need to make some decisions about what you want to hold on to, and what can get tossed. Qualities that you initially adopted from your ex that are now firmly ingrained into your true inner self do not have to be abandoned. Let's say your ex was a running fruh-eaaak (Bleh. Erica only runs so she can eat more snacks). Maybe you started running with your partner after you got married. If you ran a mile here, a mile there to (in our best Russian accent) *do the fitness*, then "runner" may not be a central part of your identity, and replacing it with a new form of exercise may be a good idea. On the other hand, if your ex got you training for marathons—something that requires far more sweat, tears, and (occasionally) blood than the casual jog—the role of "runner" might be more deeply tied to your sense of self, and you may consider keeping it. Bottom line, you should keep previously shared attributes, interests, and beliefs *only* if they are now central to your core identity. All the other ex-stuff-baggage should be tossed like a bag full of dirty diapers sitting in the summer sun and replaced with new hobbies, interests, and goals.[30]

There are also some parts of you that you simply can't change.[29] If you've always hated your elbows, you are probably shit out of luck. (Unless you can find a plastic surgeon who specializes in elbow reconstruction.) In general, when we talk about your ideal self, the focus is on internal qualities (attributes, hobbies, values, etc.) that you want to embody, not so much physical stuff. It's great to look hot—and if you want to be a healthier you, by all means pursue that value (in a balanced, healthy way please; and if you really want that Botox, knock your socks off, no judgment here)—but fixating on having the perfect nose or fewer wrinkles is not the "ideal self" we're really talking about. Sure, we want you to feel confident in how you look, but feeling confident about what's inside is the foundation upon which joy and contentment are built.[29]

I think I can, I think I can, I think I can . . .

As you try to achieve your new identity, it is necessary to maintain a full-steam-ahead-single-minded-*THIS-IS-SPARTAAAA* focus.[31] Unfortunately, anyone who has ever chased a goal (any goal, really) can tell you that it's easy to start, but it's hard to keep going. There's a reason why gyms see a flood of temporarily inspired gym-goers each January that slows to a trickle by March. There are a lot of reasons why we lose motivation, ranging from feeling hopeless about change to feeling stressed about the situation. Regardless of the reason, there are some scientifically supported suggestions that can help keep you motivated and on the path to attaining your new identity.

Ideal-you-follow-through. One of the biggest things you can do to help yourself achieve your new identity is to develop what researchers call *implementation intentions*,[32] but we prefer the more friendly term *ideal-you-follow-through*. An ideal-you-follow-through plan is a contingency strategy that helps you stay on track when life throws nasty obstacles your way. Imagine that your ideal self is to be "gracious and kind to others." You're making amazing progress, being pleasant to strangers and smiling beatifically at all around you. You didn't even get upset when the Starbucks barista messed up your order for a nonfat latte with extra foam and gave you one without any foam at all (the *horror*). Instead, you just smiled and quietly thought to yourself, *Gee, she must be having a hard day . . . poor thing.* You're basically Mother Teresa; cue the halo and angels singing. Then you meet up with your ex to discuss something; it doesn't matter what. And they open their pie hole. Words come out. Annoying ones. And you find yourself preparing to punch him/her in the throat while screaming obscenities.

Press pause. Are your thoughts toward your ex in this situation consistent with your new identity as being "gracious and kind to others"? Nope. Not a chance. But, it's a great example of how little things can derail you in the pursuit of your ideals and how an ideal-you-follow-through plan can help. An ideal-you-follow-through plan provides a pre-defined, clear-cut blueprint that you can put into action when challenges to your identity arise. You do this by having a course of action, like "if x happens, I will do y." Here, the x is the sucky thing that's happening to you, and the y is how you are going to respond to it in order to bring you closer to achieving your desired identity. An ideal-you-follow-through plan in our hypothetical situation might be: "If my ex says something obnoxious, I will take a deep breath, ignore it, and respond in a calm, matter-of-fact way."

Once you decide on the new parts of your identity, sit down and spend some time envisioning all the potential ways you could get drawn off course. Create as many ideal-you-follow-through plans as you can. Write 'em down. Post them all over your house, *Beautiful Mind* style. Repeat them to yourself as mantras. Practice them so that, when the time comes and you need those plans in place, they've become automatic to you. The cool thing about ideal-you-follow-through plans is that if you practice them religiously, they will keep you on the wagon when the road gets bumpy.[32] Trust us, a bit of preparation goes a long way when it comes to keeping you on track to becoming your ideal version of you.

I get by with a little help from my friends. Another handy way to achieve your new identity is to recruit your nearest and dearest.[33] Specifically, any friends who already embody the ideals that you're trying to achieve. Is your new identity to be an awesome ping-pong player? Hang out with that buddy who always has a wooden paddle and tiny balls ready to go. Want to be gracious and kind to others? Spend more time with the friends who remind you of Gandhi, and less time with those like Howard Stern. Friends who already embody characteristics that you're trying to achieve can serve as inspirational role models for you.[34] They also provide important backup and support to help kick your ass into gear. The people who love you are more likely to see you as you'd like to be seen—as possessing the traits that are important to you. And, by simply reminding you of who you are, they can help to shore up that shaky sense of self-clarity.[35] Even better, when people in your friendship networks encourage behaviors out of you that align with your ideal self, they actually help you to move closer to becoming that version of you.[36]

Now, remember from the last chapter: A potential problem with relying on your friends after divorce is that, on average, divorcees lose 51 percent of the friends they had when they were married.[37] Most of this loss comes in the form of mutual and married friends who withdrew in discomfort or took sides.[38] The good news is divorcees are pretty good at making friends—especially with other divorcees.[39] Having a friend who is in the same boat as you is a great idea, not only because they understand what you're going through, but also because they can help you navigate this tumultuous period in your life. Hell, that's how your authors first got to know each other. We'd been colleagues for years; but after we both got divorced, we got to know each other as friends and fellow divorce-survivors. We shared our hopes of who we wanted to become after divorce. We learned from each other's struggles and successes how to achieve our best post-divorce selves. Now, we, of course, took things to the next level, and today we share not only aspects of our identity but three kids, two dogs, and a one-hundred-plus-year-old house that always seems to have something leaking from the ceiling. We can't promise that your divorce buddies will turn out to be your identity soul mates, but they can help you in discovering and achieving your new identity.

Play make-believe. When all else fails, we're big fans of faking it 'til you make it. Ever been driving behind that car . . . you know, *that* one? The car that is covered in bumper stickers supporting [insert politician/dietary choice/deity of choice here]. Or encountered a forty-plus-year-old woman who is rarely seen without her eco-conscious travel mug with the slogan "Plant a tree = plant a life," and a "Girls can do anything!!!!" themed T-shirt? Yes, being eco-conscious is awesome. And yes, we believe that girls can, in fact, do *anything*. But we also believe that actually behaving in an eco-conscious and feminist manner does more good in the world than simply advertising these ideals on your shirt or coffee mug, which is sort of the point. When people are trying to pursue some ideal version of themselves that they haven't attained yet, whether it be environmentalism, gender equality, religiosity, or veganism, they often advertise these ideals through their public and consumer behaviors.[40] When folks feel uncertain about some part of themselves, they feel the need to show that part of them off to others so that they can confirm the ideal person that they want to be. Remember Patrick's skinny jeans? Public self-expression (of his *undeniable* self-confidence and sex appeal, both of which, let's face it, he'd felt had taken a beating post-divorce) at its finest.

Publicly claiming an attribute helps you to feel like you're embodying it to a greater extent. This is especially true if you feel a little insecure in that attribute to start with. As you become more assured about your ideal-you, these overt displays (although they still exist) become less important. And hey, your humble authors are not immune to this behavior as we both sport tattoos to advertise our ideal-self badassery, even though we're basically homebodies and card-carrying nerds.[ii] So go on, sport that shirt that advertises your awesome new identity, and plaster your car with stickers proclaiming who you are to all who motor behind you. It may feel a bit silly, but it will help you take steps toward the version of you that you've always hoped for.

Rock that new role. When kids are asked what they want to become when they grow up, the most popular responses are doctor, veterinarian, police officer, firefighter, scientist, engineer, musician, athlete, teacher, and astronaut.[41] One role notably absent from this list is "divorcee." Like these kiddos, it's probably safe to assume that you never set out to identify yourself as a person whose marriage fell apart. But here you are today—all divorcing (or divorced) and shit. Being forced to adopt an identity that you actively *didn't* want is scary and all sorts of upsetting.[29, 42]

The good news is people who can see the positive in sucky life events, like divorce, are better equipped at avoiding getting their identity all *fubar'ed*.[iii, 43] Similar to the redemptive stories we talked about in the last chapter, you need to do your best to face your new "divorcee" identity with a massive dose of positive attitude. Focus on all the great things this new self-image is going to bring to your life that we just talked about. You get to try different things and discover new and exciting interests! You can do whatever you want, whenever you want—total freedom! You will have less conflict! You don't have to have a major discussion for every decision you must make! You now have the entire bed to yourself—sleep diagonally, sprawl the hell out! You will meet lots of new people and make even better connections than your lame-o ex! It might not always be easy to see the positive aspects of your new identity—we know—but doing so will help protect your sense of who you are, which will safeguard your psychological wellness.[4, 5]

---

ii   And it's worth noting that even our attempts at badassery are nerdy . . . all of Patrick's tattoos relate to space travel or video games, and one of Erica's tattoos is Harry Potter–themed. *Expecto Patronum!*

iii   Fucked up beyond all recognition. Fubar . . . ed (past tense).

Wrapping up redefinition.

Even after you successfully Frankenstein together your old and new bits and pieces and successfully create a new self-image, you will sometimes find your old pre-divorce identity resurrecting itself, *Night of the Living Dead* style. When you are around your ex, they are going to make the old version of you want to reach its skeletal, decaying hand out of the grave and act in ways that you did when you were married. Heck, just being around someone who reminds you of your ex might cause you to start acting like you did when you were married.[8, 44] Maybe they have similar hair or the same irritating way of chewing . . . or breathing. Whatever it is, when you're around them, you feel an undead part of your identity craving some *brainzzzz*. This won't impact your daily life that much, except for when you must be around your ex and/or you decide you're ready to get back into dating. To the extent that your ex brought out your . . . shall we say, less than stellar qualities (like the tendency to murder and consume the living), you should avoid starting a relationship with someone who elicits those same patterns.

Speaking of dating, you may be tempted to jump back into dating to re-expand your sense of who you are. This might make intuitive sense because, after all, that's how you got a lot of your shared self-goodness in the first place. Why not pick up a new partner who already has some qualities you would like to adopt as part of your new post-divorce identity? Rebound relationships are good fun, and they can be a great jolt to your flagging feelings of self-worth after your divorce,[45] but jumping into a new relationship too quickly may further unravel your sense of you, especially given that you have a few loose threads already. If you're seriously thinking about jumping back into the dating pool, wait until you get to Chapter 5—there's a section dedicated solely to whether you're even ready to start the flirt-fest.

Remember that you are not going to redefine your new identity overnight. There is something to be said for the idea that time heals all wounds, and when it comes to your identity, this couldn't be truer. It can take anywhere from a few months to a year to sift through the soot of your divorce to figure out who you are and who you want to be.[15] So, give yourself the time and grace to sort it out. With some space, some focus, and some of the strategies we've mentioned, you really can be just like a phoenix, rising from the ashes as a new and improved version of you, ready to take on whatever comes your way, leaving your past (including your ex) in the dust.

Chapter 3

Can't we all just get along? The importance of being nice(ish) to your ex

Hidden on a quaint tree-lined cul-de-sac in Bryn Mawr, Pennsylvania, are two nondescript red brick homes. At first glance, the twin homes look like they are straight from a Norman Rockwell painting, with their dueling American flags swaying in the breeze and general feeling of idealistic, small-town Americana. On any given Saturday, there is a good chance a visitor might find thirteen-year-old Derek playing basketball at the lone basketball hoop hung between the shared driveway of these homes. What makes these brick houses unique is they are each owned by Derek's parents, Cindy and Mark, who have been divorced from each other for three years.

If you could have seen Cindy and Mark at the beginning of their divorce, it would have been impossible to imagine them living in the same state, not to mention being neighbors. Their animosity was so intense that during their divorce they fought, cried, and argued. They even had an epic legal battle over $150's worth of patio furniture, for which they paid over $600 in legal fees. Each. What can we say? Divorce makes illogical buffoons out of the best of us.

With time, their anger toward each other diminished while their shared love for their son, Derek, never wavered. Therefore, when the home next door to Mark went on the market, Cindy quickly put in an offer. Now they are not only divorced parents but close friends; they frequently talk, celebrate holidays together, and even confide in each other about their new romantic relationships. Mark and Cindy are still very much divorced; they are not romantically interested in each other in the slightest (the mere suggestion of a reconciliation sets them both hysterically laughing as if it is the most fucking ridiculous never-in-a-million-years idea ever). Mark is even engaged to be married to a (very understanding, nigh on saintly) woman named Mary, but their arrangement seems to be working—at least so far.

Mark and Cindy's friendship, although idyllic sounding, is not especially common among divorced couples and probably isn't a reasonable or even desirable solution for most people (more on this later). But, the overall arc of Mark and Cindy's anger toward each other after they divorced is extremely, even boringly, typical. When couples first separate, or learn they are separating, most experience an intense range of yucky emotions—sadness, regret, worry, fear, homicidal rage. In this early stage of divorce, it would be totally normal for your feelings to swing widely between hysterical crying and fantasizing about your soon-to-be ex suffering a horrific lawn-mowing "accident." You will miss them, call them every nasty name in the book (note our preference for "twat-waffle"; we feel it has a nice ring to it), consider hitting them with your car (*consider* being key here; please don't commit vehicular manslaughter . . . correctional facility orange is no one's best color), fret about your future without them, and regret you ever met them, all before finishing your first cup of morning coffee. The good news is, as time goes on, these feelings get less intense. Within just the first month of separating, most people's anger and sadness about their failed relationship, and their ex in particular, decreases by about 30 percent.[1] We aren't saying these negative feelings totally go away, or that this decrease is the same for everyone, but you will feel better with time.

Almost everyone assumes that having any contact with your ex is a bad idea and should be avoided, like frying bacon naked. Not that we'd know anything about either of these from personal experience . . . ahem . . . right? Even psychologists once warned that the "best policy is to sever all ties" with your ex.[2] And as nice as this might sound when you're stabbing a voodoo doll of your ex with needles right after splitting up, it may not be practical, necessary, or even especially healthy. After two years, approximately half of divorcees have monthly contact with their ex, and 25 percent even have weekly contact. As you might guess, those who have children interact with each other more, but even a startling number of childless exes find themselves occasionally talking. Surprisingly, even getting remarried doesn't lower the frequency of contact we have with our tool-face ex-mates. In fact, only about only 15 percent of people "sever all ties" with their ex-spouses and never have any contact.[3] What all this means is that, for better or worse, there's a good chance you are going to have *some* type of relationship with your ex.

Make love, not war.

Most people imagine that the typical relationship of a divorced couple is full of hostility, "fuck-yous," and fighting, much like the tumultuous relationship between Barbara and Oliver Rose in the movie *The War of the Roses*. Barbara and Oliver flat-out can't stand each other. "Dumb bastard!" "Slut!" "Scum!" "Filth!" "Fuckface!" Oliver kills Barbara's cat. She locks him in a sauna. They throw plates at each other. She wrecks his car. He pees on her dinner. Eventually, everyone dies. It works out well . . . for no one. The supposed conventional wisdom reflected in this movie is that divorced couples almost always hate each other long after the ink on the final legal papers dries. However, this notion was turned on its head when, in 1979, psychologist Dr. Constance Ahrons started one of the largest studies of divorced couples that would eventually span over twenty years. From this pioneering work, we learned that there are various types of post-divorce relationships. Like Mark and Cindy, some exes are in almost constant contact with their former spouse and become close friends. Others will never see their spouses again because they can't stand the sight of their stupid-ass face. Most people will find their post-divorce relationship somewhere between these two extremes and falling into one of five neat, tied-with-a-bow packages: perfect pals, cooperative colleagues, angry associates, fiery foes, and dissolved duos.[3]

Perfect pals. Mark and Cindy are the perfect example of "perfect pals." These are people who, after the divorce dust storm settled, consider each other to be good friends and engage in activities that they would do with other friends. Perfect pals seek advice from each other, ask about feelings, do activities together, and even celebrate holidays with each other. They often remain connected with mutual friends and each other's extended family. When perfect pals get into a disagreement, it rarely devolves into fisticuffs or accusations about all the varied ways in which the other person is simply a shithead. If there are children involved, each parent is involved in the child's life and assumes various responsibilities.

There is an appeal in trying to be perfect pals with your ex-spouse. After being together for so long, exes have shared memories, life events, and sometimes kiddos. Hell, you and your ex liked each other enough at one point to get married, so you must like each other enough to be friends . . . right? It certainly sounds better than the alternative of hissing at your ex like a deranged cat, and it definitely makes things like co-parenting easier.

And, after all, friendships are great. Having friends is as important to our well-being and health as exercising and eating your vegetables. Friends increase our self-esteem, life satisfaction, sense of belonging-ness, cognitive functioning, and sense of purpose.[4, 5] Not to mention, a friend is someone you can sucker into picking you up at the airport on the day before Thanksgiving. So, it seems reasonable that if you and your ex don't want to murder or fuck each other, why not try to become friends? After all, who wants the hassle of Ubering to the airport when you can just ask your friend?

Unfortunately, this type of extremely close post-divorce relationship is not for most people. Only about 15 percent of divorcees manage to be perfect pals.[6] It turns out that most people are epically shitty at being genuinely good friends to people with whom they were once legally wed. But what makes a truly good friend? Oxford psychologists Michael

Argyle and Monika Henderson examined numerous friendships from all around the world and proclaimed to have found the secret to friendship success: 13 basic qualities, or "The 13 Commandments of Friendship."[7] If these commandments are broken, the friendship is doomed to be smited (smote? smitten? eh, fuck it) with pestilence, plagues of locusts, and awkward snubbings at Starbucks.

The 13 Commandments of Friendship

I. THOU SHALL SHARE NEWS OF SUCCESS WITH THE OTHER

II. THOU SHALL SHOW EMOTIONAL SUPPORT

III. THOU SHALL VOLUNTEER HELP IN TIME OF NEED

IV. THOU SHALL STRIVE TO MAKE FRIEND HAPPY

V. THOU SHALL BE TOLERATING OF OTHER FRIENDS

VI. THOU SHALL NOT CRITICIZE IN PUBLIC

VII. THOU SHALL REPAY DEBTS AND FAVORS TO FRIEND

VIII. THOU SHALL TRUST AND CONFIDE IN EACH OTHER

IX. THOU SHALL STAND UP FOR EACH OTHER

X. THOU SHALL KEEP CONFIDENCES

XI. THOU SHALL NOT NAG

XII. THOU SHALL RESPECT PRIVACY

XIII. THOU SHALL NOT BE JEALOUS OF OTHER RELATIONSHIPS

So, how do we fall short at being good friends with our exes? In almost every, single, fucking way. Those who are friends with their exes are less likely than other types of friends (like coworkers, book club buddies, etc.) to follow 12 of the 13 commandments of friendship.[i] What all of this means is that, for almost everyone, and probably for you, trying to maintain a deep friendship with an ex-spouse is not the best of all

---

i   For some reason, friends that are ex-partners are *not* more likely to violate the commandment "Thou shall not criticize in public" than other friends. So, if you are willing to overlook the other twelve violations an ex-spouse is likely to commit, at least you don't have to worry about them talking bad about you in front of the hostess at Olive Garden.

possible ideas.[8] Unlike Mark and Cindy, most of us don't get much out of being truly close friends with our exes, aside from migraines.

Additional blows are struck against this type of relationship when ex-spouses begin to create new lives for themselves. New romantic partners enter their lives, new children are welcomed into the world, and time spent being buddies with the ex-spouse dramatically decreases. Five years after getting divorced, very few couples can maintain a perfect pal relationship: one-third eventually become cooperative colleagues and another one-third drop down to angry associates.[3]

Cooperative colleagues. Cooperative colleagues neither consider themselves friends, nor do they think of each other as enemies. Instead, these individuals view each other in much the same way you might consider a coworker. Cooperative colleagues are in business together—often the business of co-parenting or managing other shared interests, like professional projects. They are cordial, polite, and may talk or text frequently, but they stick to the task at hand, never focusing too much on each other's personal lives.[ii] The keyword here is *compartmentalize*. Cooperative colleagues don't muddy current disagreements or issues (making sure someone can pick up a child from school) with their previous marital problems (how that asshole never rinsed out a cereal bowl in his life). They frequently speak with each other about mutual areas in their lives that overlap, like children or extended family, but rarely talk about their private matters or new relationships.

Cooperative colleagues are, by far, the most common post-divorce relationship type, with almost 40 percent of exes falling into this group.[6] This setup seems to be particularly helpful when children are in the picture because it gives both ex-spouses a common goal—the welfare of their child. They represent, figuratively speaking, the board of directors

---

ii   Except for our coworker Trent. Seriously, fuck you, Trent. Who the hell eats smelly hot broccoli and tuna fish sandwiches every day, clips his toenails in the office, and spoils the end of movies before you can see them? Trent "He was dead the entire time" the moral degenerate, that's who.

of the company called *Raising Tiny Humans Not to Suck*. They share in child-related decision-making issues, celebrate major life events together (like little Timmy's bar mitzvah); and if there is a crisis (Timmy got into the bar at his bar mitzvah!), they help each other. This is probably why being a cooperative colleague is the most stable of post-divorce relationships, with 75 percent of people maintaining this relationship five years after they were divorced.[3] However, it is important to remember that cooperative colleagues are not true friends; they are simply coworkers employed together in the office of life.

Angry associates. Angry associates' interactions almost always devolve into arguments. And they interact as little as possible. Unlike cooperative colleagues, they are unable to compartmentalize the negative feelings they have toward their former spouse, and this feistiness seeps into almost every part of their relationship. For example, one member of an angry associate couple recalls how he overheard his ex-wife singing to herself *Starship*'s song "We built this city" while they were at their son's high school graduation. However, instead of "We built this city on rock 'n' roll," she kept singing, "We built this city on sausage rolls." Upon telling her that she was singing the wrong lyrics, they quickly got into an argument so epic they had to be separated by other concerned parents at the ceremony.

When angry associates attend an event, they make not only themselves, but everyone else around them, pants-squirmingly uncomfortable. A child's birthday party can quickly descend into a disaster. Angry associates bicker with each other about everything, from the theme of the party to the flavor of the cake (answer: chocolate; it's always chocolate), to that one time, two years ago, when one partner forgot to order balloons for said child's birthday. This sucks big hairy monkey balls for the exes, and for everyone around them who must listen to this nonsense. Even worse, such conflicts upset any relevant kids exposed to the competing tugs of parental loyalty. Following divorce, 25 percent of former couples are angry associates,[6] and after five years, one-third of angry associates will still be pissed as wet porcupines for all of the wrongs they perceived during their marriages, as well as those that have accumulated since. Another third of angry associates are likely to improve their relationship with their ex-spouse and bump up to cooperative colleagues. For the final third, their relationship seems to spiral even deeper into the blazing pits of hell as they enter the relational category of fiery foes.[3]

Fiery foes. Going through the litigious divorce process with your ungrateful ex—*Hulk Smash!* Seeing your slimy bowel sack of an ex's stupid oxygen-depleting face—*Hulk Smash!* Dropping off children and noticing your self-centered, jock itch ex repainted your old front door—*Hulk Smash!* Just thinking about all those years you wasted being married to your tactless-obnoxious-urinal-cake weasel of an ex—*Hulk Smash!*

Fiery foes could have easily been called *Hulk Smash!* because divorcees in this category have so much anger toward the other that there is nothing more they want to do than *Hulk Smash!* their exes into oblivion. Fiery foes view each other as an enemy and are ready to go to battle at even the slightest provocation—real or imagined.

Like angry associates, fiery foes have a heated relationship with their ex-partner. But this heat is like a blacksmith's forge poised on the ledge of an exploding volcano. Such extreme anger means that fiery foes see their ex-spouses less frequently than angry associates (which, let's be honest, is probably for the best). Fiery foes can't think of *any* redeeming qualities of their ex-spouse or remember *ever* being happy in their marriage. In what can only be said to be a stroke of good luck for humanity, this is the rarest of all the post-divorce relationships—only about 5 percent of divorcees display enough fury to be classified as fiery foes.[6] Unfortunately, for this 5 percent, they are almost all doomed to stay fiery foes, with only about 15 percent of fiery foes being able to successfully heal their relationship enough to move up to cooperative colleagues after five years.[3]

Dissolved duos. "See you later, alligator." "Peace out home slice." "Out the door, dinosaur." "Hasta la vista, baby." "Bye, Felicia." "Fuck this,

I'm out." "Hope your new neighbors are assholes." No matter how they said goodbye, dissolved duos are those ex-spouses who no longer have contact with each other. They have entirely withdrawn from each other's lives and frequently find themselves living in different geographic regions. Although not super common, such a "relationship" still happens about 15 percent of the time after a couple separates.[6]

Some dissolved duos exist because one partner found the separation so painful and upsetting that they dealt with it by totally checking out, psychologically and physically. Other times, an ex-spouse might abandon their former partner, along with any children they have, and totally disappear. In such a situation, the remaining parent is truly a single parent with no further interaction or support from the ex-partner. Often, dissolved duos occur not because of relationship strife or abandonment, but simply because partners "moved on" with their lives. Childless divorced couples, without the need to stay in touch for the sake of their children, frequently turn into dissolved duos over time. Even ex-spouses with children often become dissolved duos once their children grow older, and co-parenting gets reduced to occasional awkward encounters at weddings and baby showers.

It's over, so how to get over your overlapping lives?

Whether you are now a perfect pal or a dissolved duo, at one point you and your (now) ex shared many mutual aspects of life. You had mutual friends and similar interests; you celebrated the same holidays, lived in the same house, slept in the same bed, shared finances, went shopping together, drove in the same car, did chores together, and shamelessly released bodily gasses in front of each other. On a typical day, the average couple spends about 12.5 hours with their spouse (including snooze-time).[9] If you were married eight years (the average length of a first marriage), you would have been around your ex-spouse about 36,500 hours. This is roughly the amount of time it takes a person to have 109,500 naps, watch *Gone with the Wind* 9,125 times, have sex 438,000 times,[10] travel to the moon 506 times,[11] or do the two-minute ab workouts 1,095,000 times (and look *amaaaaazing*). In short, you spent a lot of time with your former love nugget. Regardless of whether this time was mostly happy, or if it felt more painful than doing a million ab workouts, your lives once intersected in almost every way. However, after getting divorced, the amount of overlapping life-space we share with our spouses goes down. *Waaay* down. Exactly how great a reduction occurs is mostly dependent on your new type of post-divorce relationship and how much of each other you two can stomach before feeling physically ill.

Overlapping Lives Giving You Hives?	
Perfect Pals	The lives of perfect pals overlap with each other a lot—some might say too much. They are active participants in each other's lives, turn to each other for advice, and frequently share their feelings, hopes, and dreams.
Cooperative Colleagues	The overlap of cooperative colleagues is compartmentalized. They keep elements of their life private from their former spouse but interact with their ex on issues of shared interest (like the offspring).
Angry Associates **Fiery Foes**	Angry associates and fiery foes have minimal life overlap with each other. Because their interactions tend to be full of fury and strife, they avoid interacting with each other whenever possible.
Dissolved Duos	Dissolved duos have essentially zero joint interests because they have withdrawn completely from each other. Their lives are forever separate from each other as they move on to new relationships and brand-new lives.

Little life overlap, big anger: Angry associates and fiery foes. It isn't as if perfect pals and cooperative colleagues never argue, they do. But, when they do argue, they are usually able to focus on the issue at hand rather than everything the other person did wrong in their entire life . . . ever. However, a post-divorce relationship made up of angry associates or fiery foes is so full of antagonism that both ex-spouses, and any children they might have, will experience some psychological fallout. The potential impact of such a negative relationship on children is such an important topic that the entire next chapter is dedicated to protecting these little booger monsters from their parents' shenanigans. So, for now, let's put the kiddos on the back burner and focus on how maintaining an angry associate or fiery foe relationship can fuck with *your* head.

Angry associates and fiery foes will have sporadic face-to-face interactions with each other in order to manage a range of issues, from alimony to parenting challenges. Short of moving to the other side of the world, or hiring a hitman, you're just gonna have to deal with it. Following your initial separation, you guys probably sniped at each other about the divorce itself (who gets custody of Billy's basketball . . . since no one could possibly go to the store and *buy a second one!*). However, as time passes, the nasty interactions of angry associates and fiery foes are most often about money; who gets custody of shared friends, childcare, new romantic relationships; and how much they truly hate each other.[12] Seriously, they can hate each other more than they hate burnt popcorn, animal abuse, and one-ply toilet paper . . . combined. It is probably an understatement to tell you that having such a combative relationship with your ex is going to cause a lot of stress and tears. And, like the war zone that this sort of vitriol resembles, you'll likely come away with long-lasting scars on both your identity and psychological health.[13, 14, 15]

The main contributing factor to all these problems isn't *what* angry associates or fiery foes argue about, but *how* they argue. Many adults remember the thrill of reading Choose Your Own Adventure books when they were children. In these books, the reader assumes the role of a hero, and every few pages, they must make a critical decision about how to respond to some misadventure. For example, imagine you were confronted by a giant blue-veined alien that goes by the name Russel the One-Eyed Muscle. What will you do? (a) Be fearful of the immense size of Russel the One-Eyed Muscle and fly to the moon. (b) Throw a bucket of cold water on the single-eyed alien to shrink him down a bit. (c) Give the alien a firm but loving hug. (d) Knowing your home world is low on sodium chloride, lick the blue alien to confirm if he tastes salty. In Choose Your Own Adventure books, the reader would choose one of the "adventures" and turn to the appropriate page to see what happens. Pretty cool! Except for the fact that almost all choice permutations lead you down a path that ends in your gruesome death (most likely eaten by Russel).

As a divorcee, your arguments with your ex-spouse aren't going to be as fun as fighting Russel the One-Eyed Muscle—although they will often feel like a battle with an angry, ugly creature from another dimension. However, just like Choose Your Own Adventure books, you must make some choices when you fight. For example, imagine you are meeting with your ex-spouse at a coffee shop to discuss a financial issue that involves shared children. In between sips of your iced caramel macchiato, the conversation starts to get heated, and voices begin to rise as you figure out how best to set a budget for your children's summer plans. Which adventure below best reflects how you would likely respond?

Adventure 1: Show criticism. "You were always bad with money. That's why *I* always had to handle our budget." With this option, you avoid talking about why you are having this disagreement; instead, you go right for the jugular and make it personal.

Adventure 2: Show contempt. "You are such a selfish asshole when it comes to money. You obviously don't love our kids as much as I do." Contempt is related to criticism, but with a healthy dose of being an extra dick while mocking, belittling, and ridiculing your ex. Fun? Maybe. Productive? No.

Adventure 3: Get defensive. "You are not the only one with financial issues. I have been struggling twice as much as you since we divorced, and you decided to shack up with that twenty-year-old." You defend yourself from your ex's perceived criticism, matching their blame and anger with your blame and anger. Bonus points if you first agree you did something wrong and then add in the word "but." As in: "That may be true, *but* you do the exact same thing."

Adventure 4: Escape. "..." You shut down, don't participate, and refuse to have any discussion with your former partner about this important shared interest. Maybe you even stomp out and slam the door, much like the children you were arguing over.

Adventure 5: Have a civil discussion. "I understand your concerns, so let's figure out a budget for the children that will be fair for both of us." You stay focused on the issue that needs to be resolved while also respecting your ex's concerns.

Regardless of how well you get along with your ex-spouse, everyone will go on these five different adventures at some point. However, angry associates and fiery foes are much more likely to fight in the first place and go on the first four adventures more often than other couples.[17] Collectively, the first four adventures—criticism, contempt, defensiveness, and escapism—have been given the gloriously biblical name *The Four Horsemen of the Apocalypse* by relationship researcher John Gottman.[16] While the *Four Horsemen* are often applied to marriages and marital counseling, the dangers of these negative behaviors can be seen in all types of relationships, including those with your asshat ex.

When fiery foes and angry associates *Four Horsemen* it up, it is extremely unlikely that the argument is going to end well. This is because the quarrel becomes more about the person (your selfish, no-good, cake-sniffer ex) than the issue being discussed (like the fact that you need to somehow pay for little Betty's summer camp). If you are one of these couples, make sure to be extra aware of the *Four Horsemen* next time you're fighting. It's best for your kids/friends/pets/family (whom you love), your ex (whom you don't), and even yourself (whom you should) if you move away from these patterns. Such awareness won't automatically make you select "Adventure 5: Have a civil discussion," but it is an essential first step. This isn't the last time we will be visited by *The Four Horsemen of the Apocalypse*. The four riders will make a terrifying end-of-days entrance again in Chapter 9, when we discuss how they can impact your next romance and some handy antidotes you can use to avoid a future romantic relationship Armageddon.

Lots of life overlap, questionable boundaries: Perfect pals. Depending on where you are in your divorce process, it might feel like you will never find love again. That the only spooning you will be doing is with a pint of Cherry Garcia. If you cook dinner for two on Tuesday, all it will mean is that you won't have to cook on Wednesday. The only dates you will ever get will be updates for Microsoft Windows. The most satisfying cuddles you will ever have again will be with your Bed, Bath, and Beyond body pillow (which, let's face it, is pretty stinking great—we have two . . . one for each of us). Lucky for you, most divorcees enter into a new serious romantic relationship within five years of their split.[3] Unlucky for you, you will probably have to share that pint of Cherry Garcia with your new romantic partner. (Although Erica does this very rarely—hey, Patrick can get his own damn ice cream; it's why we wrote this book: to afford *two* desserts.)

While most people do find new love after getting divorced, it can be really challenging if you're trying to find this love while staying perfect pals with your ex. In one of the largest studies on this topic, researchers found that *none* of the perfect pals in the sample were able to maintain a new romantic relationship five years after they were divorced.[3] If we take these results seriously, it means that the odds that a perfect pal will find a new lover are on par with the chances of dying from a bee sting (0.001 percent), being struck by lightning (0.0007 percent), being killed by a dog (0.0006 percent), being executed on death row as a convicted murderer

(0.0008 percent), or meeting your ultimate demise in a tragic fireworks accident (0.0002 percent).

Because so much of perfect pals' lives still overlap, even post-split, they frequently talk or interact with each other, and it's just plain inappropriate. In short, they're short on boundaries. You can imagine why this might get sticky when you insert a new lover into the warped ex-lover dynamic. Like perfect pals, cooperative colleagues also share significant life overlap with their ex-spouses; but unlike buddy-buddy-no-boundaries, this relationship type creates, enforces, and respects limits. Cooperative colleagues might discuss problems surrounding a shared child over coffee, yet they would never go to a romantic restaurant to have such a discussion . . . and they'd stay clear of talking about their personal lives. In contrast, perfect pals have very few walls between their ex-spouse and current life, and those that do exist are made of glass.

The reason why perfect pal boundary issues cause problems can be traced back to the reason why these former spouses decided to become perfect pals in the first place. In what might have been one of the great oversights in relationship research, it wasn't until just a few years ago that anyone bothered to look at why some people continue friendships with their former romantic partners. Apparently, before 2017, it was just assumed people stayed in contact with their exes because they had unresolved romantic feelings for them and might want an occasional booty call. However, by systematically asking hundreds of people why they keep in (mostly positive) touch with their exes, researchers were able to identify the six main reasons perfect pals and cooperative colleagues stay in contact.[17]

Some reasons for maintaining contact are "good" and are *generally* considered psychologically healthy, while other motivations are "bad" or even "ugly," and are responsible for the questionable boundaries of perfect pals. Ugly motives basically boil down to holding on to a connection because you still love your ex, you want to fuck your ex, or your ex buys you shit. As you might have guessed, perfect pals who are motivated by ugly motives experience a lot of negative feelings (are overly emotional,

The Good, Bad, and Ugly Reasons
for Staying in Contact with an Ex

The Good

Children or shared resources
We have children together.
We have shared property.
We work together.
I want to provide a good family environment for children.

Social relationship maintenance
We share a group of friends.
We want to maintain good relations with our friends.
We want to prevent awkwardness in our friend group.
We see each other frequently because of similar friends.

The Bad

Sentimentality
They are emotionally supportive.
We have common interests.
They understand me better than other people.
It feels normal to have them around.

The Ugly

Self-Centered
I want money from them.
They have attractive friends.
They have social connections that are beneficial to me.
They buy me nice gifts.

Romantic Attraction
I still have feelings for them.
I am still in love with them.
I don't want them to forget me.
I can't imagine my life without them.

Sexual access
To keep having sex with them.
To have a hook-up buddy.
The sex is good.
Friends with benefits.

always worrying, etc.), high antagonism toward other people (use others to get what they want, easily lie, etc.), and have a surprising lack of humility (motivated by selfish gain, have a strong sense of self-importance, etc.).[18] One study even found that those who maintained contact with their exes due to "romantic attraction" reported the relationship made them feel depressed, negatively affected their mental health, and prevented them from creating new relationships.[18] If you are a perfect pal with your ex because of an ugly motive, run—don't walk—away.

The impact of maintaining contact with your ex based on sentimentality, or "the bad" reasons, comes down to the type of relationship and dosage. It isn't necessarily bad, but it can be. If a cooperative colleague wants to reminisce occasionally and catch up with their ex by meeting at the Cheesecake Factory a couple of times a year, everything will probably be fine (not to mention there's cheesecake . . . *cheesecake,* people). However, everything isn't going to be so great if a perfect pal feels sentimental toward their ex because they can't stop thinking about them or are having trouble accepting their divorce.[19] We aren't saying you need to stop having a relationship with your ex-partner for sentimentality reasons. You just need to be careful, both for your psychological health and your waistline (seriously, who can eat all that cheesecake).

"Good" reasons for staying friends with your ex are just that—good.[18] Such motivations do not seem to create the boundary issues associated with perfect pals. However, even a perfect pal couple that began their post-divorce relationship for "good" reasons runs the risk of traipsing into "bad," or even "ugly," territory if they frequently share personal thoughts and feelings with each other. For example, a single pleasurable interaction with an ex can increase the positive feelings (how much their ex fulfills their intimacy needs, how happy their ex makes them feel, etc.) felt toward that former flame by as much as 7 percent. Equally terrifying is that such an interaction *decreases* the positive feelings a perfect pal has toward any current lovie bear by 5 percent.[20] What all this means is that regular interactions as a perfect pal places a person in danger of experiencing feelings of longing and increased emotional attachment toward their ex-partner,[21] which inevitably leads to declines in relationship quality with any current romantic partner.[22] Add this hydraulic system of feelings to the fact that most new love interests aren't thrilled when their partner shares emotional intimacy with a former spouse, and it becomes clear why perfect pals have so much trouble finding and maintaining new romantic relationships.

It is important to note that this negative impact exes have on current relationships is mainly for the perfect pal type of relationships. That is, consistent interactions between ex-lovers with lots of life overlap and few boundaries, and who remain emotionally close, often spells trouble. *Sho-ho-hocking*, we know. In contrast, it is unlikely that cooperative colleagues with good boundaries are suddenly going to fall in love again when they meet to discuss details of a child's birthday party. Nor are the angry associates or fiery foes going to experience emotions any more lusty than syphilitic rage after an interaction with their ex-spouse. This also doesn't mean that perfect pals are necessarily doomed never to be happy or to find new love. Mark and Cindy, the couple we met earlier, seem to be making such a relationship work. But nobody has talked to Mark's new fiancée about how she feels about the shenanigans. This does mean that for almost everyone, maintaining a perfect pal relationship is going to make it very difficult for them to move forward from their divorce and find their next love.

Relationship goals: The Goldilocks setup.

You can learn a lot about the ideal post-divorce relationship from the children's story "Goldilocks and the Three Bears." After committing a felony by breaking and entering, Goldilocks finds herself upstairs confronted by the bears' three beds. She lays down on the first bed, but it was too hard. Then she lays on the second bed, but it was too soft. Then she lays down on the third bed, and it was *just right.* Finding the ideal amount of life overlap with your ex-spouse is much like Goldilocks's hunt for the perfect bed. If you have any intersecting life-space with your ex (meaning, you are not a dissolved duo), you want to find the post-divorce relationship that is neither too soft and comfortable nor too hard and argumentative. The relationships of angry associates or fiery foes are "too hard," and can cause communication issues, psychological difficulties, and even physical harm. Trying out the relationship of a perfect pal is usually "too soft," and is linked to having boundary issues and dooming you to a life with your ex as your primary companion, even though you're divorced. The relationships of cooperative colleagues tend to be "just right" for most people.

Of course, you are not the only one who gets to decide what type of relationship you are going to have with your ex-spouse. You may want to be a cooperative colleague with your ex, but they'd prefer to stab you in the eye with the butter knife you two fought over in court. Figuring out the type of relationship is going to be one of the most important challenges you will face after getting divorced. Unless you are a dissolved duo, the relationship you have with your ex-twat-waffle is like ugly luggage, student loans, timeshares, and herpes—once you have them, you are usually stuck with them for the rest of your life. And nowhere is this statement truer than if you share children.

Chapter 4

The offspring: Helping your kids through this shitstorm

A t 3:29 p.m. EST on October 4, 1957, the Soviet Union successfully launched the first artificial satellite, the Sputnik I, into an elliptical low Earth orbit. It was only about the size of a beach ball, and Sputnik's simple radio transmitter didn't do much more than communicate a consistent *beep* . . . *beep* . . . *beep* signal; but, for what it lacked in modern-day technological wizardry, it made up in terms of instilling wonder (and Cold War panic) in the citizens of the United States. Coincidentally, just four hours after the fateful launch of the Sputnik, CBS aired a brand-new television comedy that would have a similarly profound impact on the lives of Americans.

"Leave It to Beaver . . . starring Barbara Billingsley . . . Hugh Beaumont . . . Tony Dow . . . and Jerry Mathers, as The Beaver." As the Sputnik satellite was orbiting overhead, viewers in the United States got their first glimpse into the innocent misadventures of Theodore "The Beaver" Cleaver and his idyllic nuclear family. During and after their influential years on the air, the Cleaver family became the nostalgia-laden archetype for American family life. The mother is the patient and understanding homemaker who does all the household chores while wearing high heels and pearls; the father is the hardworking businessman who always finds time to impart valuable life lessons to his innocent and attentive children. *Leave It to Beaver* created an image of the world that was exclusively populated by families containing two happily married parents who, along with their always obedient biological children, lived in homes on perfectly manicured lawns surrounded by white picket fences.

Well, we'd like to call it bullshit! While the Soviet Union was able to launch a satellite into space during the fall of 1957, the United States failed miserably at creating a television show that accurately reflected American families in the 1950s . . . or ever, really. During this time period, families came in all different shapes and sizes that didn't look anything like the Cleavers.[1] There was divorce. Moms went to work. Dads stayed home. Stepparents and stepchildren existed. Some families even had only one parent. Today, fewer than half of US children live in a traditional nuclear family like the Cleavers.[i] Because of various factors, including divorce and people waiting to get married until later in life, "traditional families" are on their last legs in the industrialized world.[2]

Children of divorce may no longer be members of a traditional nuclear family, but they are still part of a family. The post-divorce family typically spans at least two households, which can contain stepparents, stepchildren, and/or half-siblings.[3] While certainly not the only familial permutation, this two-household (called *binuclear*) setup has become increasingly the norm in modern American society. Now, in binuclear families, the OG (or "original gangster" according to our teens) parents might squabble a bit more with each other than in the standard nuclear arrangement. However, these extended families still usually show support, love, and care for their members, especially the pint-sized ones. Even bitter, fiery foe exes love their shared children. In short, a family continues to be a family after divorce—it just looks different.

The kids are all right . . . or are they?

"Divorce ruins children's lives."[4] "Divorce hurts children."[5] "Divorce is worse than death for children."[6] It isn't uncommon to hear claims that

---

i   In one episode, "Beaver's House Guest," Beaver befriends a child with divorced parents. In true *Leave It to Beaver* fashion, once Beaver's parents learn of this unspeakable evil, they wonder if Beaver should even be friends with a kid tainted by divorce because it might be a bad influence on poor ol' Beaver.

binuclear families are little more than "broken homes" that are going to epically fuck up the kiddos in them. But, how much does divorce actually affect children's psychological health and well-being? Given the finger-wagging and headshaking expressed by many, you might think that getting divorced tanked your kids' psychological wellness and ruined their lives. Well, you are generally wrong. Across dozens of studies, spanning several decades and thousands of children, less than 1 percent, a measly 0.15 percent, of the variation in children's psychological adjustment can be linked to divorce.[7, ii] In other words, your kids might have their fair share of issues, but only a very *verrrry* small amount of those issues are due to you and your ex parting ways.

We realize that, with kids, "psychological adjustment" is a relative term. Seriously, we once saw a child put floaties on his feet in a failed attempt to run across a pool. Well-adjusted here means a child functions generally well at school, doesn't set fire to inappropriate objects or torture small animals, has social skills to get along with others at home and school, can establish meaningful friendships, and is able to comply with rules and authority. This is not to imply that well-adjusted kids never push the boundaries and test the rules their parents set. Heck, even little Theodore "The Beaver" Cleaver once played hooky from school (considered quite shocking at the time). Some rebellion is perfectly normal for even the most well-adjusted children, so don't freak out and blame your divorce if one day you catch your sixteen-year-old sneaking a beer. Your children probably would've driven you crazy even if you lived in an alternative universe where you remained happily married to their other parent in a house full of lollipops and magical unicorns. The good news is that infrequent acts of rebellion are nearly always temporary and rarely become a consistent problem for most children, even if you're rocking the binuclear family look.[8, 9]

---

ii   For our more statistically minded readers, the average effect size (converted from Cohen's d to a Pearson r) across numerous studies examining the link between divorce and psychological adjustment was $r = .04$ (fail-safe $N = 464$).

This is all good news. As parents, our job is to protect and worry about our kids. We often (okay, pretty much always) feel like we're not doing a good enough job, and getting divorced is just one more way in which we may have scarred our wee ones for life. We get it.[iii] And there are many ways in which we may be fucking up our littles (as of this writing, whether or not Snapchat is an appropriate social media platform for middle schoolers is a current topic of debate in our home; the adults say no, the children say we're *destroying their social liiiives!*),[iv] but getting divorced probably isn't one of them.

Why then do so many people continue to believe that children of divorce are, in short, *doomed*? It turns out that people are susceptible to such a false belief for the same reason individuals erroneously believe it is bad luck to walk under a ladder, open an umbrella indoors, or break a mirror. Such superstitions or errors in judgment occur because of a psychological phenomenon known as confirmation bias. As humans, we are wired to pay attention to events that confirm our beliefs and ignore events that would challenge them. For example, if you expect that breaking a mirror will bring you bad luck, you are more likely to pay added attention to anything bad that happens after you accidentally break a mirror. Stubbed your toe—blame the broken mirror. Accidentally fart while on a date—argh . . . the fucking broken mirror! This confirmation bias creates the false sense that events are connected, when they are, in fact, not related at all.[10]

---

iii Patrick's main concern after his divorce was how his two precious monkeybutts were coping, so much so that he helped his ex-wife move into her new place (including a rather heavy bed that ultimately had to be sawed in half to make it up some stairs), just weeks after deciding to separate. He did this so that the kids could see their mom and dad working together and still being a family. Just weeks after separating from her husband, Erica (who had no monkeybutts at the time) was still trying to figure out whether there was a surreptitious way to have her ex-husband arrested for tax fraud. So, yeah. We think we know who's the better person here.

iv Update: before this book went to press, the teens won this particular battle. They harried us into submission. Snapchat for all!

When some people hear a story that a child from a "broken home" is dealing with psychological issues, it isn't uncommon to point out that the child's parents are divorced—doing so confirms the common bias that divorce is bad. What is missing from these stories are all the times that children from traditional nuclear families are fucked up . . . or turn into serial killers. Upon learning that a child from a traditional nuclear family is a bit off-kilter, no one ever mentions in hushed tones that the child's parents are still married. Equally absent are discussions about all the children from divorced families who are perfectly psychologically healthy. This isn't necessarily purposeful; it is just how we think. Unfortunately, this imbalance of information contributes to the illusion that divorce is linked to long-term harm for children.

This isn't to say that divorce has no effect whatsoever on the munchkins. You are not going to want to hear this, but getting divorced probably did really devastate your kids—at least initially. Most children have a ton of emotional yuckiness to deal with when their parents split, such as feelings of anger, confusion, shock, and sadness. Although such negative feelings are concerning, these emotions tend to disappear by the end of the second year post-divorce, as the noodles become accustomed to their new family setup.[11] What all this means is that, for most children, divorce initially sucks—and of course it does, their entire world is being turned on its head—but for the majority of kiddos, their parents' divorce ends up being just fine in the long run.[12]

We hope the news that divorce doesn't have long-lasting adverse effects on *most* children puts your mind at least somewhat at ease. The breakdown of your marriage likely hasn't broken your kids. Of course, *most* children does not mean *all* children, and for some children, divorce can be a real game changer. During those initial weeks and months following your divorce, it's important to watch for signs that your little loves are struggling.

So, how can you know whether your snuggle-nuggets are going to smoothly sail through their transitioning family structure, or whether they're in for rougher waters? For the past sixty years, scientists have been busy trying to figure out why some kiddos seem to be impacted by divorce more than others. It's analogous to a medical doctor trying to determine why the majority of people can eat tons of peanut butter with no adverse effects (other than an expanding waistline), while a small minority of individuals will experience an anaphylactic reaction if exposed to even the smallest amount of this nutty spread. In the case of divorce, these hard-working scientists have narrowed it down to several possible "allergens," which are responsible for making divorce particularly harmful to some children: financial strain, shitty peer support, self-blame, the parental relationship, and parenting style.

Cashflow: C.R.E.A.M.

The Wu-Tang Clan might be exaggerating that "cash rules everything around me" (C.R.E.A.M.), but there is no denying that lack of finances can be extremely troubling. Imagine if all your expenses suddenly doubled. There is a twofold cost increase to your weekly grocery visit. Monthly bills for utilities, phones, and cable suddenly surge. Entertainment expenses, like vacations and outings on the weekend, abruptly double. Health care and medical costs jump. Thanks to your divorce, you don't need to envision this terrifying situation because it's likely the story of your life—you and your ex's incomes went from supporting one household to two.

While you ponder that bit of fiscal suckitude, how about this extra crap-nugget from the National Bureau of Economic Research: the family income of children whose parents divorce falls by an average of 45 percent.[13] This isn't only bad for your sports-car-owning goals, but it is also troubling because there is a clear link between financial health and your family's mental health. For example, people who are depressed are two times more likely to be members of families with unsecured debt. Those with financial difficulties are also more likely to experience other psychological problems like neurotic disorder (three times more likely), psychotic disorders (four times more likely), and even suicide attempts (seven times more likely).[14] While this research isn't directly examining the effect of divorce on kids' well-being, it has led some to suggest that the economic instability that can happen after divorce is a main culprit for the negative outcomes some children experience after their parents call it quits.[15]

In addition to the financial impact divorce has on children's emotional well-being, it can also impact their educational opportunities. One of the ways that this often manifests is in moving to more affordable housing in less desirable school districts. Also, divorced parents generally have a harder time saving to support their children's future college education, simply because keeping the lights on and food on the table typically takes priority over a Harvard education.[16]

The thing that sucks is there isn't much you can do about any of this, unless you can rap like Wu-Tang or win the lottery (we are guessing your odds are probably better with the lottery). If you've been financially fortunate in your divorce, your kids are likely going to be in better shape than if the property settlement agreement didn't break your way. You can, however, try to make the most of what you've been dealt. Try to play nicely enough with your ex (check back on the last chapter for tips) that you two can shoulder the financial responsibilities surrounding your kids evenly. Watch your pennies and learn how to budget. Skip the Starbucks, get rid of cable, buy things you need secondhand. If you have a financially savvy friend or family member, enlist their help. It's important to accept that your new financial situation will likely affect your children now, and in the future, so you can plan accordingly.

The peers: Angels and assholes.

Kids can be assholes to other kids. In what must have been one of the most depressing studies to conduct, nearly one thousand assholes . . . er, we mean sweet darling children, were asked why they reject other kids.[16] The reasons these children were jerky toward other kids ranged from understandable ("She never keeps her promises," "He throws juice at us," etc.) to cruel ("She's got big ears," "He's got horrible teeth," etc.) to downright strange ("I don't like the way he runs," "He always has a runny nose," etc.). However, children were most likely to reject another kid when the kid made them feel uncomfortable or when the kid was seen as "different." Unfortunately, children of divorce are often viewed as "different" as they transition into a family structure that is unfamiliar to some of their peers. This problem only gets more compounded if your mini-you had to move to a new neighborhood after the divorce and is now faced with the task of making new friends. This unfortunate situation puts children of divorce at risk for feeling rejected and lonely, placing them in jeopardy of long-term emotional and psychological problems.[17]

Kids don't have a monopoly on being assholes; many adults thrive in this domain, too. However, this doesn't stop us from turning to close friends when we are in distress. During your own separation, there is a good chance that the support and advice you got from your friends greatly benefited your psychological health (remember Chapter 1?).[18] Kids aren't any different. Just like adults, children benefit greatly from the social support of close friends when their home is full of marital strife and conflict.[19] Even just having a supportive relationship with a single close friend promotes better adjustment after divorce than kids who do not have a bestie.[18]

So, it seems peers are a double-edged sword for kids. When other kids reject a child going through divorce, it can magnify the shittiness of having their parents split up; but when the child has supportive friends, the shittiness can be diminished. Kids' relationships with other kids have historically had this dual effect—children are both the source of great joy and great sorrow to other children—but, following divorce, children tend to spend even more time with their peers and less time at home, meaning that the double-edged sword of peers becomes sharpened.[18] Your tiny, sticky-fingered, booger-eating angel will be especially susceptible to both the negative and positive impacts of the other tiny, sticky-fingered, booger-eating devils—ahem, angels that they spend time around.

Unfortunately, your ability to influence your kids' friend situation, like your ability to influence your financial situation, is limited. You can encourage them to hang out with buddies who are kind to them, or get them involved in new activities where they can meet new children with shared interests. As a parent, you can (and should) take up school-based bullying with administrators, limit social media use if it becomes a source of distress, and (above all) be available to emotionally support your child.[20, 21, 22] As much as you'll want to, this is one boo-boo you may not be able to kiss and make all better, but you can be a haven of love and acceptance for your child through this challenging time.

Self-blame: When the sippy cup is half empty.

People worry about many things when getting divorced. 1) Will I find love again? 2) What do I do if I accidentally run into my ex on the street? 3) Will my children blame themselves for the failed marriage? The answers are:

1. Yes. And to help a bit, we've got some snazzy-ass chapters coming up on how to find love again and make it last this time.
2. Make sure there are no witnesses and then carefully wash all the blood off the car.
3. Regrettably, probably. Sorry, folks.

Somewhere between 35 and 50 percent of children blame themselves, at least partially, for their parents getting divorced.[23, 24] Children's self-blame can usually be traced back to the hatred and resentment many parents had expressed toward each other leading up to the divorce. This toxic environment spills over to the children when parents deliberately, or unintentionally, recruit their children to be allies in the ongoing wars with each other. Such a douchey tactic emotionally tears children apart, causing them to falsely believe that they played a role in the divorce itself.[22] That is just the bread surrounding the shit sandwich of the blame kids place on themselves for our marital failings. The meat of this self-blame hoagie is the psychological impact that guilt has on kids. Children who blame themselves for their parents' divorce are at heightened risk of experiencing all those numerous negative issues that we warned you to be on the lookout for: bad dreams, headaches, loneliness, anxiety, thought problems, attention problems, aggressive behavior, and social problems.[22, 25]

Ready for the final ingredient in this panini of purgatory . . . the special sauce, if you will? You probably have absolutely no idea whether your child actually blames themselves for your divorce. Yup. That's right. No. Fucking. Clue. This is especially true if your children are older (ten and up) because tweens and teens are less transparent and open with their parents when discussing divorce. The only teensy-weensy sliver of good news here is that, after about two years, the number of littles saying they blame themselves for their parents' doomed marriage drops off from about 50 to 20 percent.[22] Of course, a one-in-eight chance that your child might be suffering from psychological issues because they secretly harbor self-blame for the ultimate destruction of your marriage isn't much to celebrate. Therefore, regardless of whether you think your children blame themselves for the implosion of your marriage, you need to remind them that it wasn't their fault. Repeatedly. Over and over again, like a fucking earworm song you can't get out of your head—"Baby Shark, doo doo doo doo doo!"

Parental relationships: Can't we all just get along?

Today is a big day for six-year-old Angela. Her mom took her out of school early and has brought her to the University of Rochester. While sitting inside a tiny room on the university campus, she overhears her mom talking to her dad on the phone. The conversation is boring, something about her dad forgetting to stop by a store, but Angela starts to detect a tinge of anger in her mother's voice. As the conversation progresses, Angela's mom becomes increasingly angry-sounding until she is downright pissed at Dad. Angela stares, motionless, at her feet as she anxiously waits for the distressing phone call to end. Unbeknownst to Angela, her mom isn't really talking to her father. She is speaking with a psychological researcher in the other room because Angela is actually a subject in a scientific study. The researchers running this experiment are not trying to torture little Angela; they are studying how hearing parents fight impacts children. For Angela and the other children in the experiment, witnessing their parents argue on the phone dramatically increased their production of the hormone cortisol.[26] This kind of sucks because this "stress hormone" increases blood pressure and reduces immune responses. In the short-term, not a big deal, but in the long-term, elevated levels of this stress hormone are a big fucking problem—associated with everything from cardiac problems to increased risk of common illnesses.

If children, like Angela, can become so distressed over a minor, one-minute argument between their parents, then imagine what happens when arguments are continuous. Children with post-divorce parents who are angry associates or fiery foes with unresolved hostility toward each other face a daunting laundry list of problems associated with these types of relationships. These unlucky children are at elevated risk for depression, anxiety, low self-esteem, academic problems, and social issues.[27] We can add to this the catalog of problems discussed earlier that occur when children are drawn into parental arguments and end up blaming themselves for the eventual divorce. As a final "fuck you" outcome for the kiddos of angry associates and fiery foes, when parents consistently argue in front of their children, they are implicitly teaching their kids that disagreements should be resolved through battle rather than diplomacy.[28] This not only severely impacts their social skills but makes it more difficult for them to form healthy romantic relationships as they enter adulthood.[11]

It's essential to highlight that a child witnessing two people they love the most fight and bicker with each other is what causes the adjustment issues in children, not the physical structure of the family. The negative effects related to parental conflict are just as true in a traditional nuclear family as they are in a binuclear family. Divorce itself is something children can recover from. It's dealing with their parents' bullshit that really causes long-lasting damage. Consistent with this reasoning, children are generally better off after their parents' divorce if the marriage was full of parental conflict and strife, and the divorce actually helped remove them from this tense situation.[29] *Your job,* as the parent, as the fucking adult, is to shield your child from as much anger and resentment you might have toward your ex as you possibly can. Do not use your child as a fallout shelter for your Chernobyl marriage. That is not their job. This will be rough on you because you must play nice with your ex . . . at least when the kiddos are around. You can't let your children know your real feelings about your ex-spouse's lack of perspective, narcissism, or adulterous lifestyle. Welcome to adulting. Life is hard. And then you die.

Parenting style: 80 percent love and 20 percent trying to poop in peace.

Being a parent is hard, whether you are married or divorced. If someone tells you differently, they are full of shit. Kids are expensive, emotionally and physically exhausting, needy, smell weird, manipulative, demanding, selfish, loud, sticky, infuriating, clingy, lazy, and messy. They are this way from the moment they come into the world until you get the sweet reward of eternal sleep (i.e., death) or until they move to Baltimore with someone named Manticore whose goal in life is to become a YouTube star. It's weird that we love them so much, but we all do. And it's because we love them, and want them to grow up to be happy, functional adults who don't live in our basements, that we parent them. That said, each of us has different styles we use for dealing with our little buttmunches.

Although every parent-child relationship is unique, parents differ on two broad parenting dimensions: warmth and demandingness.[30, 31] Warmth refers to how much attention a parent pays to a child's wants and personality. Parents who are highly warm are supportive, attentive, and available when their child needs support. Demandingness addresses a parent's expectation that a child follows rules and social norms. Demanding parents set clear boundaries and are willing to dole out consequences to a child who crosses the line. By combining these parenting dimensions, we can create four different parenting styles: Darth

Vader, Veruca Salt, Home Alone, and Mary Poppins.[v] Check out the figure and the descriptions of each of these parenting styles to determine which one best matches how you generally interact with your own little snot-suckers. Keep in mind that our descriptions represent the extreme of each style for illustration (and funnies).

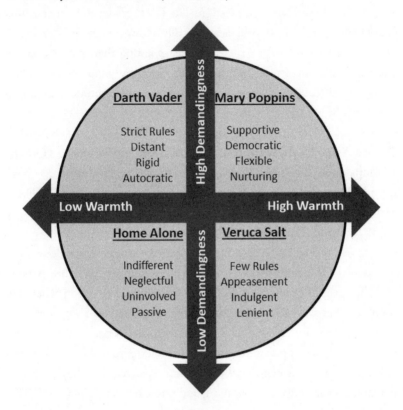

Darth Vader (Low Warmth and High Demandingness). Saying Darth Vader is a harsh parent is like saying "Mommy Dearest," Joan

---

v   Some readers might realize that we altered the names of the parenting styles from authoritarian, authoritative, neglectful and indulgent to these more memorable categories. The science is the same; only the names have been changed. Besides, it just sounds way cooler to say you are a Darth Vader parent instead of an authoritarian parent.

Crawford, had a slight dislike for wire coat hangers. Heck, Vader dismembered his own son simply because Luke Skywalker refused to follow his instructions to join the dark side. People who use the Darth Vader parenting style are extremely controlling and strict. Like the Dark Lord of the Sith, these parents are focused on obedience and expect their rules to be obeyed without question. The Darth Vader drive means that these children tend to do well academically. However, children of Darth Vader parents tend to worry about disappointing their parents, which can take a toll on them psychologically in various ways, including depression, low self-esteem, feelings of rejection, social ineptitude, and diminished independence.[32, 33, 34]

Veruca Salt (High Warmth and Low Demandingness). "Oompa Loompa doom-pa-da-dee-doo, I've got another riddle for you . . . Who do you blame when your kid is a brat? Pampered and spoiled like a Siamese cat. Blaming the kids is a lie and a shame. You know exactly who's to blame. The mother and the father."[35]

Before falling into Willy Wonka's garbage chute, Veruca Salt lived a charmed life where she was treated like a princess, and her parents gave her everything her heart desired. On the rare occasion when she didn't get her way, she would kick, scream, and stomp about until her parents gave in and she got what she wanted. The Veruca Salt parenting style is the exact opposite of the Darth Vader parent. Veruca Salt parents are warm and accepting of their precious angels, but they make few demands, dislike any confrontation, and rarely tell their child "no." This lack of discipline often causes Veruca Salt kids to have lotsa self-esteem but tinged with an unhealthy dose of entitlement that can precipitate rebellion when these children feel they are not being treated like the royalty they *obviously* are. Consequently, these children tend to be sociable but perform poorly in school, have poor impulse control, are prone to delinquent behavior, have questionable peer relationships, and struggle with alcohol-related problems.[36, 37, 38]

Home Alone (Low Warmth and Low Demandingness). In the movie *Home Alone,* eight-year-old Kevin McCallister's parents seem to pay very little attention to their son. Let's be honest: the total and complete failure of Kevin's parents to provide him with even the most basic level of care is the whole narrative of the entire Home Alone series. Seriously, how do you not notice you're missing your son until you're physically on a plane to Paris? From this parental neglect . . . cha-ching—a million-dollar Christmas franchise was somehow born. Like the McCallisters, Home Alone parents expect their children to basically raise themselves. They provide few rules and don't devote much time to addressing the emotional needs of their little ones. They probably provide the basics of food and shelter (although not always), but beyond that, these parents demand very little and give very little in return. This level of laissez-faire parenting sucks for the rugrats. Home Alone kiddos tend to experience similar negative outcomes as those with Veruca Salt parents, except with greater intensity, and they are accompanied by a risk for depression and low self-esteem.[34, 35]

Mary Poppins (High Warmth and High Demandingness). The magical nanny who soars into the Banks' home with the help of her umbrella proves to be both stern and kindhearted while helping raise the Banks children. She may value the importance of following rules, but she does so while being warm and communicative. Parents who use the Mary Poppins style take time to listen to questions from their children and explain reasons for rules. These parents have clear boundaries for their kids and are assertive without being overly restrictive. They balance using punishment while also reinforcing good behavior through praise and rewards. They are warm and engaged in their lovies' lives. Findings across various studies conducted in different countries have found that Mary Poppins children consistently experience some of the best outcomes.[39] Kids who receive this parenting style have clear advantages in the development of reasoning skills, positive peer relationships, academic performance, self-sufficiency, agreeableness, and empathetic behaviors. [33, 40, 41]

Mary Poppins's advice to the Banks children that a "Spoonful of sugar helps the medicine go down" is a perfect example balancing warmth and demandingness. With this advice, Mary Poppins is simultaneously enforcing a rule (the children must have their medicine), while also being responsive to the children's feelings (sugar will help take away the bad taste of medicine). Imagine how different this song and its charming melody would be if it were sung by one of the other parenting styles that don't emphasize the importance of being *both* warm and demanding:

Darth Vader: "The Dark Lord of the Sith commands you to take your medicine now, or else."
Veruca Salt: "Don't worry about the medicine, just have the sugar. Want some Skittles, too?"
Home Alone: "Huh . . . you're sick?"

Your ex's parenting style: Free babysitter or nightmare nanny?
When you were married, you and your ex's parenting style each had an important impact on your kids, and this doesn't change after getting divorced. Take a moment and guess your ex-spouse's parenting style. Are they Darth Vader? Maybe they are more the passive Veruca Salt? Either way, this is a more difficult task than you might think because any negative feelings you have toward your ex will taint your opinion about their parenting style. This is known as the "horn effect." When you dislike a person, you often feel as if they have a pair of horns on their head—like the devil—and this will negatively bias your opinions about everything they do.[42] This bias is why 88 percent of divorcees think their parenting abilities are perfect, but only 42 percent think the same about their former spouses.[43]

Now, if both you and your ex are Home Alone parents, your children are in real danger. In the movie, this danger took its form in a hilarious misadventure of two bumbling thieves trying to break into a house to brutally murder little Kevin in an effort to hide their crimes (again, a Christmas classic). However, in real life, kids who have two Home Alone parents are at even higher risk for low self-esteem, aggressive behavior, and depression.[44] Perhaps most troubling is that these children are 1.5 times more likely to attempt suicide than other children.[45] As you might have already guessed, munchkins who have two Mary Poppins parents are usually going to end up being the most well-adjusted. These kids are less depressed, less aggressive, less antisocial, and have higher self-esteem than any other children.[41]

About 26 percent of divorced parents are Veruca Salts, but this number dramatically increases to 77 percent when the parent does not have physical custody of the child.[41] The reason for this considerable shift is *preeetttty* obvious. When parents have a limited amount of time to spend with their children, they are usually reluctant to set strict limits or rules when they're visiting. They may also feel guilty about the divorce and the fact that they now don't get to see their littles as much as before. They want their time together to be happy, fun, and full of unicorns and cotton candy. Therefore, to avoid any conflicts, these parents employ a Veruca Salt approach by having few rules, being lenient, and indulging their children's various desires. Such as for a pony. While this reaction is understandable, Veruca Salt parenting is not ideal for your children. Although immediately gratifying to be the "fun" parent, you're actually undermining your nuggets' likelihood of developing into a happy, healthy, capable-of-adulting-without-assistance-from-you-or-your-401(k) grown-up.

The problem is you don't have much control over your ex's parenting style. You might ask: What should I do if twat-waffle-pants is Darth Vader, Veruca Salt, or (shocked gasp!) Home Alone? If you have a perfect pal or cooperative colleague relationship with your ex, you could try to convince them of the importance of the Mary Poppins style or discuss the possibility of attending co-parenting therapy. It's possible they're not going to be open to criticism of their parenting from . . . well, you . . . but they may be open to feedback from a professional, and who knows, you may learn some parenting tips in the process, too! Unfortunately, if they are not open to change or going to co-parenting therapy, there is very little you can do. *And*, sorry, unless they're putting your munchkin in real physical or psychological danger, we're not going to suggest you try to get full custody. The good news is that if *at least one* parent is Mary Poppins, children tend to do pretty darn good. It turns out that having such a warm, strong, and consistent parent seems to help negate the issues with any of the other parenting styles.[41] The bottom line is, if your ex is not a Mary Poppins, it is even more important for you to give your child both warmth and structure by taking on this supercalifragilisticexpialidocious style for yourself.

If the Poppins approach doesn't come naturally to you, you'll find that changing your parenting style isn't easy. Heck, you may have already been parenting your children for years using a certain technique, and suddenly acting like the most badass nanny that ever existed might be weird . . . for anyone. Your conversion to Mary Poppins should be gradual. Start by picking strategies in the following table that will work best inside your home and complement how you already approach things. If you're already a Mary Poppins parent—great! There really is no such thing as being too Mary Poppins (that's a level of fabulousness that research has yet to see). So, grab your umbrella and sugar spoon because you got some parenting to do.

All families have ups and downs, and kids will encounter numerous challenges during their lives. Along with puberty, SATs, and limited screen time, divorce is an ordeal faced by many children. However, it isn't some freakish experience that automatically sentences children to a life of sadness. Parents don't need to be married, or even live in the same house, to have well-adjusted and happy children. Children need loving parents who set clear guidelines and who don't constantly argue and troll each other like a YouTube comment section. Dealing with your divorce is certainly not the last challenge your children will encounter, and it's probably not the last time your love life will influence them. About 4.5 million children have stepparents in the United States, which

Mary Poppins Parenting Strategies

Good-Natured Behaviors

↑ Give comfort and understanding when your child is upset.
↑ Express affection by hugging and holding your child.
↑ Show sympathy when your child is hurt or frustrated.
↑ Be aware of problems your child has in school.
↑ Be responsive to your child's feelings and needs.
↑ Encourage your child to talk about their problems.
↑ Apologize when you make a parenting mistake.
↑ Be patient.
↑ Play with your child.

Positive Discipline Behaviors

↑ Give praise when your child does something good.
↑ Explain the reasons for the consequences of your child's negative behavior.
↑ Explain the reasons why rules should be obeyed.
↑ Calmly talk to your child when they misbehave.
↑ Make your expectations and rules clear to your child.
↑ Whenever possible, channel your child's misbehavior into a more acceptable activity.

Democratic Behaviors

↑ Be inclusive when making family plans.
↑ Allow your child to give some input into family rules.
↑ Consider your child's desires before asking them to do something.
↑ Encourage your child to express their opinions, even if they disagree with your own.

almost always introduces unique and exciting challenges.[46] We will get to the joys of incorporating a new partner into your kids' lives later in the book, but before we worry about how the new love of your life will impact your little crotch droppings . . . you have to find one.

Chapter 5

Swipe right ... no, left ... no, right: How to get back into the dating game

It may take weeks, it may take years, but at some point you're going to decide to get back out there. And by "out there," we mean out in the terrifying wilderness of dating (beware of Sasquatch: he only drinks dry-roasted, cold brew coffee, and sports a man-bun)! The average length of a doomed marriage is eight years, and you likely dated your ex-spouse for roughly two years before waltzing down the aisle.[1] This means that it's probably been a while since you had a first date, a first kiss, or a first nerve-wracking naked moment in front of someone new. During the time that you were off the market, a lot has changed in terms of how we meet other singles: Match.com, eHarmony.com, speed-dating, and, yes, even Tinder. How do you choose where to search for your new future-shnuggums, and what type of partner should you look for in the veritable smorgasbord of people that you'll find out there? We promise—there are more options than you probably think.

Red light, green light: Deciding whether you're ready to get back out there.

Get your number two pencil ready because it's test time. Don't worry about whether you know the right answers to this quiz—because there are no right answers. These are just questions about how you've felt during the past week. Ready? Set? Go!

> **Below is a list of ways you might have felt or behaved.**
> **Please tell us how often you felt this way during the past week**
> **by writing the number (0 to 3) next to each item.**

Rarely or never (Less than 1 day) 0	Sometimes (1–2 days) 1	Occasionally (3–4 days) 2	Most of the time (5–7 days) 3

1. ____ I was bothered by things that don't normally bother me.
2. ____ I did not feel like eating; my appetite was poor.
3. ____ I felt that I could not shake off the blues even with help from my family or friends.
4. ____ I felt I was not as good as other people.
5. ____ I had trouble keeping my mind on what I was doing.
6. ____ I felt depressed.
7. ____ I felt that everything I did was an effort.
8. ____ I did not feel hopeful about the future.
9. ____ I thought my life had been a failure.
10. ____ I felt fearful.
11. ____ My sleep was restless.
12. ____ I was not happy.
13. ____ I talked less than usual.
14. ____ I felt lonely.
15. ____ People were unfriendly.
16. ____ I did not enjoy life.
17. ____ I had crying spells.
18. ____ I felt sad.
19. ____ I felt that people disliked me.
20. ____ I could not get "going."

Now, add up your total score on the test. Think of your score as a traffic light that you encounter before merging onto the superhighway of dating. It's your starting point to help you decide if you should be revving your engines, idling for a bit, or just putting it in park. If you got over 16, you are at a "red light." If you're between 8 and 15, you are starting at a "yellow light." And under 8, you have a "green light."

Red Light. If you are at a red light, you are still pretty upset about your divorce and you're probably not ready to start dating. Let's be honest—if you go out on a date, you are going to be tempted to talk about your crazy ex during the entire dinner, cry, and/or make some bad life choices. It's likely to turn into a warped, regret-ridden "choose your own adventure" situation. You should probably respect this red light and just STOP right here. Go back to Chapters 1 and 2 and put some more work into getting yourself back together. Give it a little more time. Don't worry; relationship experts suggest that the average person stay single for at least a couple of months after a dating relationship ends before getting out there again, so a marriage will likely take even longer to move on from.[2] There are plenty of people out there, and plenty of time to meet them. Don't rush it. Re-evaluate yourself in a few weeks, or even months, and before you know it, you'll be ready to move forward with a new romantic interest (or at least get laid without tearfully regretting it in the morning).

Yellow Light. You no longer spend your Fridays drinking an entire bottle of wine on the sofa while simultaneously watching bad romantic comedies and sticking pins into a voodoo doll of your ex. Yay for you! You are probably ready to at least dip your toes into the pee-filled kiddie pool of dating. People date for all kinds of reasons: to have fun, to "practice," to feel like a sexy beast again, to have sex with a beast again, to find love, or to get a free dinner. For now, until you are at the green light, we suggest you don't worry so much about the finding love part. Chances are you're still licking some wounds from your divorce, or at least dealing with some moderate scarring. If love happens when you're in this stage, that's awesome! Go for it! Just be cautious about not making finding your next soul mate your primary life goal. Eventually, you will find yourself heading toward a long-term relationship, but for now, wait until you're sure you're ready. However, that doesn't mean you can't go out, meet new people, have fun, and collect some funny stories along the way.

Green Light. If you are looking at a green light, you likely have already been through the red and yellow light stages. You've probably already spent some time meeting new people, either in person or through online dating; and if not, you were fantasizing about leaving your ex years ago and are all rarin' to go. If you're in this stage, you're ready to start seriously thinking about the future Mister or Missus You. Again, don't rush it! You want to make sure that the next person you choose to blend your life with is truly compatible with your lifestyle and doesn't have any of your ex's qualities that drove you nuts (well, if we are being realistic, has only some of the qualities that drove you nuts). Take your time and guard your heart, but you're ready to get back out there.

Okay, so that's the breakdown. If you're at a red light . . . freeze, buster! Not to be harsh, but you're a hot mess and it's not as sexy as you think. No one wants to be your rebound who wipes your nose while you blubber about how you've been done wrong. Sort your shit out, work on *you* by practicing the tips in the first few chapters, give yourself more time to heal, and then re-evaluate in a little while. If you're at a yellow light . . . proceed with caution and don't take things too seriously. Think of dating as sharpening your relationship skills (let's face it, it's been a while and you're rusty) so that when the right person does come along, you'll be ready. If you're at a green light . . . what the fuck are you waiting for? You're not getting younger or prettier, so get back out there. We have faith in you!

If you disagree with your score . . . do whatever the hell you want. Who are we (besides PhD-wielding experts) to tell you what to do? We're not your mom. Just don't say we didn't warn you.

Everybody has somebody, so where can I meet anybody?

That hot guy at work . . . married. That sexy woman who just jogged by . . . married. Even the chubby, sweaty guy with food in his teeth that's doing your taxes . . . married. Dating post-divorce is a little trickier than it was pre-divorce simply because most of the people you find sexy are likely married to other people (and don't even think about playing hide the pickle with that attractive married neighbor). This is one of the primary reasons many people turn to technology and online dating to find a new partner after their divorce. Seriously, online dating is basically made for divorcees. Where else could you look at hundreds of men or women in a matter of minutes, while wearing your fuzzy pajamas and consuming a pint of Ben and Jerry's Chocolate Chip Cookie Dough after your kids are (finally) passed out upstairs? No wonder research has consistently found that people who are middle-aged, broken up, work long hours, and are single parents are most likely to turn to online dating to find a new love.[3,4,5,6] Online, you can be the best, sexiest, most interesting version of yourself without ever leaving the house, and still find yourself exposed to a plethora of other sexy, interesting, *available* people. And contrary to what your mother and Lifetime Original Movies tell you, *almost* none of them are serial killers.

You may hold out in the hopes of meeting a new love in a more "traditional" way, and that's fine, you totally might; but chances are you will end up online at some point. There's also a good chance that you've never tried online dating before. You might even have some misconceptions about what it means to find your next mate on the computer. In the 1990s, most people thought online dating was for people who were desperate, people who owned several Star Trek uniforms, or those who played Dungeons and Dragons—in other words, lonely *nerds!* However, as time has progressed (and our love of all things nerdy has become more mainstream), this attitude has dramatically shifted. Today, the vast majority (over 75 percent) of adults no longer view online dating as a sign of desperation. In fact, about 50 percent of divorced people believe online dating is a good way to meet new people, is efficient, allows people to get to know each other, and is simply easier than other means of dating (like being set up with your coworker's brother's friend and hoping for the best).[7] This is why, in the past thirty years, online dating has increased nearly 400 percent and is now the most popular way people find and meet new romantic partners.[8] So, saddle up cowboy (or cowgirl)—you are about to join this trend.

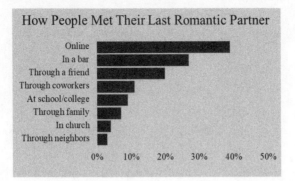

How People Met Their Last Romantic Partner

Tinder, and Match, and eHarmony—Oh my!

Before online dating existed, if you wanted to find a romantic partner, you had to wait until the weekend and then head on out into the scary real world. This would involve quite a bit of time and effort on your part to look presentable (or at least be wearing a clean shirt), and you had to engage potential lovers with your charming personality in real time (or at least not send them running away, screaming). What exactly you were looking for, relationship-wise, influenced what you would do. If you were looking for love, maybe you would ask your friends to set you up or hang out at the local coffee shop instead of that seedy dive bar down the street; although, that dive bar could be a good option if you were looking for a one-night stand. Just like in the real world, the virtual world offers different types of hangout spots that foster all types of relationships. For example, the ultra-popular eHarmony is most appealing to those seeking long-term relationships, whereas places like Tinder often attract those who are looking for more casual entanglements.[9]

Check out the table above and figure out which site seems to suit your interest, needs, and budget the best. Keep in mind that all the web-pages above have free trial versions that are worth checking out. Some of these free trials are extremely robust and you can easily start dating without having to whip out your credit card right away. For example, Tinder's free service allows a limited number of times you can swipe right in a twelve-hour period, and even sites like OKCupid allow access to most of its features for free (although your profile may get a slight

Relationship		Cost	Basic Operating Instructions
Casual	Tinder	$	Upload a couple of pictures and a few sentences describing yourself, and you're all set to start "swiping" through pictures of potential dates. Simply swipe right on your phone if you "like" and swipe left if you "dislike" a person's photo (we know, it sounds cruel . . . but it is efficient). If your potential date also swipes right on your photo, you can message each other. Don't worry—your ego is somewhat protected because you're never told when someone has swiped left on you. As an added bonus, Tinder uses GPS so you can find people that are really close to you. That means next time you have a layover in an airport, you can have a quick date with someone at TGI Fridays in Terminal G. Not that we have any experience with that or anything.
Varied	Bumble	$	Same basic idea as Tinder, but here only women can message first. Great for women who are tired of getting unsolicited "dick pics" from guys . . . bad for guys who want to send said unsolicited "dick pics."
Varied	OKCupid	$$	You submit a short bio and some pictures before you are given the chance to answer hundreds of questions ranging from "How do you feel about falling in love?" all the way to "While in the middle of the best lovemaking of your life, if your lover asked you to squeal like a dolphin, would you?" You can then filter potential partners by selecting people in terms of how they answered these questions. The trial service allows more access than most dating sites, so this leads to a huge user base with an almost wild-west type feel. Yeehaw!
Varied	OurTime. com	$$	Essentially an OKCupid type of site that caters specifically to people over the age of fifty. The same sorts of rules and dating approaches as the other sites apply here, too, but if you're over the age of fifty and not interested in dating anyone in their twenties (or competing with anyone in their twenties), this is the place for you.

| Varied | Match.com | $$$ | One of the original online dating services. Similar to OKCupid, but with a more mature and serious platform. You can narrow down potential mates based on their answers to personality, interest, and background questions. Then, just like window shopping, you browse all these profiles and send messages to anyone who floats your boat. |
| Serious | eHarmony | $$$ | Because of its cost, eHarmony tends to attract people who are the most serious about finding a long-term relationship. You first complete their *Relationship Questionnaire*, which measures "29 dimensions of compatibility" (e.g., humor, character, ambition, intellect, etc.). They then use a fancy-pants algorithm that they claim matches you only to people you are likely to be compatible with. Less window shopping and more targeted advertising is the idea. Each day you are provided with a batch of matches that you can review. On eHarmony, connecting with someone can be done the old-fashion way (by just sending them a message) or by using something they call *Guided Communication*. This interesting method is perfect for the shy among us or those who are nervous about how to initiate contact, because it allows people to communicate with each other by asking questions written by eHarmony before actually talking directly with each other. |

boost in visibility with a paid membership). Once you find a site you like, you can save a ton of money by paying for several months in advance. As of this writing, eHarmony will cost you $227 for one year, reducing your monthly cost from $59.95 to $18.95. We get it, signing a year contract with an online dating site does sound a little . . . well . . . shitty and pessimistic, but, be honest, do you really think you are going to find love in just one month? Besides, you're no stranger to upfront commitment—you were married before, remember? One final issue to keep in mind about online dating sites: because the interwebs are constantly evolving (for example, only us old folks use Facebook anymore, and what the hell is a SnapChat?[i]), the dating landscape is also always changing. New dating sites are consistently replacing old ones, so make sure to do some Googling to discover the new ways people are meeting online.

One thing to note is that some websites (cough, cough, eHarmony) claim that their matching algorithms or systems are the awesomesauce, alleging that they are more likely to find you a partner than some other online dating service. This makes for great advertising. It may or may not be bullshit. The issue here is that these sites are not open source, meaning that no one *really* knows what their matching algorithms actually do and that there isn't any peer-reviewed, scientific research to suggest that their computer systems can really match you any better than you can match yourself.[10] We're not saying don't use websites that boast this sort of technology; they can still be fantastic ways to meet people you wouldn't have met otherwise; just don't be discouraged if they don't drop your soul mate into your lap on the first try.

Marketing 101: How to sell you.

Brothers Cleo and Noah McVicker couldn't believe their luck when, in 1933, the Kroger grocery store ordered 15,000 cases of their putty wallpaper cleaner. Wallpaper cleaner was extremely important because the coal furnaces popular at this time often left a layer of soot on walls that was difficult to clean (mmmm, tasty). However, as time went on, and coal heat was replaced by oil and gas, sales of their product quickly dropped. No one wanted the now-obsolete putty cleaner, and things were starting to look bad until the company realized that nursery schoolteachers had started using their wallpaper cleaner as a modeling compound. In 1957, after removing the detergent from the putty and adding in some color and a pleasant smell, the company had a new product which children

---

i   We realize that even this joke will soon be outdated as, eventually, younger people will abandon SnapChat when their parents start to use it. This will make Snapchat something only older people use while younger people adopt some new, as of yet un-invented technology that us older folks will immediately find morally questionable (well, until we start using it, too).

could use to mold all types of objects. Advertisements soon began appearing on influential children's programs showing children how much fun they could have with this putty. As a result of this rebranding and marketing, more than 700 million pounds of this product have since been sold, and everyone around the world now knows the joys of playing with Play-Doh.

In case you haven't guessed it yet—you are the Play-Doh. You previously had a different purpose as a spouse, and now you are trying to rebrand yourself as a spicy singleton. Just like Play-Doh, you need to figure out a way to advertise your awesomeness to make sure that you will rediscover the joys of someone wanting to play with you. In many ways, the dating market is disturbingly similar to any sales market, with the exception that the product (you) is also choosing the consumer (your future love). Because of this similarity, some economists have turned to market research in order to best understand what characteristics "sell" the best. We are not suggesting you should lie when you advertise yourself. Let's face it, no one is going to believe that forty-year-old you is really twenty-five. But it doesn't hurt to use a little science to understand which of your qualities you should put on display and which ones you should probably wait to share until later in the relationship. With that in mind, boot up your computer, turn on your digital camera, and get ready to sell . . . you!

The sales pitch.

Almost every online dating service works the same basic way—you upload a picture or two of yourself and complete a profile. You use this profile to sell yourself as a potential lover by briefly telling people about your personality, your background, your interests, and what type of relationship you are seeking. A profile is like a can of soup. Soup companies put great care in selecting the perfect images and text for their cans to encourage you to buy their products. In the grocery store of online dating, there are a lot of soup cans, so you need to make sure your packaging stands out. You want to emphasize the positive qualities of your product (filling and delicious!) and maybe downplay some of the negative ones (high fat and full of artificial preservatives!), at least for now. It is important that you don't write outright lies on your dating profile. After all, your goal is to get someone to eventually pick your product off the shelf, open it up, and maybe try what you have to offer. You don't want to mislead them into thinking they are about to enjoy a delicious gourmet flourless chocolate cake when you are really just a Ho-Ho (pun intended). Although most people engage in some strategic self-presentation when making their packaging, the vast majority of misleading information is pretty minor and tends to be about height (people typically add about 1 inch to their actual height) and weight (on average, women subtract about 15 pounds from their actual weight).[11, 12] Neither of your authors is actually six-foot-one, and nobody here has been 120 pounds since college. The question then becomes what characteristics should you advertise front and center on your can of soup and which ones get relegated to the small print.[ii, iii]

Dating goals. If you are a guy and you're seeking a short-term relationship or casual sex, be ready to get about 40 percent fewer responses from women than if you are looking for a long-term relationship. Again, we cannot stress this enough: be honest about what you're looking for. You can deal with fewer options better than you can deal with a person who won't stop texting you because she thought you were interested in a serious long-term relationship when you were really just looking for a casual fling. Trust us, we know. Women's dating goals don't matter too

---

ii   A caveat emptor: *all* of the research we're talking about here is based on heterosexual daters. It's a serious flaw in the field of attraction research. If you don't identify as heterosexual, it's still possible that these ideas apply to you; scientists don't have any reason to suspect that the basic principles of attraction are all that different based on sexual orientation. Just be aware of what populations studied gave rise to these claims.

iii   Also, many (okay, most) of these findings read as supersexist. We know. We think it sucks, too, but we are just the messengers. We are simply telling you what researchers have found, so please don't shoot us!

much—women seeking long-term relationships, short-term hook-ups, and pen pals, or those wanting to find swinging couples all receive about the same number of responses from men.[13]

Income. Income is strongly related to the number of responses men receive. If a man makes more than $250,000 a year, his odds of getting contacted increase 151 percent; even making slightly above $50,000 increases his contacts 34 percent compared to those making below this figure. For women, income has almost no effect on the number of contacts they receive.[13]

Education. Like income, the more educated a man is, the more contacts he receives. Also, like income, a women's education has minimal impact on how many men contact her.[13]

Occupation. The jobs that get men the most contacts are (in order): lawyer, firefighter (mmm, yummy!), member of the military, and doctor. For women, you guessed it: her job does not seem to relate to how many men contact her.[13]

Height. Height matters, but it matters differently for men and women. Taller men (six-foot-three is the ideal) and smaller women (five-foot-five is best) get the most responses.[13]

Weight. Body Mass Index (BMI), which is a height-adjusted measurement of weight, is also related to who gets contacted the most (BMI = Weight in Kilograms/Height in Meters^2 × 703; you can also find BMI calculators online). For men, a BMI of 27 is the most popular (this corresponds to a person who is six-foot-three and weighing approximately 215 pounds). For women, the most popular BMI is 17 (this corresponds to a person who is five-foot-five and weighing approximately 105 pounds).[13] Keep in mind that BMIs under 18.5 are considered underweight and are associated with nutritional deficiencies, compromised immune functioning, and respiratory problems. A BMI of 17 is *not* something to strive for. Basically, on this one, men are shallow butt-munches. But, on the flip side, BMIs over 25 are considered overweight. A major drawback of this measurement approach is that it doesn't take muscle mass into account. We're willing to bet that men with higher BMIs are considered more attractive when they're sporting big guns and not big beer bellies.

Hair. In general, men with shorter hair and women with longer hair tend to be the most popular. Also, redheaded men and women with salt-and-pepper-colored hair might consider a change as they tend to be the least popular hair hues.[13] In the online dating world, blondes (at least for women) definitely have the most fun and get the most responses.

Age. Both men and women care about the age of prospective lovers, but the direction of this preference varies. On average, men are more interested in women who are slightly younger than themselves,[14] but report that they would be willing to date women who range from roughly a decade younger up to a whole, whopping five years older than they are. Interestingly, the older a dude is, the more tolerant he is of even younger partners, while his willingness to date older partners remains constant at around a five-year age gap.

Now, before you start thinking men are total ageist turd-monkeys, women show a similar pattern, just in reverse. On average, women are more interested in partners who are slightly older than they are but report being willing to date men who are anywhere from five years younger than they are to about nine years older. And, as women get older, they, like the gentlemen, are more willing to consider partners who are increasingly younger than they are, while their preference for older partners stays the same. We feel like Betty White would be proud.[15]

Personality. Men and women are both more likely to contact people who use words that make them sound extroverted, dependable, and trustworthy in their dating profiles. For men, it is also important to have a sense of humor.[16] Lucky for you, researchers have done the hard work of identifying which words people associate with these characteristics.[17] If you have any of these qualities, make sure to pepper these adjectives throughout your dating profile so you can draw attention to your fabulous personality and increase your marketability. If you don't see something you like here, pick up a thesaurus . . . we're all old enough here that we remember a time (ever so vaguely) before Google and we know how to use one of those.

	Extroverted	Dependable	Trustworthy	Humorous
Words to use	Talkative	Practical	Kind	Funny
	Energetic	Neat	Cooperative	Hilarious
	Bold	Efficient	Sympathetic	Playful
	Sociable	Careful	Warm	Comical
	Assured	Conscientious	Considerate	Witty
		Prompt	Agreeable	Silly
Words to avoid	Shy	Careless	Harsh	Boring
	Quiet	Haphazard	Demanding	Serious
	Withdrawn	Sloppy	Rude	Unfunny
	Timid	Disorganized	Selfish	Stuffy
	Bashful	Forgetful	Unkind	Humorless

Smile and say, "Please date me?"

Beyond merely describing yourself, you also will be given the option to upload a profile picture online. Sorry. Few people are excited about this, but everyone must do it. Men who have pictures of themselves get 60 percent more contacts, and women with pictures get over twice as many contacts compared to those who avoid uploading a digital portrait.[18] In short, there is nothing you can do to increase the chances someone will contact you more than simply uploading a snapshot—ideally of your smiling face and not your junk.

You should be highly motivated to make it the best-looking picture possible. Research (and common sense) shows that both men and women are much more likely to try to contact people who post attractive photos.[18] Now don't get too judgmental—you're no different on this one. Since the mid-1960s, psychologists have known that the best predictor of romantic interest in someone is how physically attractive they are.[18] The good news is that there is a high likelihood the potential matches you think are hotties will contact you back. After making first contact, men have a 35 percent chance of getting a response, and women have a 60 percent chance of hearing back. Heck, even people in the bottom quartile of attractiveness (research can be cruel at times) have a 20 percent chance of getting a response back from those in the top quartile of attractiveness! You need to look as good as you can, but even if you aren't Brad Pitt or Heidi Klum, you've still got a chance at a supermodel.

Pucker up, baby! Your beautiful face is now going to be evaluated by hundreds of potential suitors. You might argue at this point that beauty is in the eye of the beholder. But you'd be wrong . . . well, mostly wrong. As it turns out, there's a lot of variability across people in terms of whether they are attracted to things like piercings, tattoos, or makeup. However, both men and women generally agree on what makes up the basic aspects of a hottie-patottie's face.

Symmetry is the key word here—facial symmetry. Check out the two pictures below of good ol' Honest Abe.

If you were to draw a line straight down the middle of each picture of Abe from forehead to chin, the two halves of Sexy Symmetrical

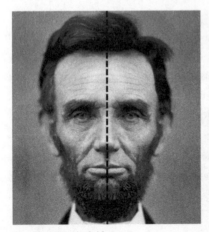 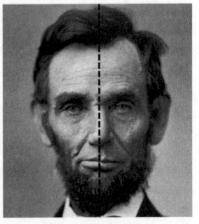

Sexy Symmetrical Abe   Frumpy Asymmetrical Abe

Abe's face are more similar than the two halves of Frumpy Asymmetrical Abe's mug. We made poor Abe more symmetrical through some basic Photoshop trickery, and most people would find this picture better looking than the picture on the right. Why we are attracted to symmetrical faces is somewhat unclear, but evolutionary psychologists have suggested the greater symmetry indicates better DNA—in other words, less mutated genes.[19] Don't panic if you aren't the most symmetrical person out there. Computer scientists at Stanford were kind enough to analyze millions of uploaded selfies to figure out the best tricks you can use to improve your overall look and make it less likely people will notice that massive asymmetrical schnoz you're working with.[20]

The Science of a Perfect Selfie

Position: Your face should take up about 30 percent of the image, centered, and at the top.

Forehead: Cutting off the top of your forehead tends to be seen as more attractive, especially with pictures of women.

Oversaturate Your Face: Using over-saturated lighting makes your skin look more uniform. Low lighting should be avoided at all costs.

Filters: Black and white filters or filters that soften the image result in more attractive photographs.

Borders: Putting a white "frame" around your smiling face will help you get more responses.

Only You: Taking pictures with your friends might be fun, but selfies of people who are alone are more popular. People don't want to play a game of I-spy and guess which person in the photo is you.

Beyond symmetry, we care about features that suggest youth combined with sexual maturity.[21] For youth, one of the key factors is making your eyes look as large as possible in your photo. For sexual maturity, you ladies should make your lips as full and kissable-looking as you possibly can. Bust out the lip liner if you must, but Google some makeup tips first to avoid looking like Pennywise from Stephen King's *IT*. For men, you should emphasize that cut jawline and strong chin you're working with.[22] Pro tip: if you have a weaker jawline/chin situation as a dude, facial hair can work wonders at giving you a more rugged appearance. We also care about other features that indicate physical health, like clear skin and good dental hygiene. So, invest in some Proactiv and brush your damn teeth.

It's worth noting that men and women differ in how much they care about this stuff. On average, men care about facial attractiveness in their partners more than women, so these tips are probably especially relevant for you ladies.[23] That said, it's not like women are completely uninterested in what their partners look like, so fellas, there's no free pass.

There you go—getting noticed on Match.com or Tinder is simple. If you are a woman, you just need to be outgoing, five-foot-five, with Angelina Jolie's lips, weigh as much as a twelve-year-old, and have long blond hair. Guys, you need to be six-foot-three, funny, with a well-defined jaw and short hair, and an income like Bill Gates. Easy, right? Of course, no one meets all (or even most) of these criteria. Not even our sexy selves (shocking, we know). The point here isn't to depress you, but to show you the market research for online dating so you can best understand what characteristics of yourself to promote. Once you meet up with the people who express interest in you (provided you are also interested in them), a lot of this appearance-based stuff falls away in favor of things like a stellar personality. But the trick is, you have to get people initially interested. If you're a woman with blonde hair and symmetrical features, emphasize those elements over your six-foot-two height. If you are a guy who is five-foot-four, but saves lives as an ER doctor, talk about your job. You want to sell yourself, not by being deceptive, but by playing up the qualities that are going to encourage people to swipe right. This self-marketing will help increase the number of potential mates that *you* then get to pick from. Because really, at the end of the day, isn't that why you're here?

Life is like a box of chocolates . . .

Okay, so you've posted your profile, and the potential matches are rolling in. Depending on your website of choice, you may be getting ten to fifty new people thrown at you on the daily. This sounds awesome, right?

Mr./Ms. Right, or even Right-Now, is bound to be in there somewhere. But, to quote everyone's favorite Tom Hanks character, "Life is like a box of chocolates; you never know what you're gonna get." In the world of online dating, this couldn't be more accurate.

Chocolate is awesome. We're going to go out on a limb here and say that chocolate, especially really good quality chocolate, could possibly compete with some orgasms. So, imagine this: The salesperson at your favorite candy store asks if you would like to try a sample of Godiva chocolate (and saying "yes" *is* the only correct response). What would you rather do—pick a single piece from a box containing six different flavors or from a box with thirty different flavors? Most people report that they would rather have more options and prefer picking from the thirty-piece candy box. However, when this exact situation was presented in a research laboratory, people found it about 38 percent more frustrating and difficult to decide on which chocolate they wanted when they were given the choice of selecting a piece of candy from the larger versus smaller box.[24] We get overwhelmed when we have too many options to pick from. After we make our decision, we start to wonder if any of the other delicious-looking chocolates would have been better. Maybe that one with the raspberry would have been tastier. Or that one with the caramel, or the mint, or the salty, salty nuts. Argh!

In many ways, online dating is like the box of thirty chocolates . . . but instead of thirty delicious candy options, you have hundreds, if not thousands, of potentially delicious mates to select from. And, just like with the chocolates, as our number of potential online choices increase, we start to overthink our choices and make mistakes.[25] We forget if profile 231 was a lumberjack poet or an English teacher with a motorcycle. When there are a lot of choices, we tend to select potential mates based on easily observable qualities (like appearance) and not those qualities that require a little more effort to learn about but are better predictors of relationship success in the long run (like personality). This is why, when browsing many profiles at a time, we are more likely to end up choosing people who are not at all similar to what we say we are looking for in a partner.[26] Before you turned on your computer, you might have been looking for a person in their thirties with a good job and a witty disposition, but after looking through hundreds of profiles, you quickly find yourself overwhelmed and ultimately strike up a conversation with a twenty-two-year-old who is unemployed, quotes Nietzsche like an angsty teenager, and fancies himself (or herself) the next great misunderstood philosopher.

Some dating websites help this situation by limiting the number of choices they show you. Earlier, we mentioned that eHarmony purports to employ an undisclosed algorithm that matches you only to (and thus only lets you choose from) people with whom you are likely to be compatible. Although the benefit of their exact matching algorithm is questionable, this does mean that instead of fifty-plus new matches per day like you get on some sites, you may only get ten. Other dating websites offer similar services to narrow down your choices, but still . . . ten matches times seven days in a week . . . this is still a pretty damn big box of chocolates.

What's a guy or gal to do? The answer is that you have to become a pro at knowing what you're looking for so that out of the potential lovers who swiped right for you, you only spend your precious and limited free time interacting with ones who have real potential. Not Nietzsche guy. No one likes that guy. So what do you look for? Say it with us now— Looks, Location, Personality.

Looks. You are a shallow, appearance-driven goat. But it's all right, pretty much everyone else is a goat, too. Most people rate physical attractiveness as one of the key things they look for in a partner. As we warned you earlier, men are a bit shallower in this domain than women, but no one is immune.[27] Since everyone is more or less in this boat, there's no harm in judging a potential date's physical looks. After all, what distinguishes a romantic relationship from a good friendship is primarily the desire to do sexy-naked things with that person that would embarrass your mother. Just be aware that what you see in their profile picture is likely to be the most glamorous version of themselves.

What's interesting here is that there's a similarity effect when it comes to looks. On a scale of hotness from 1 (Jabba the Hutt) to 10 (Princess Leia in her gold bikini), let's say you're a 7. Maybe an 8.5 on an exceptionally well-groomed evening. You are more likely to end up in a relationship with someone who is also in that ballpark.[27] This is known as assortative mating. Let's just say relationships research has put the "ASS" in *ass*ortative mating. Cheesy, terrible pun—we know, but we couldn't resist. The idea is that we all think that super-hot people are . . . well, super-hot. But, we also have an understanding of how attractive we are in comparison to the people around us. Think about it—you have a sense of whether you're a 4 or a 9 based on both the mirror and your past romantic entanglements. Because of this understanding, we tend to pursue partners who are similar to us and thus likely to be interested (rather than cruelly laugh) when we ask them out on a second date.

Location. In the fall of 1960, a group of researchers began a survey of students living in a brand-new male dormitory on the University of Chicago's campus. The new Pierce Hall housed 320 students and offered a novel opportunity to investigate how people formed new friendships. At the end of the fall term, the researchers discovered that how much the residents liked each other was primarily predicted by living proximity.[28] If a person lived on the first floor, they liked other people on the first floor more than people on the fourth, et cetera and so forth. People were also more likely to report that their friends, and even best friends, in college were shacked up in close proximity to them.

Smelly college residence halls can tell us a lot about dating. It turns out, the principle of physical proximity applies to romantic attraction just like it did to the friendships created in that university dormitory more than fifty years ago. You are more likely to form a romantic relationship with someone who lives near you. Some of this is psychological: you tend to have more in common with someone who lives close by. You may come from similar backgrounds, both appreciate the same local traditions (woo, cheesesteak!!), or both laugh at jokes that are common in your region. A dear friend of ours used to visit Italy for months at a time on vacation but never availed herself of, shall we say, the locally made sausage. When we asked her why, she said that she didn't understand any of the jokes Italian men made, and they didn't seem to understand hers. One of the things she was looking for in a partner was someone who could make her laugh. It just wasn't going to work out. The distance between them was too great.

Some of the power of the proximity effect is purely practical. It's less of a hassle to date someone who lives ten minutes from you than someone who lives an hour away. Think of the gas money you'll save! When your two authors were each on the singles meat market, neither of us were willing to date people who required more than a half-hour drive or required us to pay tolls to get there. It was a deal-breaker for us both. The ironic thing is that after we first started dating, we realized that we lived over an hour away from each other. Oops. However, because we worked together, we still had a lot of proximity time during the workweek.

This leads us to the other environmental factor predicting attraction—frequency of interaction. We met at work, meaning that we saw each other almost every day. This was good news for us because humans tend to like things more the more that we encounter them. This is true of everything from novel images, to food, to people. It's called the *mere-exposure effect*.[29]

When it comes to evaluating potential lovers online, both factors mean that you should probably opt to strike up a conversation, or swipe right on people, who live within a fairly small geographic range, focusing on those closest to you first. It's far easier to get together, meaning you'll see each other more, and that, dear friends, can only be good for your sexy self.

Personality. Ever heard the idiom "Opposites attract"? This little bit of folk wisdom about what makes for a successful romantic pairing is extremely common—and mostly wrong. Yes, yes, we all know that one couple where each partner couldn't be more different from the other and yet they are as happy as a basket of bunnies. But, on average, dating research as far back as the 1960s tells us that similarity, or *not* being opposite, is second only to physical attractiveness when it comes to predicting who you want to snuggle up to.[30] This means that, as you evaluate potential dating partners, you want someone who is more similar to you than not. When it comes to online dating, you'll get more information about your dreamboat's personality from websites like OKCupid or eHarmony than from Tinder. With Tinder (or a blind date arranged by your sister's boyfriend's aunt) you'll have to wait to make your personality judgments in person (check out the next chapter for advice on this front).

At this point, you might be wondering what types of similarity matter (or at least you should be . . . come on, work with us here). After all, it's one thing to have one partner love pad Thai and the other hate all forms of Asian food; it's quite another to argue about whether you should save for retirement or purchase several Maseratis. Or is it? As it turns out, similarity of all kinds predicts romantic attraction. People are more attracted to others who share their demographic or background characteristics. People are also more attracted to others who share their political values, religious beliefs, morals, personality traits, goals for the future, hobbies, and even speech patterns.[31, 32] So . . . we basically love everything that is just like us. Like the Greek myth of Narcissus, we want to hook up with ourselves.

One notable exception to this rather self-involved pattern is the personality trait of dominance. Social dominance is—you guessed it—how dominant and take-charge a person tends to be in their social interactions. When you're out with your friends, who does most of the talking? Who picks the restaurant when you go out to eat? Who wants to be the center of attention? Who interrupts when others are talking? If the answer to these questions comes up as "you," chances are you are a fairly dominant person. This isn't a good thing or a bad thing; it's just *a* thing about who you are. When it comes to romantic attraction, more dominant people tend to have more successful relationships with more submissive people, and vice versa.[33] Now, we're not talking some *50 Shades of Grey* shenanigans here (although we *will* talk about that in Chapter 7); we're talking more about simple coordination of social activities and daily interactions. If both you and your partner are dominant, and thus both of you insist on picking the movie you are going to watch . . . that would suck. You'd probably spend more time arguing about what to see than actually watching anything. Similarly, if you and your partner are both submissive, and both of you want to defer to the other's movie choice, you'd likely spend most of your night saying, "I don't care, what do you want to watch?" in a herp-derpy voice and not actually get around to watching anything. That would also suck.

The take-home here is that you should look for somebody who is like you in pretty much all ways; but who, when it comes to that good old take-charge attitude, is the peanut butter to your proverbial jelly. Doing so can help to fan any early sparks you feel into a fragile fledgling flame. That said, early sparks on paper will only get you so far. After you've identified a handful of profiles that look promising, it's time to start getting to know the real live humans behind those profiles. Even the most enticing person on paper can turn out to be a total fucking dud in real life. It's easy to come off as fascinating when you have the time (and sound advice from us) to craft the perfect Internet version of yourself; it's far harder to pull that off in person. This means you need to start interacting with these potential objects of affection. Not to fret my friends, we've got you covered. Surviving that first contact is not only possible; we're here to help you make it probable.

Chapter 6

The audition: Surviving the awkwardness of first dates ... again

If you've gotten to this point in our fabulous-tastic book, chances are you've encountered at least one attractive (and, hopefully, sane) person whom you'd be interested in getting to know better. Maybe you've mastered the art of swiping right on Tinder, met someone in a bar, were introduced to your friend's cousin's cute brother, or found a hottie in the frozen foods section of your local supermarket. No matter how you were first clued into the existence of the potential object of your affection, it's now time to get up close and personal. The chemistry between two people in real interactions is way more important when it comes to predicting lasting lovey bliss than the first impressions formed from a brief encounter next to the frozen carrots or from reading an online dating profile.[1] So, it's time to get comfortable with a four-letter verb that you're about to engage in again ... and again. No, not *that* word, although hopefully you will be doing that, too—we mean get out there and *date*.

Have you ever had that dream where you were auditioning for a high school play, and when you stood in front of the whole school, you realized you were completely naked? Yeah, dating is kind of like that—with the exception that your naked body now is likely not as glamorous as it was in high school. Think of the first few interactions you have with a new love interest just like that audition (although we recommend you wear clothing, at least initially). Things are going to be nerve-wracking, exciting, and more than a little awkward. You're standing up in front of a relative stranger and allowing them to pass judgment on all aspects of you . . . voluntarily. But, one thing that makes dating different from an audition is that you are doing the same thing to your date. In your first conversations, you're sizing each other up, and both of you are trying to decide whether there's enough interest and compatibility to warrant putting yourselves and your bruised hearts on the line again.

Jumping back into dating can seem so intimidating that you might be tempted to give up and become a hermit and live the rest of your life in an apartment full of cats. But, choosing to stay single forever is not the best decision for you long-term. Giving up your clowder of kitties and finding a new love means that you will probably be more content with your life, have better cardiovascular functioning, have a stronger immune system, and be much more likely to still have all your teeth. You also will be less likely to suffer from drug addiction, rheumatoid arthritis, neurological disorders, dementia, ulcers, and depression.[2, 3, 4, 5] In terms of mortality rates, staying single basically means you're screwed. If you are a woman who stays single, you will likely die about seven to fifteen years earlier than if you couple-up again. For men, it's about eight to seventeen years sucked off your lifespan.[6] So, the choice is simple: find love and live about a dozen years longer, or die alone, unhealthy, depressed, and surrounded by cats . . . who will, let's be honest, eat your face off after you've keeled over and they haven't been served their tuna pâté. Harsh? Yes. Backed by science? Also yes . . . except for the cats part; we just threw that in for fun. Turns out cats are either the least loyal, or the most practically minded of all pets. What other house pet do you feed dinner to until you *become* dinner? But we digress.

In dating, there are a million questions whose answers will determine whether you will ride off into the sunset with your newly discovered dreamboat to the tune of "Take My Breath Away," by Berlin. How do you keep a conversation going, which isn't focused only on your ex or kids? How soon do you "officially" ask out someone you've been messaging? What are good (dinner) versus bad (strip club) ideas for your first few real dates? And, when should you wear that new sexy underwear (or the Spanx that will increase the likelihood of getting to the point that the sexy underwear is recommended)? Lucky for you, we're here to help! Scientific research allows you not only to understand those initial interactions with the new object of your affection, but it can also help you learn how you can behave around them in order to make them fall madly in love with you (or at least increase the probability for another date).

Reach out and touch, um . . . we mean message . . . somebody.

You're ready to start dating! Possibly. You've found the perfect person! Maybe. You're not 100 percent sure, but they seem promising—and ohmygod they have the sexiest . . . smile (come on, get your mind out of the gutter!). At first glance, they seem to possess all the qualities you want in your future mate—hot, funny, charming, lives nearby, and shares your fascination for collecting garden gnomes. So that's it. The hard part is over, right? You will now have hours upon hours of hot monkey sex, laugh at each other's jokes, find all their quirks charming, [insert all other romantic comedy clichés here], and live happily ever after. Easy-peasy.

You wish! This is where the hard part actually starts.

How people start getting to know each other can vary a lot from person to person and situation to situation. But, in this day and age, a large portion of your early interactions with potential romantic partners will happen before you even go on an honest-to-goodness date. You'll likely start by sending a few text messages to test the waters before committing to dinner, drinks, or that honeymoon in Maui. Messaging gives you a chance to figure out if that new subject of your fantasies is worth getting to know further, or if they have the personality of pee-soaked cardboard. Of course, they will also be passing judgment on whether they want to get to know you better, or if you have the personality of . . . well, you get the picture. This means that your potential future and love life with this new person is based almost entirely on the next few messages you send. No pressure.

Messages can take many forms. If you found the perfect match using an online dating format, you may exchange your first few flirtations via the service's dedicated communication platform. If you were given a potential lover's contact information via friends, you might jump straight to emailing or texting. No matter how the connection begins, the rules are more or less the same in terms of how to fan those early flames. If you get contacted first (you stud muffin, you), you don't want to wait too long to reply. On average men reply to an initial contact within sixteen hours, and women reply within nineteen hours.[7] Any longer and you will find your odds of making a connection going steadily downhill. For each day you wait to respond after that first wink comes your way, the chance that the person who initiated contact will stay interested drops by about 1 percent. In the world of dating, there is no such thing as replying too quickly. Don't try to play it cool. The good old "two-day rule" where you don't call your crush back for two days does not apply anymore in our modern, instant-gratification world.

Messaging with a potential romantic partner is like a dance; we move with our partners to the rhythm of a song. When dancing, if you step left when your partner expects you to turn right, it could spell trouble for the dance and your partner's toes. When communicating, if you say or do something that is too unusual, inappropriate, or drastically different than what your partner expected, it could also spell trouble and possibly sabotage your chances for a first date. There are definitely a few taboo topics that should be avoided when first messaging, such as religion, politics, sex, or money. These are important issues if you want to pursue a long-term relationship and you should talk about them eventually, but not just yet. However, there is one thing that you are going to find extremely difficult not to bring up in early conversations post-divorce: your ex-spouse.

Bringing up your twat-waffle ex is the equivalent of not only stepping on the toes of your dance partner but also breaking their leg . . . probably in several places. Repeat after us: *I am not allowed to talk about twat-waffle. I am not allowed to talk about twat-waffle. I am not allowed to talk about twat-waffle. I am* allowed to talk about waffles. Because waffles are fucking delicious. Talking excessively about your ex is going to cause the person you are texting to question if you are really over your previous partner and whether you are truly ready to start a new relationship. Also, do you really think your potential romantic partners care if your ex was terrible in bed or had bad breath? You might care, but when you start speaking badly about your ex, your match is going to think you are a downer. And, really, who wants to be around Negative Nancy? If you need to talk about your ex, go see a therapist or call up a friend; don't do it with that hottie you just met. If you eventually start dating this person more seriously, your ex will ultimately be worked into the conversation. But, just like your opinions on current political drama, religion, or whether Red Vines are better than Twizzlers, save that shit for another day.

There are some great advantages to messaging at the start of the relationship. Because messaging is typically asynchronous—meaning that you're not responding in real time to each other's statements—it allows you to better edit and revise what you say to your new love interest. This is helpful because you are less likely to say something too quickly without thinking and end up embarrassing yourself (you'll do plenty of that later). You can write it out ("I love the titsburg feelers"), read it over, edit it ("I love the Pittsburgh Steelers"), and then send it off. This allows you to present yourself a little more strategically as the best, most suave version of you. Like building your online dating profile, it is important to remember that you shouldn't lie. Instead, you just want to wait to reveal some of the more undesirable information about yourself until a bit later into your relationship. Really, do they need to know, at this early stage, that you collect Star Wars figures or followed Nickelback on tour?

One drawback to messaging, compared to in-person interactions, is the number of words used during any given conversation. When talking to another person, we usually speak about 125 words per minute. That's a lot of information—seriously, that is basically the number of words in the previous paragraph. When we text people, our messages are much shorter: "Do you like going to the movies?" "Any interesting hobbies?" So, the amount of information we can get and give to a person is limited.

The good news is that this finite information will cause your new hottie to fill in the gaps of your limited messages with their own hopes and dreams. It's sort of like a Rorschach texting test—your match sees what they want

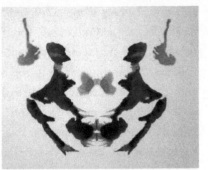

The Rorschach: Children playing? Two large-breasted women? A terrifying cow? You choose.

to see.[8] Imagine that your potential love enjoys long walks on the beach, but you prefer going surfing and playing volleyball. If you messaged "I love the beach," your new love is going to interpret this as indicating that you like to do the same thing that they like to do at the beach—going for long walks—even though this may not be the case. Psychologists call this *hyperpersonalization,*[9] and it reflects our tendency to interpret ambiguous information in a positive light when we like a person (or at least when we hope we are going to like a person). The halo that hyperpersonalization casts is powerful and means that initially talking to a person via some sort of messaging paradigm usually results in them liking you more than if you had first met in person. We encourage you to use these powers for good rather than evil because, in a fun twist of fate, you are prone to making the same mistake when interpreting your crush's nebulous comments about "liking boats and seamen." Maybe they're really into sailors, or maybe . . . hmm.

When crafting your witty banter, you also want to be careful to avoid a few major faux pas. DO NOT USE ALL CAPITAL LETTERS. We have no research to back this up, but let's be honest: you don't need a PhD to know that this just comes off as unnecessarily shouty. Research does tell us that you should be somewhat liberal with your use of exclamation points. We tend to view people who use them as more positive, and we like happy, positive people! For realsies!! We're serious!!!! Yay, happy people!!!!! (Although you might be able to overdo it at some point . . . !!) Make sure you remember the differences between *your* and *you're*, *whose* and *who's*, and *then* and *than*, because almost half of the people online think poor grammar or spelling is a deal-breaker.[10] Avoid using too many negations like *no*, *not*, or *never* as you will come off as inflexible and unpleasant. People who type using more, versus fewer, words in their messages, and those who use first-person singular pronouns like *I*, *me*, and *mine*, are often seen as more honest.[11] So don't be scared to talk a bit about yourself while you are trying to learn about your future love.

Finally, emojis—know them . . . use them . . . love them. Over 50 percent of us regularly use these little characters to convey our squishy sides, and most of us think they are helpful to this end.[12] You will also encounter some people who are a little more creative and combine various emojis together in order to craft not-so-subtle sexual invitations that often involve giant eggplants, tacos, and doughnuts. Heck, in 2016 the American Dialect Society even named the eggplant emoji as the "most notable emoji" due to its . . . um . . . sexual innuendo (penis, guys . . . it's a penis). Knowing the language of emojis is half the battle and will give you a leg up on the competition.

867–5309.

According to the smash hit from the eighties, getting someone's number (in particular, Jenny's) is the surefire way to make them yours (seriously, if you don't get this reference, do the Google . . . also, we're judging you). Today, phone conversation is a dying art. As teenagers, we remember spending hours on the phone just listening to our soul-mate-du-jour breathe. There was some talking about the meaning of life, a lot of giggling, and a nauseating amount of "you hang up . . . no, *you* hang up." Depending on your age when you divorced, you may remember the good ole days of phone conversations lasting for hours with your latest crush, or you may be from a slightly more youthful demographic and are a bit uncomfortable with the whole principle and would prefer to keep communication at the level of the text message.[13] It doesn't really matter. Chances are you will end up having to talk to potential partners on the phone or Facetime with them at some point. The amount that you chat is really up to you and your comfort level, but you should at least have the basics of modern phone chitter-chatter etiquette down, so you don't blow your chances with your future sweetie-pie.

The good news is that we really don't have to totally reinvent the wheel here. Most of the same rules that apply to texting also apply to phone and Facetime conversations. Although, if you're talking on the phone, you don't really have to worry about interpreting the eggplant, doughnut, and winky face emojis your Tinder match just texted you. Here's the simple version of the things that hold true for both messaging and phone calls: (1) Don't be flaky. If you say you're going to call at a particular time, honor that commitment. Not doing so is rude as fuck and will likely end with you all alone. (2) Similarly, reach out or return calls (which might mean checking your voicemail!) in a reasonable amount of time. With the phone, you can wait a bit longer than with texts. A day, maybe two, but no longer than that. The same logic as with text messages applies here. If you're interested, let the poor sucker know. Keeping them guessing is likely to backfire on you. (3) Finally, keep conversations positive and light-hearted. Remember, twat-waffle ex, politics, and religion talk = NO! Waffles-are-yummy talk = YAY! Ask questions about your potential date, try to get to know them, but keep the conversation focused on neutral, positive topics for the time being. Travel, hobbies, and movie/music preferences are all safe choices.

Despite these similarities between messaging and the phone, which basically boil down to "don't be an asshat," there are some differences. Phone calls are a synchronous rather than an asynchronous form of communication. This means you're responding to each other in real time. For this reason, not letting the conversation stall is super important. Too many awkward pauses give the impression that the conversation isn't going well. This also means that you really should be giving your phone date your full attention when you're talking to them. The TV, your emails, and the texts from other potential lovers can wait. If you sound distracted, it does *not* give off a good first impression, and it decreases your likelihood of making it to the first, official, real-life first date stage (or of getting another date if you've already met in person).

The way you interact with a potential romantic partner on the phone has a major influence on whether they feel the proverbial flames of passion for you. One of the ways that you can do this is through mimicking your crush's style of talking. Now, we don't mean mimicking in the childish playground sense where you repeat the things they say in a whiny, weirdly high-pitched voice. We mean matching how you talk to how they talk. This type of mimicry increases the odds that the person you are talking to will find you attractive. This mimicry is not about *what* you say, it's about *how* you say it. How do you structure your sentences? Where are the pauses in your speech, how do you include prepositions and clauses, how complicated are your sentences, etc.? Greater similarity in communication styles increases the odds that you're going to get the romantic butterflies, so you want to maximize it as much as you can.[14] The key here is not to overthink it. Don't start diagramming your crush's sentences while you're on the phone like some crazed high school student. Rather, just notice how they talk. Do they pause frequently? Are their sentences simple, or more complicated? Do they use fillers like "um" a lot? Just try and match them in these simple ways, and you'll have a leg up on any competition.

Another trick you can try to increase your chances of love is changing the tone of your voice when you talk.[15, 16, 17] People tend to talk in a slightly lower pitch when speaking to someone they think is a sexy beast. Third-party observers can even tell when someone is talking to an object of their desire compared to a friend they're not interested in through this lowering of tone. Now, don't go all James Earl Jones here, but aim for the sultriest version of your natural voice rather than Minnie Mouse on helium. In addition to sounding a little deeper, people's voices also become subjectively more "pleasant" when speaking to someone they're romantically interested in. What "pleasant" means is a bit vague in the research, but generally people come off as warmer and more approachable when talking to romantic partners (desired or actual) than when talking to other people (like their mom). Coming off as warm and approachable is also to your advantage because people rate those with more pleasant voices as more interesting, sexier, suave-er (our spell checker tells us this is not an actual word, but we don't care), and even more physically attractive . . . and all of this is true without ever having seen the person talking in real life.

A final word of caution about phone conversations. Remember, they can hear everything (and we do mean *everything*) you're up to. When you're on the phone with your match from Match.com or your best friend's cousin's neighbor or whomever, make sure you're not doing anything that you'd be embarrassed to be heard doing. This includes peeing, pooping, masturbating, and/or eating (although simultaneously doing all four would be impressive). Let's keep it classy, folks. There's nothing that kills the mood faster than hearing someone flush the toilet while you're in the middle of a flirty conversation.

In the beginning stages of relationships, texting and talking are necessary steps in getting to know that potential love interest who seems to have so much, well, potential. At some point, though, you will need to progress from the virtual or telephonic world to the "real world." Fortunately, the positive impressions you get from messaging and phone calls tend to only get stronger after you meet in person.[18] The bad news is that the same is true for negative impressions . . . so if it's not going well via text, meeting in person will not turn your romantic Titanic around. Just make sure you don't wait too long to make face-to-face contact. Messaging and talking can increase positive feelings between two potential sweethearts, but this benefit disappears if you wait too long . . . about three weeks seems to be the expiration date.[19] Meeting in person means you can not only build on the positive feelings established by flirty texting and late-night pillow talk, but you can also get a better sense of fit and chemistry. Going on that first date is a necessary part of the process, even if it does entail the inconvenience of brushing your teeth and putting on real pants. It sucks, we know. But we have faith in you; you can do this. So, get on out there! It's time to audition for the leading role in a new romantic comedy, (hopefully) starring . . . you!

Figuring out the first few dates: When Harry met Sally, then Julie, then Molly, then Susan . . .

In romantic comedies, the "meet-cute" is the first time that two characters, who will eventually become romantically intertwined, meet each other. They're meeting, and it's typically cute. Get it? If this were a romantic comedy, this would be the part where the protagonist enters a small Italian restaurant to meet their date. It's a rainy spring night, when our hero (who is drenched from the rain) looks up after walking inside and notices their stunning date sitting at a private table with a bottle of the restaurant's finest wine. They welcome each other with a hug, and as they gaze longingly into each other's eyes, they see their future together, and our hero realizes this is truly The One. A person who will always be there, who listens, who is kind, who is generally interesting, as well as promising amazing sex and everlasting love . . . basically the protagonist's soul mate. The gaze quickly turns into a long lingering kiss as the camera pulls away, romantic music begins (*deep breath* . . . And *IIIIIIIII* will always love *YOUUUU*)—end scene.

First, the bad news. None of this is going to happen. Most likely, your first dates are going to be more "meet-awkward" than "meet-cute." Consider the case of John (name has been changed to protect the unfortunate). Wearing a blazer and a newly purchased pair of post-divorce skinny jeans, John found himself standing in front of an unmarked office building in downtown Philadelphia. It was 10:38 p.m. and his date, a woman named Heather whom he had encountered on Match. com, was running late for their first date, which she had arranged. John was nervous not only because of the date, but because this was going to be his first date since he separated from his wife six months previously. Finally, Heather walked around the corner, grabbed his hand, and led him inside a small elevator in the strange office building. As they made small talk, John began to wonder what was going to happen—dinner, dancing, a first kiss, sex, or maybe he was about to get murdered. Whatever, he was ready for anything. Then the elevator doors opened, and John realized that he actually wasn't ready for *anything*. His date had decided to take him to one of Philadelphia's premier BDSM (bondage-domination-sadomasochism for the uninitiated) clubs. There were chains, belts, masks, and leather . . . oh-so-much leather. John, deciding he wasn't quite ready for nipple clamps, quickly made a few polite excuses and exited the building.

Although your first date probably isn't going to have the makings of a popular romantic comedy, it is equally unlikely to be on par with John's bondage adventure. By examining data from 1.5 million people, it appears that, in America, the most common place to meet for a first date is, drum roll puh-lease . . . Starbucks![20] Next time you get yourself a pumpkin spice latte, be sure to look around for awkward first-real-official-date couples. You might be witnessing the beginning of true love, or you may just get a good laugh at someone else's discomfort and potential misfortune. "Guess the first daters" is one of our favorite games to play when out and about. Say what you like, a little schadenfreude never hurt anybody. Meeting for something like coffee on a first date is a great idea because it is inexpensive, most people can find something they like on the menu, and it gives you a quick exit if you discover (as Erica did on an early Starbucks date) that your potential beloved takes enough psychotropic medications to tranquilize a rhinoceros and lives in his grandmother's basement with his (literal, not figurative) pet snake. Yup, that happened. The coffee shop setup makes it easy to say sorry, you have to go home and "wash your hair." Other popular places for first dates include Olive Garden, Panera Bread, Barnes & Noble, Topgolf, Whole Foods, Yard House, and Red Lobster. Obviously, someone must pay for all those unlimited breadsticks from Olive Garden, and that someone is usually the man. Sexist? Yes. But surveys consistently find that 80 percent of both men and women think the man should pay for the first date, which tends to cost, on average, about fifty dollars.[21]

As you can tell from these popular date locations, people tend to opt for casual places where food and drinks are typically involved. These locations are ideal because they allow you the chance to talk and get to know your potential partner. However, if you want to increase the chances of making your partner find *you* irresistible, you should consider doing something for your date that is a little offbeat and get your date's blood pumping a bit. Think indoor rock climbing, kayaking, paintballing, racing go-carts, or riding roller coasters. When humans experience things that are physiologically arousing—that is, they get your heart racing and your palms all sweaty—our brains sense these bodily changes and turn them into emotions based on what is going on around us. If you're riding a roller coaster, your date might be terrified, but then they look over at your oh-so-sexy self and instead unconsciously misinterpret their racing heart as being due to their increasing attraction to irresistible you. *BOOM!* Infatuation boost.[22] Patrick even used this knowledge while attending graduate school in California. Whenever a small earthquake would strike, he would quickly go out onto the campus quad to find unsuspecting coeds who might misattribute the physiological response they had from an earthquake to feelings of romantic interest in this nerdy little scientist-in-training. The bottom line is if you want to do something *a little extra* to get your date to like you, consider going to a place that offers some thrills or excitement.

Another trick of the trade when you go on dates is to subtly copy the behavior of your partner. Remember when we talked about mimicking your crush's vocal style on the phone? This is *exactly* like that, except now you're copying their physical movements. Just like on the phone, we are more romantically attracted to people when their behaviors are like ours.[23] If your date leans back, wait a few seconds, then lean back yourself. Cross and uncross your legs as your date does. Smile when they smile. Scratch your junk if they do. You get the idea. There is a cautionary statement here though—*for god's sake be subtle about it*. It turns out that if your date catches you copying what they do, it gets super creepy super fast. They are then much *less* likely to be interested in you than if you hadn't mimicked them at all. Gotta be smooth on this one, folks.

No matter the location or activity of your first date, at some point during the outing, you will inevitably talk with the potential object of your affection. We know, there is nothing more terrifying than first-date small talk. That said, most first dates last a couple of hours, so you have to manage *some* chitchat. Bear in mind that this is a first date—it really is just a screener to determine if you want to go out with this person again. The best advice we can offer is to know that you are only responsible for half the conversation; don't feel the need to carry the whole thing. Ask questions, let your date answer; and answer the questions you are asked. Just like with those early texts and phone calls, keep the conversation light and fun. Remember our earlier advice about not talking about your twat-waffle ex-spouse . . . yeah, that applies here too. Talk about your hobbies and what you like to do. If you get stuck, or the conversation lags, bring up one of these safe topics: What sort of vacations do you like to take? What are your friends like? Do you like your job? What were you like as a child? What is something you've always wanted to try? Be yourself, and you will probably do great.

To date, or not to date (again): Figuring out if there should be a second date.

Remember that dating is not about getting *everyone* to like you; it's about getting the *right one* to like you. It's important that you are true to who you are . . . just maybe the friendliest, most engaging version of that person, with the best hygiene. If your date doesn't like you, they're probably not right for you. Furthermore, you need to check them out a bit. Yes, you will make some questionable dating decisions driven by loneliness, not wanting to hurt someone's feelings, or the need to get laid. But remember that at the end of all of this, you want to find someone who you believe is a good fit for you and your life. The light chatter that happens on first dates is a good way to start figuring this out. The key here is to build on what you might already know about this person to see if there are any glaring red flags (like your date is into collecting handcuffs, making lamps out of human skin, or dressing up as a clown) and to get as much information about your future snugglebutt as possible. This sets you up to best assess whether you two are a match made in romantic comedy heaven, or if this is the start of a serial killer horror flick.

So, what does science say you should look for on your first date? It turns out that you already know the answer to this question; we talked about it in the last chapter. Say it with us now: looks, location, personality. The factors that you used to decide whether or not you even wanted to swipe right for your date are the exact same factors that you will use to decide whether or not you want things to progress to a goodnight kiss, a second date, nakey-nakey time, etc. For looks, keep it hot (or about as hot as you are anyway). For location, keep it close (remember: proximity breeds frequency of seeing each other, which breeds warm fuzzy feelings).

As for personality, remember to pay attention to similarity (you have the best shot of long-term relational success when you find someone who is like you). But also pay attention to traits that you value. These are the traits that may or may not have made it into their online profile, and so they're the ones you'll have to judge in person. And you may have to pick and choose a bit. No one person is going to embody everything you're looking for. That would be like finding a needle in a haystack, or Sasquatch in the forest . . . you get the idea. No one is perfect (including you, cupcake). So, you need to decide on your deal-breakers. Will you tolerate dishonesty if he or she is charismatic? Are you okay with someone who doesn't like spicy food if they like the outdoors? What is the balance you're willing to strike?

But how good are we at judging the personality of another person in a short(ish) time frame, like a date? After all, the personality judgments made during a first date have a significant influence on whether you will see the person again next weekend or run screaming from the room. You might wonder whether you can actually judge a date's personality in just a couple of hours. Seems like hokum, right? Wonder no longer, because you can; and you can do it *really* (disturbingly) quickly. Heck, just looking at a person's face and dress is enough for you to accurately judge some personality characteristics. For example, people who look healthy, energetic, happy, and relaxed are likely to be extroverted. Whereas individuals who are messy, not very stylish, tired, and tense are probably lonely. People who are chatty and a little loud are often socially dominant, and people who smile and laugh a lot are likely warm.[24] We also are remarkably accurate at judging things like sexual orientation (important on the dating market) in very short time frames—we're talking high levels of accuracy in under thirty seconds of looking at a person.[25] First impressions definitely matter.

As your date progresses, your personality judgments become increasingly accurate the longer you are talking to your prospective love over dinner. To give you some help in identifying the personality of your date, the table below displays the behaviors that people tend to exhibit during conversations when they have certain personality characteristics. So, if you are looking for that dominant but warm partner, keep your eye out for someone who is a little bit loud and ambitious but still able to be relaxed and sociable.

Social Dominance	Social Warmth
Speaks in a loud voice	Is not hostile
Tries to control the interaction	You find yourself seeking advice from this person
Shows high enthusiasm	Not irritated
Talks to you a lot	Seems to enjoy the interaction
Volunteers a large amount of information	Expresses ideas well
Displays ambition	Offers advice
Is not fearful or timid	Is relaxed and comfortable
Does not seek reassurance	Makes or approaches physical contact
Is not reserved	Talks with partner, not at them
Likes attention	Is not condescending
Compares themselves to others	Exhibits social skills
Is competitive	Is reassuring

Remember, this is a first date, so you will only have limited information (one more time for the cheap seats in the back: looks, location, personality!!!!) to use in order to determine if you want to have a second date. Of course, we are all for trying to find out extra info about the person based on what you can learn about them from others or even a good Google stalking session. Gathering as much information on this first date as possible will increase the chances of weeding out the frogs—the people who are totally wrong for you—and leaving yourself only with a pool of potential princes or princesses. Presumably, at least one of these people is perfect for you, and you two will end up riding off into the sunset together. Or at least have mind-blowing sex.

Speaking of sex, there is one last thing that you should be paying attention to during your date. Chemistry, baby![1] Chemistry is hard to define; it's the butterflies in the stomach, sparks-flying feeling that you get when you're with someone and you just click. It's sexual attraction (often driven by looks) and things in common (um . . . personality, anyone?), but it's also more than the sum of those parts. Whether or not you'll have chemistry with someone is hard to predict ahead of time. You're more likely to have chemistry with a person who ticks your boxes on paper, but a good fit on paper is in no way a guarantee that you'll want this person to tick your boxes, so to speak, for real. This means that you might be out on a date with someone who seemed perfect for you when you viewed their eHarmony profile, but in person there is just something missing. They probably seem nice and all but . . . meh, you're just not that interested in making out with them. Pay attention to this feeling! Chemistry is an important part of any relationship, you sorta want to have it. Trust us on this! Look for someone who is the three scoops—looks, location, personality—for your ice cream sundae, but ultimately go with your gut to make sure you get the chemistry cherry on top (and maybe a few nuts, too, if that's your thing).

"You still here? It's over. Go home. Go!"

The iconic Ferris Bueller couldn't have said it better—all good things must come to an end. Or, sometimes in the world of dating: "Thank God that's over, I was about to scoop out my eyes with this dessert spoon!" Either way, at some point it will be time to say goodbye to your date. Before this awkward interaction begins, ask yourself whether you thought this was a good date. If you don't see any future between you two, be honest but not cruel. There is no need to explain to this poor schmuck that you thought their story about their childhood pet hamsters was beyond boring and their breath smelled. Simply tell them you had a wonderful evening (even if you didn't) and it was great meeting them (even if it wasn't). Do *not* tell them that you can't wait to see them again (if you don't). Just cut it off there and move on.

If the date went well and you actually *can't* wait to see them again, don't be shy about letting your partner know you are interested. Tell your date what a wonderful time you had and that you would love to do it again. If they seem interested, lean in for a kiss and see what happens. We get it. That first kiss can be scary, but let's be honest—this ain't exactly your first rodeo. You've kissed before, you can do it again. Just keep it short (ish . . . more than a peck, please) and go easy on the tongue. Inspecting your date's tonsils may not go over well at this point. Easy there, cowboy (or girl).

Speaking of bucking broncos: if you are going to have sex on your first date, we won't judge (although you should definitely check out Chapter 7). That said, do know that dating couples who had sex on their first date tend to view their relationships as less satisfying and stable than couples who waited to have sex.[26] This is correlational, so it is unclear if having sex actually *causes* a relationship to be less satisfying in the long run, but there is an association here. We suggest to just play it safe and keep it in your pants until that second, third, or fourth date. That said, neither of your authors are exactly *not* guilty in this particular area, so it may be more of a do-as-we-say, not as-we-do situation. Any way you choose to handle it, make sure you and your date are on that same page.

Be sure that everyone is happy and comfortable with the level of physical intimacy that's happening, and, for heaven's sake, use a condom (more on all of this later).

Regardless of how you felt the evening went, you are going to text or call your date the very next day. You just are. We command you. You don't want to "ghost" anyone! Ghosting is when a person suddenly stops texting and contacting another person they were dating. It is a dick move that happens because the person doing the ghosting is a chicken shit and just hopes the person being ignored will "get the hint" and stop being interested. The problem is the person being ghosted will be uncertain as to why the relationship ended. Did they do something wrong? Did they have lettuce in their teeth? Did they smell? Are they a horrible human being? What's wrong with them? This ambiguity only causes additional distress to the rejected person and can cause them to question their self-worth.[27] To avoid this problem, if you are not diggin' a love connection, just drop the person a quick text to let them know that you enjoyed your time out, but you are not feeling it. Most people will appreciate this honesty and, if they don't, then fuck 'em—you made the right choice by rejecting them! If you did enjoy your date, make sure you text them soon. Research finds that contacting your date within twenty-four hours is a good strategy. All you have to do is reiterate that you had a great time and ask if they would like to go out again. If they do, set up a concrete time and place. Something like "Let's meet up for dinner next Saturday" or "Want to check out that new exhibit at the museum on Thursday?" Whatever you do, make sure they understand you are interested without being too pushy. A follow-up text or two to set up the next date = good; a text every hour about everything you ate that day = creepy.

Alrighty. now comes the tough love. You might think that your post-divorce single days will be short-lived. That you'll date a couple of people casually before lightning strikes and you meet your soul mate version 2.0. In truth, it rarely works like that. The average divorced person who remarries does so within about five years, and over 75 percent of divorcees are remarried by the ten-year mark.[28] The good news here is that, even if it doesn't feel like it right now, the odds that you're going to find love again are very high. The bad news is the odds that you'll find that love with one of the first few people you go out with are very low. You're gonna have to kiss some frogs or frog-ettes before finding your prince or princess. So, pucker up, buttercup! Hopefully, the tips and tricks we've offered will make navigating the early days of your dating experience less overwhelming and a bit more fun. Remember . . . at first, keep it fun and light. Invest in getting to know people who are worthy of your time, and treat others with respect. Before you know it, you'll be ready to figure out how to be all in loooooove again with someone new. In the meantime, though, let's talk about the next logical step in the dating process—humpin'.

Chapter 7

Fuck it. No . . . seriously: Navigating your newfound sexy time

You were young. You probably didn't have much experience. Most people only have sex with one or two people before they get married for the first time.[1] Let's face it, you and your ex probably weren't that great in bed. Sex was vanilla and routine . . . if not at first, it probably became this way. For heterosexual couples: kiss, missionary, cowgirl, rinse and repeat. By the end, a little doggy style on special occasions was likely as wild as it got.[i] But guess what? That's all about to change! One of the hidden chocolate chips in the shit-cookie of divorce is that you have a unique opportunity to rediscover and possibly even redefine your sexual identity. Interested in a little variety? You are about to enter the thirty-one flavors of . . . blond, brunette, older, younger, hairy, smooth . . . whatever twirls your sexual beanie. How about a fantasy you've always wanted to try? If it involves consenting adults, almost anything is fair game.

This is not to say that divorced people are only focused on sex, but there is a lot of sex happening out there. Considering you've likely been

---

i   Just like the research examining romantic attraction, almost all of the research on gettin' busy has also focused on people who identify as heterosexual. While some of the findings may not be applicable to all people, there is no reason to believe that many of these juicy tidbits won't apply to people in the LGBTQ community. As we warned earlier, just be aware of what populations studied gave rise to these findings.

"out of the game" for a while, it's best to know what to expect and be ready before you get off the bench. We get it, your ultimate goal is probably to find love again. That's why we cover love, in all its sugar-coated tastiness, in the next chapter, but this chapter is strictly about doin' the dirty. So, buckle up buttercup because we are about to get n.a.s.t.y.

Post-divorce sex: A trip to Space Mountain or the Thunderdome?

Did you ever go to Disneyland (or any other amusement park) as a kid? The night before your adventure, you probably had trouble sleeping due to the excitement of all the anticipated thrills. When you arrived at the park, you lost your little mind as your churro-fueled adventure sustained the adrenaline rush of bouncing from ride to ride. There were just so many rides to cram into that day. Post-divorce, you might approach sex the same way. Maybe you are excited about all the thrills that lie ahead of you. You may find yourself bouncing from "ride" to "ride" in Divorceeland, trying to jam as many opportunities as you can into your new single lifestyle.

Alternatively, instead of an adventure to the "Happiest Place on Earth," your new sexual freedom might feel like a journey to the "Scariest Place in the Entire Frickn' Universe." It's been a long time since you've had sex with anyone other than your ex-spouse, so the prospect of getting naked with someone new could be more than a little terrifying. Your body looks different (where did that twenty-year-old body disappear to?). You are not sure what to expect when you get out there (what are the norms of body hair removal these days anyhow?). Emotionally, it might even take you awhile to adjust to the idea of being naked with someone new without feeling like you're being unfaithful. Hell, with so many issues to deal with, you may feel like skipping the post-divorce orgy altogether. Seriously, what good is sex? It can be sticky, messy, squishy, sweaty, smelly, and produces . . . ummmm . . . interesting sounds.

At least if you're doing it right.

Stickiness aside, it's common for some divorcees to feel they are too old to start over, and so they seriously consider putting their sex life out to pasture. We cannot emphasize enough—do not fall prey to this mistake! You'll be missing out on oh-so-much-fun. By examining what is called your "sexually active life expectancy," it's possible to estimate the number of years of ass-slapping good times you have in front of you.[2] The news is entirely good, like *When Harry Met Sally* "I'll have what she's having" good.

As you can see in the following figure, thirty-year-olds can expect approximately thirty-four to thirty-seven more years of an active sex life. Even if you're sixty, you have at least a decade of sexy time left. Unless you're over eighty-five (and then, bless your heart, do whatever the fuck you want), retiring that black lace (or leather) thong means that you could be missing out on years, even decades, of incredibly fulfilling sex. Worst of all—you will almost certainly be missing out on the best sex you ever had. For starters, divorcees have sex for longer periods than their married peers. No more we're-tired-as-fuck,

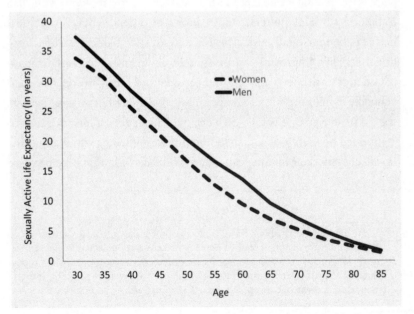

the-kids-just-fell-asleep, for-the-love-of-God-hurry-up, humdrum sex for you, my friend. An impressive 29 percent of divorced people's most recent sexy-time lasted longer than an hour, compared to a mere 8 percent of married people.[3] Not only does the sex last longer in Divorceeland, but it might also be better. After getting divorced, men's testosterone spikes,[4] which is linked to increased interest in sex, sexual arousal, and sexual activity.[5] Women hit their sexual peak in their early thirties[6] (which is approximately the average age of a person going through their first divorce) and are not only more interested in getting it on but report enjoying it more, too.

Not only is missing out on all this sex a bummer because sex can, and should, be amazeballs, but there are also psychological and physical benefits associated with sex. While we learned from the nursery rhyme that "an apple a day keeps the doctor away," it appears that "sexual relations might lead to longer life expectations."[ii] Doing the nasty might be sweaty, but having more sex is linked to a whole host of wonderful, life-affirming outcomes, including (deeeeeep breath . . .) satisfaction with one's mental health, emotional awareness, lower depression, less likelihood of schizophrenia and neurotic disorders, reduced pain, less body fat, better overall cardiac health, lower resting blood pressure, emotional stability, improved testosterone levels in men, decreased menopausal heat flashes in women, lower prostate and breast cancer risks, and generally living longer[7] (. . . gasp, phew!). We aren't telling you that you should treat everyone you go on a date with like a ride at Disneyland—to be hopped on with glee and abandon. But we are telling you that healthy sexual activity after divorce can be an awesome thrill that may be good

---

ii   Lame attempts at rhyming aside, while an apple a day might not actually keep the doctor away, it might lead to better sex. Research published in the *Archives of Gynecology and Obstetrics* has found that women who eat an apple a day report higher levels of overall sexual functioning (desire, lubrication, orgasm, satisfaction, etc.). It turns out, an apple a *day* will keep the bad sex *away* with some good *foreplay* for the *divorcee*.

for you. So, grab that "E" ticket (or "O" ticket) and get on board because you're about to go on a roller coaster.

Fifty Shades of . . . whatever frickn' color you'd like.

"A non-credit series of twelve lectures on legal, economic, sociologic, psychologic, and biological aspects of marriage will be available for the first time during the Summer Session."

—*Indiana Daily Student* newspaper (June 22, 1938)

It was the summer of 1938 at Indiana State University when students first learned about a series of lectures on marriage from the advertisement above in their school's paper. In response to what many at the time saw as a breakdown in traditional life—which some felt began with granting women the right to vote (oh, the unimaginable horror!)—such "marriage" classes were slowly becoming more popular on college campuses around the United States. Probably not too surprisingly, most of these marriage classes focused on teaching traditional morals and values with a heavy emphasis on hygiene. Sex was only discussed in strictly biological terms—usually only after separating students by gender—and specific sexual behaviors were never, *ever, ever*, discussed. The general philosophy of most people who taught these courses was that couples should only learn about sex through trial and error, and even then, only after they were married (and preferably with the lights off).[8]

Back in Indiana, it was unseasonably warm, with temperatures in July nearing 100 degrees, as ninety-six students entered the auditorium of the school's chemistry building for their first "marriage" lecture. To the surprise of many students, the professor leading the lecture was not a psychologist but instead an entomologist who, up until this class, was best known for his research on gall wasps. It didn't take these students very long to realize that this class was going to be as hot as it was outside. Soon, the professor, sporting a bow tie and oversized trousers, was wildly drawing graphs on the chalkboard showing the average penis and clitoris lengths. He quickly showed slides of different sexual positions and informed them (much to the amazement of many men in the audience) that the primary source of women's pleasure comes from the clitoris and not the vagina. Seeking to learn more about this taboo topic, some of the students would meet privately with the professor to discuss their own sexual desires and questions. This professor quickly recognized the immense diversity of sexual interests among his students.[9]

Inspired by this diversity, he soon ventured around the United States to interview individuals about their sexual behaviors. The bowtie-wearing professor, Dr. Alfred Kinsey, eventually interviewed over 18,000 men and women about sexual behaviors ranging from run-of-the-mill (petting) to a little kinky (anal sex), to bat-shit crazy (bestiality). This work eventually taught people that most of their sexual behaviors and fantasies were completely normal. Most women masturbate, and often—yes. Men masturbate, basically always (seriously, we didn't know this already?)—yes. Most women have overt sexual dreams—yes. Women tend to have sexual relations before marriage—yes. Oral sex is pretty great—yes. By bringing all kinds of sexual behaviors out of the closet, Kinsey helped teach the world that almost everyone is a little kinky.

Building off Kinsey's legacy, modern researchers have continued to ask people about all sorts of sexual behaviors. While sex might basically be about inserting "Tab A" into "Slot B," exactly how someone goes about that can range from plain old missionary to some kinky Kamasutra shit involving pulleys, clamps, and a shiny new bottle of KY. Not to mention, people will have diverse definitions for what is meant by "Tab A" (dick, dildo, fist, etc.) or "Slot B" (vagina, mouth, anus, etc.). Since sexual behaviors and desires involving tabs and slots are not typically discussed during water cooler conversations, we tend to be oblivious about the sexual world of the average divorcee. Luckily, modern-day Kinsey-type researchers have been busy interviewing numerous divorcees from around the United States to enlighten us.

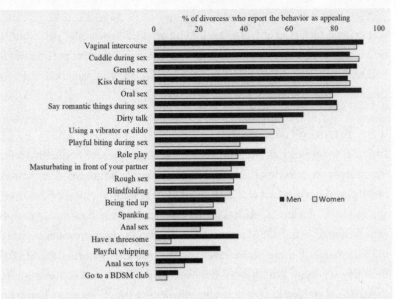

% of divorcess who report the behavior as appealing

To gain insight into this hush-hush world of sexiness, the previous figure shows how desirable divorcees found twenty different sexual behaviors, ranging from kissing to playing with anal sex toys.[10] It turns out the sexual behaviors divorcees find most appealing are behaviors that are typically associated with romance—gentle sex, kissing, and cuddling.[iii] However, this does not mean that a sizable number of divorcees aren't also interested in behaviors that are a little kinkier. About half enjoy talking dirty, role-playing, and even playfully biting during sex. Heck, if you go out on dates with ten different people, there is a good chance that at least two of them are into BDSM and enjoy being tied up, spanked, or even whipped. Given this diversity in sexual interests,

---

iii   Want something to do on a slow Saturday night? Want to know what sex behavior thirty-something, divorced, college-educated women who live in Colorado find most appealing? The authors of this research were kind enough to make their data available to the public here: http://doi.org/10.3886/E100426V1. This means that you can check out the common sexual behaviors for just about any demographic you are interested in learning about. This is how we were able to compute the sexual behaviors divorcees find appealing as well as create and standardize the Kink-o-Meter.

it is crucial to figure out how kinky you are and how kinky you want to be so that you can set yourself up to get naked with new partners who will be into the same shit you're into. Luckily for you, we created a tool that will help!

The Kink-o-Meter.™

In 2011, soccer moms attending book clubs everywhere suddenly found themselves in a fictional world of millionaires, bondage, domination, sadism, and masochism (a.k.a. BDSM) after reading the book *Fifty Shades of Grey* by E. L. James. Although it is unclear exactly how many people experimented with BDSM after reading this book, there are clues suggesting that many of these housewives tried on some handcuffs for size after their literary foray. Following the release of the book and related movies, there was a sudden increase in the sale of sex toys,[11] ropes at hardware stores,[12] and even reports of BDSM-related injuries.[13] Like Kinsey's earlier research, what *Fifty Shades of Grey* exemplified is that everyday people, even those you wouldn't expect (like your child's second-grade teacher) have private desires, some of which don't get expressed until some catalyst instigates thought about what truly and honestly gets them hot and bothered down in their pantaloons. With this in mind, it is time to introduce you to the Kink-o-Meter.™ [iv] The Kink-o-Meter™ was designed to get you thinking about how kinky you want to be in order to help you find a person who matches your desired level of kink. It is important to remember that the Kink-o-Meter™ is not a game where you are trying to get the highest kinkiest score. Instead, you want to be as honest as possible to allow the Kink-o-Meter™ to best figure out your kinkiness level.

---

iv We thought it would be obvious that it was a joke to irritatingly keep putting "TM" after each time we said "Kink-o-Meter." However, Carol, from legal, informed us that we need to inform you that the Kink-o-Meter is not really trademarked. As E. B. White said, "Explaining a joke is like dissecting a frog. You understand it better, but the frog dies in the process." Thanks, Carol, for killing our frog.

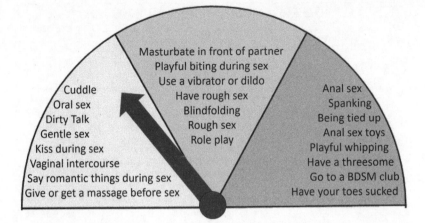

Cuddle
Oral sex
Dirty Talk
Gentle sex
Kiss during sex
Vaginal intercourse
Say romantic things during sex
Give or get a massage before sex

Masturbate in front of partner
Playful biting during sex
Use a vibrator or dildo
Have rough sex
Blindfolding
Rough sex
Role play

Anal sex
Spanking
Being tied up
Anal sex toys
Playful whipping
Have a threesome
Go to a BDSM club
Have your toes sucked

Completing the Kink-o-Meter™ is easy. All you do is select the behaviors on the Kink-o-Meter™ that you find desirable. It's okay if you've never tried these behaviors. Pick behaviors you find most appealing, even if only hypothetically (so far!). For example, hypothetical Suzy has always enjoyed kissing, cuddling, oral sex, and genital intercourse, but she is also really interested in trying role-playing, biting, and spanking. On the Kink-o-Meter™, Suzy would circle these seven behaviors. To get her Kink-o-Meter™ level, all Suzy has to do is add up her score. She gets one point for each activity she circled in the light grey area, 2 points for the medium grey area, and 3 points for the dark grey area. So, hypothetical Suzy's final score would be 11. Now, it's your turn to add up your score on the Kink-o-Meter™ and find your Level-o-Kinkiness below.

One thing you might have noticed is that the Kink-o-Meter's™ Level-o-Kinkiness only goes up to 3, but there are even higher levels of kinkiness. For example, level 4 behaviors include things like feces play, bestiality, and necrophilia fantasies. However, only a very tiny percent of the population has engaged in, or are interested in engaging in, these behaviors.[14] The Kink-o-Meter™ is designed to cover most, if not quite all, individuals' sexual appetites. Therefore, even if you got a score over 33 (which would put you in the top 5 percent kinkiness on this scale), don't worry that you are some crazed sexual

The Kink-o-Meter's™ Level-o-Kinkiness

Score	Level	Description
0–7	Vanilla	Your score puts you in the bottom 25 percent of people's kinkiest scores. You are not really into fetishes or kinks. Instead, you're pretty vanilla in the bedroom. This doesn't mean you don't enjoy sex or are not good in the sack. It just means that you like to keep things simple, and you have no need for all those whips and chains.
8–20	Spicy Meatball	You are in the middle 50 percent of people's kinkiest scores. Your bedroom activities are a little kinky— you're like vanilla with sprinkles. There are some things you are interested in doing to take your lovemaking up a notch, but nothing too extreme. For you, these activities add a little adventure and spice to your lovemaking, but they are not the main course.
21–40	Kinkster	Your score puts you in the top 25 percent of people's kinkiest scores. You make porn stars blush. Let's be honest, the nightstand by your bed is probably full of all types of toys, ropes, clamps, and a ball gag. For you, *Fifty Shades of Grey* is a children's book. There is very little you won't try in the bedroom.

deviant. We mean, you might be a crazed sexual deviant, but there are likely people out there who are more crazed and sexually deviant than you. Receiving a low score is nothing to be worried about, either. High versus low isn't bad versus good here; it's just about the style of sex you prefer. And all styles of sex can be fabulous. This is all about what you want to do and what will, hopefully, make you most fulfilled in your next relationship.

When comparing the kinkiness of married people to divorced people, it quickly becomes apparent that those of you who ditched the wedding ring are kinkier. Divorced people score about 12 percent higher on the Kink-o-Meter™ than married people. What exactly do divorced people like to do more than married folks? Well . . . divorced people report more interest in masturbating in front of their partner, playful biting, being blindfolded, role play, anal sex, spanking, being tied up, whipping, having a threesome, and going to a BDSM club. Okay, before you get all worried (or all excited) that everyone suddenly becomes a fuh-reaak after they get divorced, there are a couple of things to remember with these statistics. First, most people who are into kinky behaviors also report being into more gentle behaviors, too. Second, just because divorced people are kinkier than married people, it doesn't mean divorcees are maxing out the Kink-o-Meter™. Just as it is unlikely that your Kink-o-Meter™ score suddenly jumped from a 7 to a lasciviously naughty score of 40 after you got divorced, the average divorcee has a score of about 15 on the Kink-o-Meter™, placing them squarely inside "Spicy Meatball" territory.

Matchmaker, matchmaker, make me a (kinky, but not too kinky, maybe some light bondage, but nothing too heavy) match.

In the last chapter, we talked about why you should try to meet romantic partners who are similar in terms of various characteristics. We are more attracted to people who share our personality traits (well, except for dominance), political values, goals, morals, religious beliefs, and hobbies.[15, 16] And nowhere is such similarity so crucial as in finding a romantic partner who shares your kinkiness level (except, again, for dominance). In the bedroom, kinky opposites do not attract, but birds of a feather do fuck together.

Kinky similarity is essential because it provides people with a sense of self-validation. We understand the term *self-validation* might sound like some psychobabble that you would hear on Oprah, but it's just the straightforward idea that we are most comfortable and happy when we find someone who allows us to act in a manner consistent with how we see ourselves.[17] For example, a person who sees him or herself as a hipster will be most happy with another hipster who encourages them to hang out at obscure coffee shops, wear non-prescription glasses, watch nothing but foreign films, stroll farmer's markets, and own a cat (because dogs are simply too mainstream). Because this hipster's romantic partner is allowing them to behave in a manner consistent with how they view themselves, they will feel understood and have confidence that their crazy hipster thoughts and emotions are being accepted.

In much the same way that the hipster found validation and satisfaction with another hipster, a person who is similar to yourself in terms of kinkiness will also produce the most validating and satisfying experience for you in the bedroom.[18] Two kinksters in the bedroom will feel accepted because they allow each other to behave in the manner that they both desire. By the same token, two vanillas together will experience the same validation, as they are unlikely to encourage wild behaviors they do not desire. Problems in the bedroom happen when there is a drastic mispairing of desires. For example, a kinkster will feel like a pervert and a pain in the ass (literally) when they attempt to convince their vanilla partner to try out their shiny new butt plug. This will then cause the vanilla person to feel like an uptight asshole (literally) because the thought of a butt plug scares the shit out of them (again . . . literally), but they are also worried their relationship might fall between the cracks (one last time . . . literally) if they don't give it a try.[v] The point is, in such a mismatch, both partners will likely feel bad (one will feel like a sexual deviant and the other like a prude), and at least one of them will be forced to act in a manner that is not consistent with their sexual desires and how they view themselves—by either using or not using said shiny new butt plug.

You might be thinking that finding someone similar to you, sexual interests–wise, isn't that big of a deal. That you'll get to know what your partner likes as the relationship progresses, and so even if you start out with different interests, your sex life will become increasingly hot over time. You might be thinking this. But you'd be wrong. Feelings of passion decline over time in the average relationship (more on this in the next chapter)—sure, you might have a relationship that is the odd exception, but this is the rule of thumb.[19] This means that if your sex starts out lackluster, perhaps because you and your partner aren't on the

---

v   Seriously, Carol? You have a problem with the whole "TM" thing, but five butt plug jokes in a row don't even raise an eyebrow.

same kink-wavelength, it's unlikely to suddenly improve to be the most awesome sex you've ever had. Sorry, darlings.

He found his tight end! Penetrate the hole! Go deep!

We are talking football here, you little perv. Philadelphia is known for Independence Hall, cheesesteaks, the Liberty Bell, pretzels, and, above all else, football. So, in 2018, it wasn't too crazy that a couple of Philadelphia Eagles fans got married on Super Bowl Sunday in an Eagles-themed wedding. As you might expect, there was tailgating before the wedding, the groomsmen wore Eagle's jerseys, and the wedding was presided over by a friend dressed as a referee. After the ceremony, guests enjoyed beer and stadium food while they watched the bride toss a football to the awaiting arms of eager bridesmaids.[20] Everyone witnessing the wedding agreed that the bride and groom, who shared an overzealous passion for football, were lucky to have found each other.

But what are the actual odds that two people with the same love of football would randomly find each other? Here are a couple of statistics. In the United States, 39 percent of men and 37 percent of women watch football. If you remember probabilities from middle school, you might recall that you can multiply the probabilities of the two events (39 percent of men and 37 percent of women) together to figure out the odds two people who randomly bump into each other would both be interested in football: 14 percent. The good news is, if a person has an overzealous passion for football, he or she can dramatically increase these odds by not just relying on random chance. Football lovers could increase their odds of finding a like-minded fanatic by going to sports bars during games. They could wear the jersey of their favorite team to advertise their interest in football to potential mates. Maybe such a person could go to a game and be surrounded by thousands of people with their exact same passion for the pigskin!

While there are numerous things a person could do to increase the odds of finding another football fanatic, what can someone do if they seek another individual who shares their love of anal sex or being spanked? Wearing a jersey that says "Eagles" isn't really frowned upon but sporting a jersey that says "I Love Butt Stuff" to the local grocery store might land you in some trouble. Because our Level-of-Kinkiness is usually not revealed in public, or even during the very early stages of dating, it is very unlikely two people will be randomly matched in terms of their sexual interests. For example, there is only a 25 percent chance that two random people will both be Spicy Meatballs and have average levels of kinkiness. The odds that two people would both be Kinksters or both be Vanillas are even lower, at around 6 percent.

Lucky for you, there are a few things you can do to increase the odds you will find someone who shares your Level-o-Kinkiness. We didn't really cover it in Chapters 5 or 6 because we didn't want to freak you out,

---

Example sex questions from online dating sites

* *Would you ever consider making a sex video with your partner?*

* *Which pubic hairstyle do you prefer for a partner?*

* *If a partner asked you to have sex in a sex shop booth with others watching, would you?*

* *Do you like to be dominant in the bedroom?*

* *What are your thoughts on tickling in the bedroom?*

* *How many sex toys do you own?*

* *Would you enjoy watching pornography with your partner?*

* *Would you consider having an open relationship?*

* *Do you enjoy it when someone uses ice or cold items on you during sex?*

* *Do you think the romantic aspect of a relationship is more important than the sexual aspects?*

* *While in the middle of the best lovemaking of your life, if your lover asked you to squeal like a dolphin, would you?*

---

but it involves going online. One advantage of online dating is you can pick people who have qualities you desire. Want someone who is outgoing? Just click! Educated—click! Tall—click! Funny—click! Loves butt plugs—click! That's right, on many of the online dating sites, you can pick not only your date's personality but also their sexual interests based on their responses to questions ranging from kissing preferences to their opinions on BDSM.

With all this information, you don't need to hang out at sex dungeons and questionable bars or wear that inappropriate jersey to the grocery store. You can find your kinky match in the exact same place you find dates. Best of all, even before your first date, you will know whether you two have similar levels of kinkiness. We get the romantic notion that some people want to wait for the relationship to naturally progress before discovering sexual compatibility. But let's be honest here: you are not getting any younger. If sexual compatibility is going to be a key component of your love life, then it's best to know this information before you get too involved. Besides, with this knowledge, you will potentially avoid that awkwardness when, after dating for a month, your partner tells you that they really need to hear you squeal like a dolphin while having sex.

Doing the dirty in a post-marriage world

Let's say you played your cards right and followed our advice. You were able to find someone online (Chapter 5), you impressed them with your awesome dating skills (Chapter 6), and you have similar levels of kinkiness. You like this new person, and they seem to really dig that you just ordered a venti-iced-skinny-caramel-sugar-free-double-pump-syrup-light-ice-extra-shot-with-soy. Think you are going to get laid at the end of the date? Probably not with that coffee order. Of course, the real answer is, maybe, depending on what you both want. But what are the odds? If this was a sexual slot machine, how many times would you have to pull the handle (that is, go on a date) before you hit the sexual jackpot? Turns out, you don't need too many quarters before you are likely to hit it big.

Back in the day, there was the familiar "three-date" rule. This was the popular guideline that you should wait until the third date before, um, engaging in gland-to-gland combat. It seems like no one ever told men about this "guideline," because 33 percent of men want to have sex on the very first date (or maybe this means 66 percent of men are lying, but let's stick with the research). For women, this number is a bit lower at 10 percent, meaning there are a lot of sexually disappointed men after that first date. Luckily for this group of men, by the third date, about 33 percent of women are also ready to have sex. Most of the remaining men and women are ready to have sex by the seventh date.[21] However, there are a few romantics out there who want to wait to have sex until they fall in love. As you might have guessed, most of these romantics are women. About 15 percent of women want to wait to be in love before they have sex with their partner, which is about double that of men who want to wait for the "Big L."

Obviously, "counting dates" until you have sex is more than a little silly. It's not like a rocket launch where you are counting down to a blast-off. This ain't NASA. You and everyone you meet will have different "rules" that they use to decide when they are ready to have sex. Some wait ninety days (suggested by "relationship guru" and inept Miss Universe host Steve Harvey), others use the three-date rule, and some just say "fuck it" and start fucking. The point is, you will be faced with the option of having sex early on while dating, most likely *waaaay* before either of you are feeling in love.

Before you get ready for all that sexy time, it is important to keep in mind that the actual amount of sex you have after you get divorced will probably be less than when you were married. About 40 percent of married people have sex two times a week or more, but once you get divorced, this number drops to 23 percent.[3] The main reason for this decline is not due to decreased sexual desire, but simply because when you're married there is usually another person right next to you in the bedroom, which makes access to another's naughty bits pretty easy. If anything, it seems divorced people are a bit hornier than their married peers—divorcees spank the monkey and paddle the pink canoe (i.e., masturbate) twice as frequently as married individuals.[22]

With all this sexual interest, you are going to see a dramatic increase in your number of sexual partners. When you were married, if you behaved yourself, you probably had about one sex partner a year for the length of your marriage. After getting divorced, you can expect that number to increase significantly. The average sexually active divorced person has sex with a different partner every six months.[3] With this increase in sexual partners, we want to help you to avoid some pitfalls associated with sex. We don't want to be a killjoy here, but we feel obligated to remind you of some key issues to consider as you navigate the sexual post-divorce minefield.

STIs: They're not just for kids anymore. The Villages is the largest retirement community in the United States. It has a population of over 75,000 residents who can enjoy the thirty-four golf courses, numerous country clubs, and series of bars and restaurants. Some have called it the "Disneyland for seniors," but the naughty behaviors that go on inside and outside the bedrooms of this senior community would make Minnie Mouse look away in shock. Residents have been arrested for having sex in golf carts. There are suggestions of an underground "black market" for Viagra. And health officials have expressed alarm at the increasing rates of STIs (sexually transmitted infections) among the residents.[23, 24] We shit you not. All this senior sex is not just limited to the Villages— across the country, seniors living in retirement communities are having more and more sex, which is leading to an increase in STIs.

Seniors who are recently widowed and younger people who are freshly divorced share something in common when it comes to sex. It is very unlikely that either of these newly single groups has given much thought to the potential dangers of having sex with other people in years. Here is a fun bit of trivia for you: people over the age of thirty experienced the greatest increase in STIs in the last five years. Even among those over the age of sixty, rates of gonorrhea, chlamydia, hepatitis B, trichomoniasis, syphilis, and herpes rose 23 percent during this time period. Within the United States alone, there are over 110 million STIs.

Heck, each year, there are 20 million new infections, and people older than twenty-five account for a substantial bulk of them.[25, 26]

The good news is that many of these STIs, like chlamydia, gonorrhea, syphilis, and trichomoniasis, are easily treated and cured if diagnosed early. The bad news is that many people don't know if they have one of these STIs because they often have no symptoms. Even HPV, which accounts for the majority of newly acquired STIs, will go away on its own 90 percent of the time within two years and cause no harm. Of course, a serious HPV infection can lead to major health issues, like cervical cancer.[24] Which means you need to start thinking about STIs.

Say it with us now: *condoms are non-negotiable.* Unlike your last marriage, herpes lasts forever. Until you are in another committed monogamous relationship and are sure everyone is non-infectious, remember to cover that stump before you hump. You also want to start getting tested. Being tested for STIs is not only fundamental for your health, but it's a nice thing to do for any future sex partners. Be sure to talk to your doctor about becoming sexually active outside of marriage again, and they will have recommendations about the types of tests you need. We get it, the idea of planning and thinking about STIs is a drag. But being sexually active and not taking precautions will end up being so much worse . . . and warty . . . and with a funky smell.

Yes, YES, YEEEESSSSSSSS! Consent, bitches! Let's talk about it. In the newfound era of #MeToo, everyone is talking about what consent means and how to get it. Countless public figures have had their lives, and careers (typically oh-so-rightfully) shattered because they fucked up in this area. We want to help you avoid being a less famous version of one of those assholes and/or avoid falling prey to an asshole.

Simply put, consent is one person's uncoerced agreement to engage in some form of sexual activity with another person. Most common conceptions of consent focus around the idea that you say a firm "no" to anything that you don't want to do. Further, you check in with your partner before engaging in any sort of sexual contact to make sure that they have the chance to say "no" to anything they don't want to do.

We want to expand on this idea a little bit. And this challenge is based on some lessons from the folks who we imagine score high on our Kink-o-Meter™: members of the kink community. People who are part of the kink community are those who engage in some of the more extreme sexual behaviors out there on a regular basis . . . the Kinksters plus. As you might imagine, consent becomes especially necessary if you plan on doing something like ball-gagging your partner before slathering them in peanut butter and letting your dog lick it off. Anywho, this means that the kink community has given a lot more thought about consent than the more vanilla among us, and you can put their advice to good use, even if you never plan on owning a ball gag.[27]

One of the techniques that kinky folks routinely put into place is the use of a safe word. This is a word, or a few words, that can be used at any point during sex that means *NO, STOP, DESIST,* or at least *WHOA.* It gives partners a way to communicate, without confusion, when they want things to slow down, or completely stop. It's best if your safe word is non-sexual, because it's more likely to grab your partner's attention. If your lover yells "Brussel Sprouts" in the middle of a sexy moment, it's pretty jarring and likely to promote a stunned pause. Whatever you've agreed upon, if you hear it, stop and check in. If you say it, expect your partner to stop and check in. A popular approach is to use the words "Yellow" and "Red." Yellow indicates that you're iffy on what's going on—you're okay, but you'd like things to slow down so that you have time to process your feelings. Red means immediately stop and check in with each other. No matter what you and your personal sex god decide to go with, remember that you (and your partner) have the right to put your safe word into play at any time, for any reason.

Beyond creative ways to say, "no thank you, sir or ma'am," consent should be more than not saying no—it should be about saying yes, yes, *ohgodyes!* Rather than focusing on a partner telling you what they don't want to do, focus on what they *DO* want to do. Make them beg for it. What's hotter than that? To achieve this, you and your partner need to communicate about your preferences. Like a lot. Start talking about sex as soon as you can in your relationship without feeling like a pervy weirdo. You may not want to bring up the fact that you like your toes licked on your very first date, but before you even consider putting this little piggy in your lover's face, you need to discuss it. Make the conversation fun, make it foreplay. As a prelude to the act itself, consent can be hot. Beyond that, make sure you check in as things, ahem, progress. Consent isn't a one and done thing; you need to keep the conversation going. You or your partner are allowed to change your minds, about anything, at any point in the process, and that's okay. But again, there are ways to make this incredibly sexy. Try saying, "I want to [insert dirty fantasy here]," and pause. See how your partner reacts. If they're all about it, go for it. If there's even a little tiny moment of hesitation . . . don't. Let them take charge from time to time in order to express what they're interested in. You get the idea.

Finally, in order to be able to talk about what you want to do and don't want to do in the sack, you must know what you do and don't want to do in the sack. This means that, before you consent to anything with another person, you need to understand what does and doesn't turn you on. See the Kink-o-Meter™. This is why we were so insistent that you be honest with yourself when tallying up that kinky score. Think seriously about what you like. Check out some porn (seriously dudes, it's the twenty-first century, get over it), and see what works for you and what might make you gag a bit . . . or just feel uncomfortable. Masturbate often (you're divorced, we already covered that you're doing this more now anyhow, so make the most of it). And more important, tell your partner what you want. Shit, being bossy in the bedroom from time to time is pretty hot. Right?

Ex-sex. It's another Saturday night and recently divorced Betty finds herself home alone, again. Opening a bottle of her favorite red wine, she relaxes on her couch to catch up on her favorite show, *Game of*

Thrones. "Oh God—has Jon Snow always looked that good?" "Has Jaime Lannister always been so bad . . . oh so very bad." Great, Betty thinks, now I'm alone, drunk, and horny. She still has some feelings for her ex, and the temptation is strong as she stares at her cell phone and decides— maybe just one more night together.

The next morning, Betty calls her friends, and they all agree that Betty just screwed the pooch. She quickly goes online to seek advice, only to discover headlines like "Sex with your Ex: Don't Go There!", "Why Having Sex with your Ex is a Bad Idea," and "Why Sleeping with your Ex-Husband Will Only Hurt You." Clicking on one of these articles, she reads the same disapproving sentiment echoed by her friends:

> Having sex with your ex forces the separation into a gray area no matter what because you're still bonding intimately. This gray area provides a bridge for emotional expectations. One or both people will develop expectations that will keep you from moving on.[28]

Now before we get all judgy on Betty, we'd like to point out that ex-sex is a common activity. About 25 percent of people will have sex with their ex-spouses at least once.[29] The good news (for Betty and the 25 percent of you who will have a night of ex-sex) is that you are probably not in any danger of developing "expectations that will keep you from moving on." Doing squat thrusts in the cucumber patch with your ex-spouse one time is unlikely to produce more psychological distress the next day or even months later.[30] Contrary to popular opinion, and what Betty learned on the Internet, ex-sex doesn't typically cause people to feel worse about their relationship ending, nor does it hinder them from accepting the end of the relationship.

We are not suggesting you should make active plans to go out and screw your ex. As we mentioned in Chapter 3, if you are maintaining a relationship with your former spouse simply to have sex (e.g., friends with benefits), this is going to lead to all types of boundary issues and should be avoided. Sure, if you are like Betty and it does happen once or twice, it doesn't mean that you failed or that you're doomed never to move on to find new love. But while a night of ex-sex might not hinder you from getting over your past relationship, it could mess up any new relationship you're trying to start. Just because you did the four-legged foxtrot with your ex-spouse while married doesn't mean ex-sex isn't cheating on a new partner. Finally, the "why" (oh god, *whyyyy?*) behind your choice to have ex-sex could certainly impact your psychological health.

Having sex for the "right" reasons. Think about the last time you did the dance with no pants, and not just by yourself. Maybe you were still married, or perhaps it was after a hot date. Why did you have sex? People

Examples of Approach Goals for Sex	Examples of Avoidance Goals for Sex
I have sex to . . . *pursue my own sexual pleasure *please my partner *promote intimacy in my relationship *satisfy my sexual needs *have a thrilling time *express love for my partner *have an emotional connection	I have sex to . . . *avoid conflict in the relationship *prevent my partner from becoming upset *stop feeling disappointed with my life *avoid feeling unattractive *cope with upset feelings *prevent my partner from losing interest in me *avoid feeling lonely

have sex for various reasons: to feel less lonely, express their love, relieve tension, boost their self-esteem, or simply for pleasure.[31] Even though there are numerous reasons a person might have sex, we can classify all these varied reasons as either "approach goals" or "avoidance goals." Approach goals are go-get-em-tiger goals. They focus on having sex in order to obtain a positive outcome like pleasure or to feel emotionally closer to a partner. In contrast, avoidance goals are run-awaaaaay goals. They emphasize having sex in order to evade negative things like feeling lonely or depressed.[32] Check out the table below for some other examples of approach and avoidance goals for sex.

One thing you might notice is that approach goals are not just lovey-dovey reasons to have sex. Heck, having sex simply because you want to satisfy your own selfish sexual needs is as much an approach goal as having sex to express your deep emotional love for your partner. What approach goals have in common with each other is that achieving them will lead to obtaining a reward—either physical (e.g., experiencing pleasure) or emotional (e.g., experiencing love). In contrast, the best-case scenario for accomplishing an avoidance goal (like "preventing partner from losing interest") is a temporary relief that some negative event was avoided (phew, my partner didn't just leave me), and worst case, it will produce the very anxiety it was trying to avoid (I can't stop thinking that my partner might leave me if we don't have sex . . . ugh).

Now is a good time to ask yourself again: Why did you have sex last time? Was it for an approach goal or an avoidance goal? Be honest with yourself, because the reason why you had sex probably impacted both the quality of the sex and how you felt about it afterward. Having sex for approach goal reasons is much healthier for you and your budding romantic relationships. People who have sex for approach goals feel more satisfied with their relationship, experience more positive emotions, and even have better sex. As a bonus, having strong approach goals helps maintain your sexual desire across the course of a new relationship. In contrast, people who have sex for avoidance goals have worse sex, more relationship conflict, and feel distressed, upset, ashamed, and even guilty.[33, 34, 35]

In an ideal world, you would only have sex for approach goal reasons, but one major problem is that it is difficult to control why someone wants to have sex at any given time. It turns out, some people just tend to generally pursue sex for approach goals, whereas others are more inclined to pursue sex for avoidance goals.[36] It is hard to suddenly flip from wanting to bone that hottie to "avoid feeling lonely," to wanting to do the horizontal mambo in order to "have an emotional connection." But you can choose when and when not to have sex. That is something that is completely under your control. The basic rule of thumb is to try to maximize the times you are having sex for approach goals and keep it in your pants if your desires are being driven by an avoidance goal. We understand that this is not easy. However, in the long run, if you try to have sex for the "right" reasons, you will likely not only boost your overall sexual pleasure but will also feel much better about it in the morning.

Putting a lace (or leather) bow on this whole thing.

Okay, so we know that having sex to have an emotional connection is a good thing. We all want to love and be loved, and, hopefully, have mind-blowing coitus in the process. So have great sex while you're dating, and lots of it. Be safe, be kind, be mindful of consent, be aware of motives, and you'll be fine. Amazing sex is a big deal in the early stages of relationships because it helps to build trust and closeness. We even produce more of the hormone implicated in emotional bonding, oxytocin, after orgasm.[37] And that's the end goal, isn't it? To fall in love again? We think so.

Chapter 8

When you've met "The Next One": What to do now that you've found love again

M aybe it's a month after divorcing, or maybe it's five years and many dates later, but you've gone and done it. You're officially off the market and in a new relationship. You're either the bravest, most optimistic person alive, or a massive fucking idiot. We'll cut you some slack and say it's the former. We love being in love. It's exciting, gut-wrenching, wonderful, and horrifying all at once. It's also complicated. And it's going to be more complicated this time around. If you're hitting the stage where you're "Facebook official" with your new sweetie, you should think about what you're getting yourself into and what issues (especially those unique to your post-divorce life) you need to tackle. It's best to do this before getting in so deep that it will take another painful bout with lawyers and alimony payments to pry yourself free.

To everything there is a season.

The Byrds recorded *Turn! Turn! Turn!* as a plea for world peace in 1965 while tensions surrounding the Vietnam war were escalating. However, the song's consistent reminder that "to everything there is a season (turn, turn, turn)" can also be applied to romantic relationships. Although there is no calendar that predicts how every relationship progresses, relationships generally go through four stages or seasons: Passion

(Spring), Attachment (Summer), Adaptation (Autumn), and Termination (Winter).[1, 2] Understanding each season of your relationship will help you better understand where you're at with your new love and what you should be focused on doing.

Spring passion. Passion peaks early on, in the spring. Think about it . . . all those birds chirping in the April trees aren't doing it just for fun—they're trying to get *laaaaaid*. Feeling like a horned-up blue jay is common during the spring stage of dating. These early, heady days of a relationship are almost always marked by intense feelings of infatuation, obsession, and something researchers call *limerence*. Limerence is a psychological state characterized by an intense rush of emotions, extreme sexual attraction, and swings in romantic feelings.[3] During a spring relationship, we find ourselves feeling on top of the world when things are going well, and then suddenly chained in the pit of despair[i] when they're not.

At the extreme end, this can venture into unhealthy territory. Shakespeare's *Romeo and Juliet* (or really, any Lifetime Original Movie with the word *obsession* in the title) is an excellent case of how infatuation gone crazy can lead to heartache and hysterical sobs of "O happy dagger! This is thy sheath; there rest, and let me die." While this is a dramatic example, over-the-moon-can't-live-without-you is a totally normal way to feel at the beginning of a relationship.[4, 5] It would be a bummer if early relationships weren't characterized by butterflies in the stomach, constant fantasies about the other person, and the general belief that they are perfect in every way (including that they simply don't poop). These powerful emotions are what make things exciting and help encourage us to put extra effort into a new union in order to stabilize it into something more profound . . . like love.[6]

This intense feeling of passion even changes the way our brains work. In those first months of a love affair, our brains pump out extra

---

i *Princess Bride*, bitches!

doses of the neurotransmitters serotonin and dopamine.[7, 8, 9] Serotonin helps regulate our feelings of joy and happiness, while dopamine helps control our experience of pleasure and reward. These neurochemical changes are similar to the changes that happen when a person is addicted to drugs, meaning you can literally get hooked on somebody.[10, 11] Terrifying, we know. But this cocktail of chemicals is a big part of why we feel euphoric, energized, and happy to sit up all night talking or . . . not talking (wink, wink) in the early days of a spring relationship.

Summer lovin'. As the soft glow of spring passion begins to fade, you enter the heat of the summer season. In the summer of love, you become more emotionally attached to your partner, more bonded, more interested in supporting your partner's needs and goals, and more comfortable sharing your true self.[12, 13] This early stage of love means that you share with your partner personal details about your life and past, and you trust that they will understand where you're coming from and make you feel seen and validated.[14] When you fall in love, you also get another nifty neurochemical boost that adds to the toe-curling cocktail brought on by your feelings of passion. It's a hormone called oxytocin, and it's the biological glue that bonds us together.[15, 16] Lovers get boosts of this neuropeptide when they snuggle, kiss, and have sex (well, when they have an orgasm, anyway—so ladies, make sure to get yours!).[ii] So, as your relationship matures from spring to summer, you get more of this closeness enhancer pumping through your system, and it helps to cement your bond.[14] These changes are crucial if your relationship is to continue, because it's this newfound emotional bond that allows you to deepen your relationship and begin contemplating what it would be like to feel like this, with this person, over the long-term.[12]

---

ii Pregnant and nursing mommas also get massive hits of this hormone in the early days of their baby's life, and both moms and dads release it in spades when listening to their little one's cry.

When we're in relationships, we're always considering the extent to which the relationship meets our expectations (more on this in a bit) and comparing what we'd like to be getting out of our relationship (in terms of lust, trust, intimacy, and whathaveyou) with what we're actually getting and what we could get elsewhere.[17] *Buuuttt*, what we base those comparisons on changes as our relationships move through their seasons.[18] In spring, we might base our evaluations on whether we have fun with the person, or if the sex is good, or if the person shares our taste in movies or music. In the summer of love, your evaluations become based on different, often deeper, things. Does this new partner possess personality qualities that are essential for a long-term relationship? Do you both share similar expectations for living together? Are future goals compatible? Do you have similar expectations for any current or future children? These are the judgments that will determine whether your relationship burns out like a scorching hot day in August, or whether it develops into an even deeper, more stable union.

True summer love takes time to build; it rarely occurs instantaneously.[10] That's why "love" at first sight really isn't a *thing*. Lust at first sight, yeah, sure; but not real, honest-to-goodness love. Most people don't even report saying "I love you" until a few months into a relationship. It typically takes an average of 88 days for the fellas to say those three words, while it takes women about 134 days to communicate that lovin' feeling.[19] When someone first drops the "L-bomb," it usually means that they are ready to move from the magical fairy dust stage of an infatuated romance into the beginning of a summer relationship. However, it is extremely unlikely, at this early stage, that two people actually share a true, deep consummate love.[2, 11]

Psychologist Robert Sternberg argues that for love, *twue wuv*,[iii] to exist, it needs to contain three basic components: passion, intimacy, and commitment.[20] Passion is that infatuation stew where we can't get enough of our partner—we crave them like a kid craves candy on Halloween.

---

iii   Again, *Princess Bride*, bitches.

Intimacy is feeling close and bonded, our emotional attachment to our love. Commitment is our choice to stay with our boo-bear through thick and thin. Each component is an important part of love, and missing one of these elements impacts the type of love we feel. For example, as you can see in the following figure, having only passion, but missing the other elements, is what most people experience during a spring relationship—infatuation. Whereas, having both passion and intimacy but no commitment is the type of love usually felt at the beginning of a summer relationship—romantic love. This love is great, but it is missing long-term commitment and future plans. These pieces of the puzzle take a little bit longer to develop. For a relationship to experience the deepest type of consummate love possible, all three elements are needed. When couples achieve this type of love, they are fulfilled and couldn't imagine themselves ever being happier with anyone else.[21]

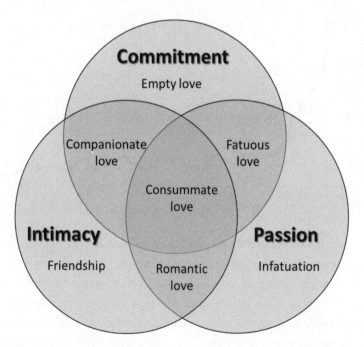

Autumn adaptation. On the calendar, autumn starts three months after summer begins. Around this time of year, everything begins to wither away. Formerly lush trees are suddenly left barren as their lifeless leaves litter the ground. Once green lawns turn into ugly patches of brown grass. The air grows cooler. The days become shorter, and you suddenly become aware that the whole world has a weird obsession for pumpkin spice *everything!* In the world of love, autumn usually hits a couple of years into a relationship. Just like in the outside world, come autumn, most relationships experience a cooling of their passionate temperatures.[1]

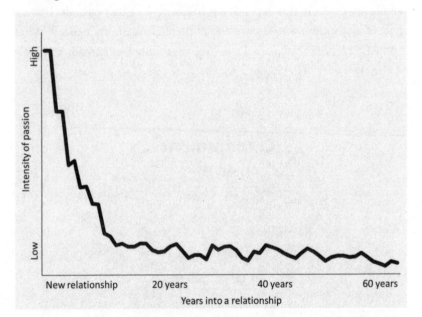

As you can see in the previous figure, passion is at its highest during a relationship's spring period before it drops, like a lead balloon, as time marches on.[22, 23] If you look back at Sternberg's model of love, this means that many people's relationships move through infatuation and romantic love, and then into something called companionate love as their bonds mature.[19] This love is characterized by deep friendship, trust, and mutual respect (intimacy), coupled with plans for a future together (commitment).[22] By no means is this a bad thing. The drop in passion that occurs as relationships get older is normative—it happens to most people and isn't necessarily a sign that something is *wrong* between you and your love. Couples who experience companionate love can have satisfying relationships that last for decades.[22]

When you decide to begin another long-term relationship, you want to start it with a partner who will be able to adapt, with you, to these changing feelings. If you both panic and bail at the first sign of changing leaves and crisper air, you'll be missing out on what can continue to be a very fulfilling relationship. That said, it never hurts to try to infuse a bit of heat into your autumn. This is greatly helped if your partner has similar sexual interests as your own (you two have similar Kink-o-Meter scores).[24] Additionally, because a good sexual relationship is bolstered by emotional intimacy, maintaining an emotional connection with your partner over the years is extremely important for keeping the fires burning, or at least glowing warmly.[14] How you do this is a little beyond this chapter—you are just at the start of a summer relationship and autumn isn't going to hit for a few more years—but we wouldn't leave you hanging. In the next chapter, we'll give all kinds of advice on how to maintain your connection and help keep your passion alive.

Winter: The terminator. "Winter is coming" is the motto of the House of Stark in the blockbuster series *Game of Thrones*. Its meaning is simple—you need to prepare if you are to have hope in surviving the hardships of this freezing cold season. During your divorce, you experienced "winter coming" firsthand when your marriage ended up dying of hypothermia. You want to avoid repeating this unpleasant bit of history at all costs, which is why it's essential to prepare and winterize your new relationship now. The very best time to prepare for winter is at the start of a relationship (during the summer phase), as a romance is starting to become serious.[18] Preparation at this stage will help you figure out if your new love is a bond that will bring in a fruitful fall harvest, or if it is best left at the beach after Labor Day weekend with the other well-loved, but not so sturdy summer things . . . like boardwalk-purchased flip-flops. This also means that, right now, you should focus not only on enjoying your current lovie-dovie feelings of passion and intimacy, but also on whether this relationship is worthy of your commitment and effort over the long haul. There are three major factors to mull over here that can be real killers as your relationship's temperature drops: whether your new love lives up to your expectations, whether your sweetie fits in smoothly (mostly) with your existing post-divorce life, and whether there are any major red flags in your relationship indicating that you should make a hasty run for it.

Expectation vexation.

Whether a relationship has the staying power to avoid winter is largely determined by how well it lives up to the expectations of its members.[25] We stay in relationships where the benefits outweigh the costs, and our outcomes are in line with our expectations.[26] When what we expect is more or less what we get from our partner, we're satisfied and happy with our relationship. On the other hand, when reality doesn't live up to our fairy tale, we become dissatisfied and, eventually, go our separate ways. During the early summer of a relationship, there are three expectation vexations that are crucial when deciding whether a relationship should progress and become more serious: partner expectations, home expectations, and future expectations.

Partner expectations: Prince(ss) Charming? Or just a frog? We all have an ideal romantic partner built up in our heads.[27] This fairy tale figure is created out of what we expect our partners to be like, from our experiences observing romantic partnerships out in the world (our parents, our friends, *The Notebook*, Cinderella), as well as our experiences with past partners. Your particular ideal vision of a romantic partner helps you evaluate your actual partner's fabulousness (or lack thereof), explain relationship events (like how you expect Valentine's Day to go down), and know when you need to make adjustments in your relationship (like asking your partner to bring you flowers more often).[28]

Because expectations of partners are so strongly influenced by the outside world, it is important to first consider whether your expectations are even realistic. In the age of Facebook and Instagram, people often compare their relationship to the relationships they see on social media.[29] When browsing through an Instagram feed, you'll find lots of pictures of happy couples, who all seem to possess perfect partners and are living fabulous lives. Of course, in reality, all these Insta-couples have just as many pimples, dark circles, and splotches as your relationship . . . they're just using filters. People tend to share the best parts of their lives on social media, so comparing your "real" partner to these other "filtered" partners sets up unrealistic expectations. This is just one reason why people who constantly check the activities of other couples on social media tend to have more relationship issues.[30]

Having realistic expectations is important because when flesh-and-blood partners don't match our expectations, the discrepancy is pretty upsetting and can lead people to respond in various negative ways.[28] For example, you might distance yourself from the relationship. The downside here is that if you are too hasty, you could end up missing out on a great person. Maybe instead of running away, you decide to try to change your partner to be more like your romantic fantasy. Romantic comedies are rife with this sort of approach—the guy isn't so sure the girl is his type, but with a change of wardrobe (typically taking down the hair and ditching some glasses) and of heart (she comes to appreciate his caveman-like ways), she suddenly morphs into his perfect fantasy woman. Gag. Not only is this way of handling things pretty cringeworthy, but it also tends not to work that well.[27]

When your romantic partner isn't quite matching up with your ideal expectancies, but you want to keep them around, it's often better to try altering your expectations to be more in line with what your partner is actually like.[28, 31] Of course, this should only be done if the quality your partner lacks isn't super important to you. If it's critical that your partner never cheats and they are always "working late," "plowing the neighbor's field," or "hiking the Appalachian Trail," then fuck 'em—you probably should walk away. However, if your ideal partner is "musical," and your new love can't play any musical instruments and sings like a dying cat, you need to decide if that quality is important enough that it is worth losing the relationship over. Another trick is to try to reinterpret the characteristics your partner *does* possess to be more in line with your expectations.[28] Sure, your partner might not be able to play a musical instrument, but they might love listening to songs. By changing your viewpoint, you are better aligning your fantasy with reality, without asking your partner to be anyone other than who they are . . . and we're willing to bet that they are pretty awesomesaucy.

Home expectations: Adulting is hard. One area that often fails to live up to expectations is the division of adulting responsibilities in the home.[32] During the early summer of a relationship, romantic partners are usually living apart, handling the practical shit of their lives mostly on their own—kings and queens of their own little kingdoms, beholden to none. But, if all goes well, these separate kingdoms will eventually consolidate into a single castle. Trust us when we say that sharing a living space with another human is really fucking hard. Erica had no idea how much laundry Patrick and his kids produced until she unpacked her bags. She previously washed clothes weekly but quickly found that now there was laundry to be done (and folded . . . ugh!) on the daily. Pat did not expect that Erica would be as concerned as she was about wholesome food choices. Out went the chips and cookies, in came the whole grain crackers and fruit. There were many complaints lodged.

How couples divide household labor is a major source of conflict and disillusionment in many relationships. Most couples expect the job of maintaining a house will be split equitably, and everyone will pull their half of the weight.[33, 34] That said, this nifty fifty-fifty is rarely a reality. When it comes to managing the messiness of daily living, the sexist truth of the matter is that women often disproportionately bear the burden— even when they are also bringing in their share of the dolla dolla bills y'all.[35, 36] Women simply execute the majority of the daily tasks required to keep a household running (like cooking, cleaning, and shopping for toilet paper), in addition to shouldering the invisible burden of managing which tasks need executing (like even noticing that the home is almost out of toilet paper). This is why, on average, women complete about sixteen hours of household chores a week, while men average approximately six.[37]

An imbalance of household chores isn't automatically a bad thing—some couples are happy to maintain such an arrangement. The problem is that resentment and grief can occur when your *expectations* for the division of household labor aren't matching up to your reality.[38] The best way to avoid this problem is to be proactive and communicate expectations during the early summer of your relationship—before moving in together. Understanding and discussing any differences that exist in how you both run your lives and homes is a critical step to take before shacking up. It might not be the most romantic thing to talk about, but it will be helpful to know if your partner is happy to wash clothes or if they are just going to continually buy new underwear to avoid doing a single load of laundry.

After moving in together, if your mate deviates from your informal housework agreement, and you find yourself thinking, *That fucker acts like running laundry might actually kill him* (or her . . . but most likely him), be sure to share your concerns. Partners are often unaware when they aren't doing their fair share of household tasks.[38] Of course, telling a partner to do more work isn't always going to automatically fix the problem, but it is a step in the right direction. Both members of a romantic couple need to share and listen to each other's perspectives on what each believes they are doing for the household. For all the things we notice that our partner is *not* doing, we might be missing many of the things that they are. Maybe our partner doesn't remember to put the toilet seat down (or leave it up) like we'd hoped, but perhaps they do remember to replace the toilet paper roll when it gets low. They even put it on the right way (the paper goes *over the roll,* you monsters, not under). One thing *not* to do is keep a detailed record of who does what. "I emptied the dishwasher, so you need to do the dishes." "I went grocery shopping, so you walk the dog." This tit-for-tat approach, as tempting as it might be, is a recipe for disaster and will quickly smother any affection you have for each other.[39]

Future expectations: Be a goal digger. What are the goals you hope to achieve in the future? Maybe you want to retire at sixty. Perhaps you are hoping to have kids for the first time or the sixth time (Brady Bunch style). Or, maybe you want to live large and drive around a Jaguar or six (wannabe James Bond style). Goals are important. They help determine how we allocate our resources and time most effectively. Goals provide the basic blueprint for how we hope to achieve a happy and fulfilling life.[40] They are essentially a list of expectations you have for your life—five, ten, or even twenty years from now.

Goal compatibility is a big deal in relationships. When our lives are wrapped up with someone else's, we are never truly chasing our goals in isolation—we're part of a unit, a team, a collective.[41] Exactly how we go about achieving or abandoning a goal is highly influenced by our partners. These special people also affect our goal pursuits by shaping how we evaluate the value, likelihood, and importance of a goal.[42] Where we can get into trouble with our goals is when we assume our new sexy love cocoon's goals are the same as our own. You know what they say happens when we assume, right?[iv] Therefore, by the early summer of your relationship, you and your new partner should be clear on the goals that are important to each of you. Rejoice in the similarities that are already there and seriously consider what it means if any of your goals conflict with each other.

We're not suggesting that the goals of partners need to be carbon copies of each other. You are allowed to have some different future plans than your partner.[41] If your goal is to eat lots of tacos, but your partner wants lots of pizza, you will probably be okay. Your partner just needs to be supportive of your unique goals (and vice versa, friends). So, be

---

iv Ass-u-me? When you assume you make an *ass* out of *u* and *me*.

sure your love is down with Taco Tuesdays. However, there are some areas where compatibility is usually mandatory[40]: how money is handled, where everyone lives, children (none, some, or tons), retirement timing, etc. A summer relationship, where one person wants to raise a large family on a farm in Kentucky, and the other dreams of living as DINKS[v] in a penthouse in New York, is probably doomed to eventually run aground in the ice of winter.

During an early summer relationship, communication is essential to avoid problems associated with expectation vexations. It is crucial to share and discuss the expectations you have about your partner, how you will share adult responsibilities, and your dreams about the future. Share what matters to you and listen to what matters to your new person. Create a plan for what you want your life to look like that reflects both of your expectations in a realistic manner. That said, expectations change as time passes, so keep talking about your hopes and dreams for your relationship even after the initial deal-breakers have been tackled.

Kids, future-stepkids, and exes . . . oh my!

Having an ex-spouse and/or children is probably the biggest difference between your dating life today and your dating life before you initially got married. In earlier chapters, we discussed the difficulties of ex-management and post-divorce parenting. Unfortunately, adding a new summer relationship to this situation is only going to make things a whole lot more complicated. Navigating this territory can be as painful as walking barefoot on the hot sand of a beach in August. But, just as bringing the right shoes will prevent your tootsies from baking, careful preparation is your best weapon when your post-divorce dating world begins to merge with the world of your previous life: your kids and your ex-spouse.

Your babies and your baby. If children exist from your previous marriage, it is crucial that you never, we repeat, *never* rush into introducing

---

v   D.I.N.K.s—Dual income, no kids

your children to people you are dating.[43] You need to avoid exposing your children to a revolving carousel of lovers. They've had enough upheaval in their lives already with your divorce; you don't want to add to it. You want to introduce your littles to a new partner *only* once you're pretty damn sure they are going to be sticking around for a while . . . so at least wait until the summertime of your relationship. Furthermore, you and your new sweetie, *and* you and your kiddos, need to have some serious conversations about expectations for how things will go down beforehand.[44] This is true both for the first few meetings and long term. Have a plan, Stan.

Make sure your partner knows a bit about your children and their interests before the big reveal. Imagine the awkwardness if your partner shared their distaste for *My Little Pony* to your son who is an aspiring bronie.[vi] By the same token, explain to your children that you would like them to meet the person you are dating. Let them ask questions and be honest (but kid-friendly) in your answers.

Keep the first few interactions casual. If you both have kids, it is best if you meet each other's munchkins separately before introducing the kids to each other.[45] Patrick first introduced Erica to his offspring at Chuck E. Cheese. The food was questionable and the children likely caught some sort of undiscovered virus, but the outing was relaxed and lasted just a couple of hours (including the time it took to apply hand sanitizer). During these initial outings, partners should go easy on overt physical affection (no smoochin' or ass grabbin'). Children, especially teenagers, often feel upset when they witness displays of affection from their parents, especially early on in a relationship.[45] By keeping things low-key for a while, everyone can get to know each other at their own pace. Save more intense time spent together for later. No overnights. No big trips.

There is a prevailing view, which many recoupled parents are guilty of, that their new partner and their kids will love each other instantaneously,

---

vi   A bronie is a person (typically male) who is an extreme fan of the television program *My Little Pony: Friendship is Magic* . . . we could not make this up.

and everyone will instantly skip off into the sunset as a happy family. Reality check time. Caring relationships between any two (or more) humans take time to evolve.[46] You didn't fall immediately in love with your partner (probably). Your new partner is not going to fall immediately in love with your children. And, your children are not going to fall immediately in love with your partner. There might be some bumps in the road while both sides of your love equation warm up to each other. During these early days of hanging out as a quasi-trying-it-on-for-size stepfamily, the most anyone should hope for is that everyone is on their best behavior, and all are comfortable in each other's presence. You can't rush or force this. Let your kids and your new love create their own relationship, on their own terms, and in their own time.

It is totally normal for children to have mixed feelings about their parent being in a new relationship. For many children, this new relationship represents the final nail in the coffin of their most fervent wish—that their parents will get back together.[45] Be clear with your children that, although you love them to the moon and back, you and their other parent will not become a romantic couple ever again. Don't mislead or give them false hope . . . it will only fuel resentment toward your new sweetie. Listen to their worries and concerns. If they're too tiny for deep conversations, spend extra time with them, and keep reminding them how much you love them. That they are the most important thing to you. That you think they're more special than any other special thing ever invented, including Santa Claus and wine.

As time passes, if everyone seems on board for this crazy adventure, you will need to figure out the practical details of bringing your new sweetie into your daily lives . . . including where everyone is going to live. Communication with everyone is, again, key.[44, 47] Talk to your love about what they'd like to see happen. Talk to your kids about what is going to happen beforehand. Many couples prefer to move into a new, neutral space. We didn't; we stayed in the home Patrick shared with his ex, but we painted and remodeled and de-ex-wifed the shit out of the place. We also created excitement for the children by redecorating their rooms however they wanted to do them (mostly, black paint was a non-starter). Regardless, if you move into a new home or revitalize an existing home, when blending two families with children, it is best to have a fresh start so that it becomes "our home" rather than "mine" or "yours." [47, 48]

Other issues to address at this stage include: How will you and your partner handle finances, especially as they relate to the children? [45, 47, 48] What rules are in place for your munchkins, and how might they change with the addition of a new person into the home? What role can your children and their new stepparent expect to play in each other's daily lives? There aren't necessarily *right* answers to these questions. There are only *right* answers for *your* family. Some stepparents "step up" and share in the lives of their stepkids in almost every way: financially, helping with homework, bandaging scraped knees, and showing up for every ballet recital and basketball game. Other stepparents "step back" and function more as support staff rather than major players in the lives of their partner's kids. Both approaches can be completely healthy for both your children and your relationship.[48] The key is to start talking about these expectations during the early days of a summer relationship to avoid "missteps." The more everyone involved communicates, the easier it will be to find the path that best fits your family.

When there are children involved, you don't have the luxury of keeping a summer relationship perpetually light and fluffy. If introducing your partner to your children sounds too heavy, you may want to rethink whether you're ready to bring your romance into the lives of your children. By the same token, if it seems unlikely your children and partner are going to get along, it might be best to let your summer relationship end in a wintery frost. However, if everyone seems onboard, you could be on your way to joining the fastest growing family structure in Western, industrialized society: the binuclear stepfamily.[49]

Out with the old (spouse), in with the new (lover). When you were casually dating, your rendezvous, booty calls, friends-with-benefits relationships, or Netflix and chill-ing[vii] trysts are none of your ex-spouses' business. Nor were their post-divorce escapades any of yours. However, this might change when you find someone you want to make a permanent part of your life. Except for divorced couples who are dissolved duos and who never speak, it is usually best to tell ex-spouses about new serious relationships instead of letting them learn about it on Facebook or through friends.[47] When notifying an ex, you are *not* asking for permission; instead, you are stating a fact: "I have been dating Keanu Reeves for a while. He is a great guy. I am going to introduce him to our daughter next week at his movie premier of *John Wick 8*." The secret is to be honest, straightforward, and aware that a new love interest will almost certainly impact your relationship and co-parenting with your ex-spouse.[50]

Two issues will affect how an ex responds to a new partner: the type of relationship between exes and whether there are children. A contentious relationship with an ex (angry associate or fiery foe) usually results in a poorer reaction from a former spouse than couples who have an amicable relationship (perfect pals or cooperative colleagues).[47] And by poor reaction, we mean with anger, recriminations about how much everyone sucks, and other assorted dick-tastic behaviors. Regardless of the type of relationship you have with your ex-spouse, it's completely normal for your ex to have *some feelings* about your summer relationship.[51] Even in the best of circumstances, it's hard to see someone you thought you were going to spend your life with thinking about spending their life with someone else. Try to afford your ex, no matter how much they might irritate you, some understanding during this time. Take a few deep breaths, set solid boundaries, and focus on keeping any interactions you must have with each other task-focused (like, who is going to shuttle little Suzy to her fourth ballet class this week). If you need a refresher on how to manage difficult ex dilemmas, go back to Chapter 3.

---

vii Unfortunately, Patrick was a little slow in learning that "Netflix and chill" is a euphemism for sex. This was made painfully clear when he first introduced Erica to his best friend and suggested they all go back to his house and "Netflix and chill."

If there are children in the picture, your ex will have additional concerns about the role your new partner will eventually play in the children's lives. They may have strong feelings against your new love being involved in discipline matters or feel yucky about sharing special events like holidays with your new partner.[51, 52] Now, some of these concerns fall into the "tough shit Sherlock" category. Your new love is likely going to have thoughts and feelings about how these things will go, too, and your new partner is now the person whose side you should be on . . . not your ex.[48] The idea that your new partner should have no say in the rules in their own home, or would never get to spend an important holiday with their step-kids, is frankly ludicrous. Of course, you need to do what's best for your children, but make sure your ex's requests are really about the children, and not their own issues, before seriously entertaining them.

What's ultimately best for your family will depend entirely upon your situation. There is no one-size-fits-all remedy here, and there are a lot of people's needs to take into account. You will quickly find that focusing on your children's needs while also not neglecting your new relationship *and* not pissing off your ex is a challenge of Herculean proportions.[51] Factor in other extended family members' needs, and good lordy, it's a mess. Our holiday plans in any given year look like a middle school math class word-problem from hell: You have three kids, split across two binuclear households, meaning two of them have four parental units. You also have eight grandparents, six sets of aunts and uncles, two grown children of one stepparent, one of whom also has a child, and three dogs. Everyone's extended family lives in different states at least five hours, by car, from each other. How do you make sure that everyone gets to see everyone, every holiday, and no one is ever left out or has their feelings hurt?

Initial response: Fuck this shit, you don't. Pass the scotch.

Correct response: Communication, compromise, and patience . . . and, still, pass the scotch.[viii, 45, 47, 48, 50, 52]

---

viii While we can't supply you with alcohol, in Chapters 3 and 9, we do stock you up on advice about how to communicate with all interested parties so neither hurt feelings nor law enforcement get involved.

Red flags . . . run, don't walk, away.

Navigating your new relationship through the minefield of a post-divorce life can be tricky. One moment everything might be sailing along smoothly, then suddenly, an unexpected object strikes you and . . . *KA-BOOM!* These are the deal-breakers, the red flags, the piles of dog shit in the love yard that, once stepped in, will stank up shoes and carpet forevermore. Some of the shit is your new partner's. Major run-don't-walk-away red flags include: a partner who knowingly hurts you in any way, even if it's just them lashing out when angry;[53] a partner who keeps you on edge by not returning your calls or reciprocating your affection . . . fuck'em.[54] You deserve to be with someone who makes you feel like you are the best thing since *Reese's* peanut butter cups. Similarly, you need to think twice about keeping a budding summer romance alive when your partner doesn't live up to your expectations. Red flags include a person who doesn't possess qualities you think are important,[28] has different expectations for adulting,[32] has goals that are incompatible with your own,[40] or doesn't seem to be invested in your children.[45]

Some of the shit is yours. Are you ready to be in a serious relationship? Have you moved on from the pain of your divorce? Do you have a solid post-divorce identity? Have you achieved a sense of self-efficacy and self-compassion? Are you prepared to have serious discussions about expectations with your children, new partner, and ex-spouse? Go back to Chapter 5 and retake our Red Light, Green Light quiz—this time envisioning yourself in the hot, sticky summer of love, rather than when you were just thinking about jumping into casual springtime relationships. If you're not at a full-on-go signal, reevaluate whether you want to deal with all the heavy stuff that comes when lust turns into love. Shit tends to get real pretty fast, especially in the land of divorce aftermath.[47] If moving this new relationship into the heat of summer feels like too much work, and you'd rather sit on the sofa in your fleecy pajamas watching *Law & Order,* you're not ready. On the other hand, if you know, deep down in your boner (or lady boner), that you're so flippin' ready to be in love again, and to make that love happy, fulfilling, and lasting . . . read on, you starry-eyed romantic, read on. We're going to wrap this whole crazy acid trip of post-divorce life up with a bang and a bow—and advice on how to keep your new love thriving for many, many seasons to come.

Chapter 9
Divorce-proofing: Keeping marriage 2.0, or 3.0, or 5.0 together

Congratulations! You've made it! You picked yourself up off the post-divorce floor, dusted yourself off, applied more than a couple of Band-Aids, and got back out there. You've dated, mated, and found yourself someone with whom you want to spend the rest of your life. You dream about sitting on your porch with your love in your later years, looking out over your garden, watching your children and grandchildren frolic in the flowers, and fondly reminiscing about the time gone by. We can't be the only ones who have that fantasy . . . right? The good news is, if you are going to jump back into marriage with both feet (or at least serious, long-term monogamy sans matrimony), we can teach you how to 100 percent divorce-proof your new relationship.

Cue the raucous laughter. Gotcha, suckers! If you've learned one thing from your last marriage, it's that there's no such thing as a divorce-proofed relationship. Like unicorns, Sasquatch, and garden gnomes, a marriage or long-term relationship that is completely invulnerable to implosion is the stuff of legend. And, unfortunately for you, the odds are not in your favor. The average length of an American marriage is just over eighteen years, and just slightly less than half of all first marriages end in divorce.[1, 2] That's *first* marriages. Your chances do not improve with version 2.0 or 3.0 . . . or 5.0. In fact, according to 2010 US Census data, 67 percent of second marriages and 73 percent of third marriages end in tears and legal fees.[1, 3]

Multiple marriages: Why practice doesn't always make perfect.

"First divorce: wife's hidden sexuality, not my fault. Second divorce: said the wrong name at the altar, kind of my fault. Third divorce: they shouldn't let you get married when you're drunk and have stuff drawn all over your face, Nevada's fault."

—Ross Geller, *Friends*[4]

Just like Ross Geller from the television show *Friends*, it isn't uncommon for people to wonder why later marriages become increasingly likely to fail. Luckily, researchers like us have spent countless hours working out reasons why second and third marriages are more difficult to maintain. The first reason is, after successfully navigating the end of a marriage, people learn that divorce is an option that they can survive.[3] The fear around the "Big D" becomes diminished, which makes divorcees (like you), a little more trigger happy when it comes to executing and exiting their unhappy unions the next time around.

Second, your divorce likely left you with some baggage that you will carry into your next relationship. We've tried to help you sort through some of this in the previous chapters, but chances are you'll still carry some of the horseshit into your next relationship.[3] Did your spouse cheat on you? Great, now you have a big ol' suitcase holding all kinds of trust issues. Did the spark just sort of fizzle out? Now you are the proud owner of a duffle bag full of anxieties and worries about any (remember: normal and inevitable) signs of waning passion. Beyond the psychological baggage caused by your past divorce, there's also practical messiness.[3] There might be children or stepchildren to factor into the mix (including ongoing, oh-so-fun contact with ex-spouses and the complications of a blended family).[5] The merging of assets is trickier for later marriages than first marriages. For example, Patrick was just a college student who didn't have two nickels to rub together when he got married the first time. However, by the time we got together, we both had mortgages, retirement funds, children's college savings, and investments . . . oh my! The more life you've lived, the more complicated it becomes to merge that life with someone else's. Your past makes you who you are, but it can be a risk factor for later-life marriages.

Finally, these first two issues become compounded by the fact that you probably are still going to make the same silly matrimonial mistakes in your new relationship that you made in your past one.[3] Let's face it, even if your ex was the worst person on the planet (we mean, we wouldn't go so far as to liken him or her to Satan, buuuut . . .), there were times in your last marriage when you weren't exactly an angel. Maybe you fought dirty, were neglectful of your partner's needs, forgot a birthday, monopolized the TV remote, or left dirty socks on the floor. Unfortunately, if you don't learn from those mistakes, you're bound to repeat them. It's way too easy to pin all the blame for your divorce on your ex and their shitty self. In order to give your new love a solid chance for success, you need to own your share of the shenanigans and commit to doing better this time around—and for God's sake, put your dirty laundry in the hamper.

Mary, Mary, quite contrary, how does your garden grow?

Keeping a long-term relationship thriving is like tending a garden. You've already chosen the perfect spot in your yard, carefully selected the seeds, and placed them lovingly in the ground. Now, the hard work of keeping it alive starts. But, before you launch into tending your love garden, you need to know what it needs. What stifles, chokes, and chews holes in love? And, what gives it the light, air, and food to flourish?

There are many things that people *think* contribute to the breakup of relationships that actually don't.[6, 7] Your ex being a crazy fuckwit, or your own personality shortcomings, didn't cause your last divorce; and your new partner's quirks (or your own) are unlikely to cause your new relationship to fail. Personality matters in relationships because it can exacerbate challenges or conflict, but in and of itself, it is not a root cause of relational failure.[8] We'll talk more about conflict in a bit, but suffice to say, if either you or your partner are a neurotic sorehead or a disagreeable curmudgeon, you might have a harder time keeping your fights above the belt. Further, things like affairs are often perceived as causes of a failed relationship, when in reality, they are usually the symptom of a garden that is in trouble—the manifestation of a deeper, festering disease within the union. Extramarital trysts generally happen because people seek something that is lacking with their partner, whether it's sex, respect, love, attention, friendship, support, or understanding.[9] We're certainly not advocating that you hook up with other people after you start a serious relationship. But, we want you to focus on protecting and nurturing your new love garden, rather than being fixated on simply avoiding infidelity.

For approximately thirty years, scientists from around the world have spent countless hours discovering what makes couples' affectional plants more likely to wither and die, and what makes them grow like untamed zucchini in July (if you've ever grown zucchini, you *know* what we mean . . . that shit takes over *everythiiiiing*).[10] It turns out that managing the problematic pests and applying the right fertilizer on an ongoing basis will keep your garden flourishing. Specifically, you want to make sure to keep a keen eye on your love garden's critter situation (conflict), sunshine (positive focus), trellising (support), and fertilizer (love).

Love pests: Conflict.

Let's start with pest management: What are the varmints and bugs that you need to control or (preferably) ruthlessly eliminate in order to keep your newfound love on the lifelong track? The key vermin to manage here are destructive conflict behaviors. This doesn't mean that you need to totally avoid conflict. Heck, conflict is a normal part of all close relationships. Couples most commonly argue about money, sex, communication, children, household responsibilities, and time together.[11] And that's okay. Say it with us now: *conflict is OKAY*. Fighting, or not fighting, with your new partner is not a reliable predictor of whether you'll stay together. It's *how* you and your partner behave during your conflicts that matters. Just within the first *three* minutes of an argument, it is possible to accurately predict whether the fight is going to end on a positive or negative note.[12] If you start with negativity and harshness, that's where you'll end up.

To learn what negative conflict behaviors you need to avoid with your new baby-cakes, we want you to think about how you handled conflict with your ex-spouse. In Chapter 3, we briefly talked about four conflict patterns that rock star researcher John Gottman and his research team found cause problems in relationships. They are *The Four Horsemen of the Apocalypse*: criticism, contempt, defensive, and escape![5, 13] When interacting with your ex, avoiding these tendencies are important for keeping peace; when interacting with your new love, avoiding them is important to keep your current lover from becoming your next ex. To keep your relationship from having as many holes chewed in it as the fruit in Eric Carle's *Very Hungry Caterpillar*, you need to identify and exterminate the pesky conflict critters.[13] Check out the following chart to help identify what creepy crawlies you might have in your new love garden.

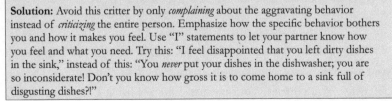

Pesky Conflict Critters

The "Critical" Caterpillar
If you spend a lot of time with someone, chances are they are going to have some behaviors that annoy you. Chews loudly—egads! Left dirty dishes in the sink—yikes! Using the word *literally* incorrectly—literally, the worst thing ever! Instead of acknowledging an irritating behavior, the critical caterpillar attacks the whole person, which makes them feel as if there is something fundamentally wrong with who they are. This pest likes to use the phrases "You always" and "You never" when being critical.

Solution: Avoid this critter by only *complaining* about the aggravating behavior instead of *criticizing* the entire person. Emphasize how the specific behavior bothers you and how it makes you feel. Use "I" statements to let your partner know how you feel and what you need. Try this: "I feel disappointed that you left dirty dishes in the sink," instead of this: "You *never* put your dishes in the dishwasher; you are so inconsiderate! Don't you know how gross it is to come home to a sink full of disgusting dishes?!"

Pesky Conflict Critters

The "Contemptuous" Cockroach

The filthy contemptuous cockroach communicates nothing but disrespect for their partner. At its core, this pest attacks a partner's moral fiber (which is just a dick move). Contempt can take the form of name-calling, sneering, nasty sarcasm (not the funny kind), eye-rolling, or mocking. It's anything that demeans and dehumanizes the person you claim to adore. This critter's contempt usually stems from long-simmering, unresolved anger. Harboring resentments is going to make anyone feel more than a bit snarly, so it is important to squash bitter feelings under your foot as soon as possible.

Solution: Be concrete and factual about your expectations and needs on an ongoing basis to keep festering upsets at bay. Keep reminding yourself of all the good qualities your partner possesses. But, once you've started being nasty, there's no magic bullet here to redirect contempt. You just need to take a deep breath, grit your teeth, and stop.

The "Defensive" Dung Beetle

The poop-encrusted defensive dung beetle tries to deflect any complaint a partner has about it (legit or not) by using righteous indignation. This pest will sometimes whine as if it is an innocent victim to deflect blame. The defensive dung beetle's behavior will cause a partner to feel that their concerns are not being taken seriously, and all the blame is being unjustly shifted onto them.

Solution: Avoid this smelly pest by resisting the urge to defend yourself when being criticized. Take responsibility for what's bothering your partner and focus on tackling the issue at hand.

The "Escapist" Earwig

Even when you don't want to hear what your partner has to say, it's important you stay tuned in. During conflict, when you start to feel overwhelmed with negative feelings, there is a good chance you will see the escapist earwig scuttle across your garden. This annoying pest withdraws from confrontation and stops responding to its partner. When the earwig starts to check out  of important (albeit unpleasant) conversations, it will often build walls in other places in the relationship. Avoidance becomes a habit, and soon you will be infested with escapist earwigs as they chew through your feelings of love and affection.

Solution: Neutralize this pest the first time you notice it in order to avoid making your partner feel consistently unheard and neglected. If you feel the need to step away from confrontation tell your partner you need to take a twenty-minute break. Breathe. Relax. Psychologically self-sooth yourself and then return to the conversation.

Pesky conflict critters feed into an escalating cycle of nastiness in your arguments. You complain about something to your partner. They get defensive. You criticize. Your partner criticizes back, a bit more harshly.

You roll your eyes. They call you a jerk. Before you know it, you are both in a full-blown screaming match, or you are so close to *reallllly* losing it that you shut down and refuse to talk about the issue anymore. Your garden is now infested with every type of conflict critter, and they're happily chomping away at your plants and destroying your new relationship.[5] The escalating ugliness that these critters enable leaves everyone feeling hurt, misunderstood, and neglected. This anger and resentment builds and festers to the point that the relationship becomes unsalvageable. These pests are so damaging to your garden that it is possible to predict if a couple will divorce, with over 90 percent accuracy, based exclusively on how many of these pesky conflict critters emerge during an argument.[14]

You're probably sitting there freakin' out right about now. Maybe it's dawning on you that you have a little bit of blood on your hands when it comes to how you fought in your last marriage, and you're worried that you're going to bring the same issues with you into your new relationship. In short, you're doomed! Except you're not. Not by a long shot. There are several conflict pesticides you can try, before and after a fight, to help alleviate the problems caused by those pesky conflict critters and prevent them from swarming all over your new relationship.

Patch-up pesticide. The special ingredients in Patch-Up Pesticide are designed to de-escalate an argument and repair any damage done to the relationship.[15] To apply Patch-Up Pesticide to your garden, all you have to do is say or do something—silly or otherwise—that prevents further infiltration of those pesky conflict critters and halts the infestation before it spirals out of control. You could make an (appropriate) joke or put your hand on your partner's arm. You could simply take a deep breath and say, "I think that this is getting out of hand. I am sorry for my part in that—can we start again?" As a bonus, Patch-Up Pesticide can also inject some positivity and warmth into a tense situation. Check out the list below for some ideas . . . but make this your own—get creative! It could just help to save your relationship.

ACTIONS	WORDS
Smile.	I'm sorry for my part in this.
Make an appropriate joke.	Can we start over?
Hug your partner.	Can I try to say that differently?
Sit next to your partner.	This isn't your (my) problem; it's our
Turn to face your partner.	problem.
Uncross your arms and legs.	I see what you're talking about.
Make soft eye contact.	I feel blamed, can you rephrase that?
Hold hands.	I don't like fighting with you, can we
	just talk?

Step-away argument spray. Another strategy to try is to take short breaks from arguments.[6] Rather than getting overwhelmed to the point that you totally shut down and escape, when you feel yourself starting to crave a vacation away from all other humans in Greenland, grab a bottle of Step-Away Argument Spray and tell your partner you need a time-out. Take ten minutes apart to regroup and calm down, then come back to the discussion. Focus on addressing things calmly and staying as present as possible. Make sure not to use too much Step-Away Argument Spray because you don't want to totally run away from a disagreement. You must deal with the issue at hand at some point, so using too much repellent will likely turn a shit-sprinkle into a full-on shitstorm.

This pesticide works best if you and your schmoopy have an agreed upon signal that you've decided on ahead of time to use if you need a breather. We prefer funny step-away safe words, like "bananas foster," "Liechtenstein," or "Hoobastank." It's hard to stay angry when your partner shouts dessert words, obscure countries, or the names of alternative rock groups from the nineties. After you have both had your ten-minute break to calm down, make sure to come back to the conversation; don't ignore it and hope it goes away. Like a stubborn weed, the anger will always return if not addressed after applying Step-Away Argument Repellent.

Perspective-changing conflict repellent. This handy repellent works by changing your perspective about the fight. Make sure to follow the steps listed on the products label (see below) for best results.

A two-year study of Perspective-Changing Conflict Repellent found that when couples used this product once every four months, they

> ## Perspective-Changing Conflict Repellent
>
> **Directions**
>
> *Step 1:* Think about a specific disagreement that you recently had with your partner. Think about this disagreement with your partner from the perspective of a neutral third party who wants the best for all involved, a person who sees things from a neutral point of view. How might this person think about the disagreement? How might they find the good that could come from it? (Please write about this for three minutes.)
>
> *Step 2:* Some people find it helpful to take this third-party perspective during their interactions with their romantic partner. However, almost everybody finds it challenging to take this third-party perspective all the time. In your relationship with your partner, what obstacles do you face in trying to take this third-party perspective, especially when you're having a disagreement with your partner? (Please write about this for two minutes.)
>
> *Step 3:* Despite the obstacles to taking a third-party perspective, people can be successful in doing so. Over the next week, please try your best to take this third-party perspective during interactions with your partner, especially during disagreements. How might you be most successful in taking this perspective in your interactions with your partner over the next week? How might taking this perspective help you make the best of disagreements in your relationship? (Please write about this for two minutes.)

became happier in their relationships in almost every way (they felt more satisfied, intimate, passionate, trusting, *and* committed).[16] The best part is, Perspective-Changing Conflict Repellent only takes seven minutes to apply, meaning that you can improve the conflict and your relationship in twenty-one minutes a year. No matter how busy you are, we're willing to bet you can spare that. So, give it a try! Set aside seven minutes every week to reframe conflicts with your partner that make you nutty.

The power of sunshine: Focusing on positive memories.

Anyone who gardens will tell you that keeping the bugs out is not the only thing that's important for plants to flourish. You also need to make sure your love-garden gets a lot of sunshine and positivity. If you think of your relationship as a positive force in your life, it becomes a self-fulfilling prophecy where you feel more positively about your relationship . . . and round and round the cycle goes. Making sure your garden is basking in positive sunlight will contribute to you feeling more committed and satisfied in your relationship.[17] It will make it more likely that you will recall past difficulties with your current partner as less crappy and past fun-times (like vacations) as more amazing.[18] Heck, when the sun is really shining, you even tend to reconstrue your partner's faults as indicators of their *obvious* virtue.[19] A partner who is a little boring to almost everyone will be given the benefit of the doubt by their loving partner and be seen as a "strong, silent type." In contrast, those whose gardens are constantly covered by clouds and negativity are unlikely to grow anything beyond a withered turnip.[6, 13]

A favored approach by horticulturalists and marital therapists for adding sunshine to a garden is to have couples tell the story of how they met. Sit down with each other, look into each other's eyes, and take turns telling the tale of the first time you saw each other, or your first date, or when you first realized you were falling in love. Let your partner talk uninterrupted, and then switch. You might be surprised at what your snugglebutt remembers about those early days! When we share things about ourselves with our loves, and they share with us, it boosts our feelings of closeness and happiness.[20, i] Spouses who are happy in their marriages typically enact five positive behaviors for every one negative behavior.[5] Marriage researchers refer to this as your "emotional bank account" in your relationship—the more positivity and sunshine you put in, the more you have stored up for a rainy day.

In addition to encouraging feelings of intimacy and boosting your emotional bank account, sharing your positive memories provides an extra dose of sunshine by encouraging eudaimonic well-being. This crazy-ass term refers to the sense that your life has purpose and meaning. And, one way to get it is by feeling that you and your partner are part

---

i In some weddings, couples write a letter about what they love about each other and then seal it up in a box with a bottle of wine. The idea is to open both letters and the wine after their first major fight in order to remind each other of why they got married in the first place. It's the same idea as what we're talkin' about here. Although, we'd suggest focusing on positive memories more often than just when you fight . . . but we're totally on board with the wine. *Yesss* . . . yes, we are.

of a larger, cohesive unit striving toward the same long-term purpose.[6, 21] Eudaimonic well-being can be contrasted with hedonic well-being, which is the feeling of pleasure that comes from experiencing satisfying yet superficial things (e.g., eating homemade chocolate chip cannoli).[22] Both types of well-being are good for you, but eudaimonic well-being is more stable (that chocolate chip cannoli is only so big). We get spikes in hedonic well-being when we do fun stuff or eat awesome foods, but then reality kicks in—we lose a job, get injured, fail, run out of chocolate chip cannoli, get divorced. Hedonic well-being tanks. However, if we find purpose and meaning with our partners, we will be better able to keep the sun shining on our garden and maintain an eudaimonic sense of well-being even when we hit occasional rough patches.[23]

Recollecting the happy past with your partner is a great way to start increasing a sense of eudaimonic well-being, but you also want to consider what your mutual garden is going to look like in the future. Make a two-, five-, or even ten-year plan together. Be sure to include what you each hope your individual lives will look like, but also what you hope your life together will include. You can even go so far as to create a joint vision board (for the uninitiated: a literal piece of poster board with your *vision* for the future displayed in quotes and images, often endorsed by the likes of Oprah)![ii] This exercise serves the purpose of creating shared meaning for you as a couple and more of that sunny eudaimonic well-being; plus it helps clarify expectations for the future. Building a relationship that is full of meaning involves prioritizing your time, resources, and each other. Think of it as your legacy—the memories, goals, beliefs, and culture of your family that you create to last far into the future.

---

ii   Full disclosure . . . we think vision boards are silly. They're basically fourth grade art projects made by adults. We're bigger fans of skipping the glue sticks and just writing down your vision—but hey, you do you. We promise we'll only judge a little.

Trellising your beans: Support in bad and good times.

"Beans, beans, good for your heart
The more you eat, the more you fart
The more you fart, the better you feel
So eat beans for every meal!"

As we learned from the popular child's playground song, beans can give you butt burps while also benefiting your loving heart.[iii] It's important to build trellises in your love garden to support all those needed beans. Just as emotional support from family and friends helped you out at the beginning of your divorce,[24, 25] you and your new love's support for each other will be the trellis that lets your relationship grow to towering heights. When challenges in life arise, feeling supported by your partner will enhance your ability to cope. Perceived support from a partner is associated with a plethora of positive individual outcomes, from greater happiness and optimism about the future to lower blood pressure and stress hormone levels.[24] What's extra cool is that perceiving your sweetie as supportive also has nifty benefits for your relationship. You'll feel more loved, valued, and accepted by your partner to the extent that they support you. Plus, your relationship will be more satisfying and last longer if you have this support.[26] Like support from family and friends, your *perception* that your baby-schmoopins is there for you in a sensitive and appropriate way is what matters; neither you nor your relationship gets much benefit if you think your partner is leaving ya hanging like an unsupportive bra.[27]

It turns out that a strong trellis of support matters not only when the shit is hitting the fan, but also when we are on top of the world, kicking ass and taking names. When life is going well, and you feel supported by your partner, you get all the same relationship benefits as when life is

---

iii   Okay, this song is probably alluding to the fact that beans are good for your physical heart because they contain lots of minerals and fiber with no saturated fat. But, cut us a break here; it's hard to keep coming up with garden analogies!

smushing your face in the dirt, but you get the extra perk of upping your emotional bravery. Specifically, people who are supported by their partners are more likely to try new things and opt for challenging, rather than easy, tasks.[28] This means, through the proper trellising of your beans, your partner can actually help you move closer to achieving your personal goals and ideals.[29] Pretty cool, especially with that new sexy identity you have been putting together since Chapter 2.

It's crucial to remember that support in relationships is reciprocal—or two halves of the bean trellis. If one half is missing, the whole structure collapses. Not only does your partner need to support you, but you also need to return the favor for your relationship to harvest the benefits. When two people in a relationship can create a cycle of responsiveness, they are happier, more content, have fewer physical issues, less stress, and even sleep better.[30, 31, 32] Dual support in a relationship creates an atmosphere where *both* members feel understood, validated, and cared about. So, as you embark on your new (hopefully) lifelong journey with your smushykins, make sure that you have each other's backs, for better and for worse. Of course, with all those beans in your love garden, you might want to be a little careful about getting too close to each other's backs.

Love fertilizer: Keeping the devotion and passion alive.

Staying focused on your affection for your new love over the long-term probably sounds pretty easy—we mean, you think your partner is the bee's knees now . . . why would that change? Alas, as we discussed in the last chapter, the unbridled, can't-live-without-each-other, crazy-passionate-sex-all-the-time intensity of the early days of your relationship is unsustainable. No matter how affectionately you feel with your snuggly-bear-smoochikins right at this moment, this is likely to fade over time. The ugly truth is that most markers of marital quality (passion, satisfaction, love, and intimacy) decline as the years march on, and the once rich soil in our love garden becomes a barren wasteland.[33] To combat this problem, you need to break out giant bags of love fertilizer to help revive your barren patch of dirt and revitalize your feelings of affection, admiration, and love. The two best types of manure for this job are Love Guano and Creative Compost.

Love guano. Spreading love guano onto your garden every few months is sure to help keep your relationship growing. This amazing fertilizer was created by John Gottman (man, when it comes to marriage hacks, this dude is the *shit* . . . and so is Love Guano!). You apply Love Guano to your garden via a series of exercises that help you and your partner focus on and communicate your feelings of affection and admiration toward each other.[6] These exercises teach couples to cherish one another. And now, we bring them to you, free of charge (well, almost free—you did have to buy our book, but we're cheaper than therapy)! We've distilled these exercises for you in a handy-dandy set of instructions to help create an environment where you and your partner both feel L.O.V.E.D. in your relationship.[6]

Making Each Other Feel L.O.V.E.D.

List five reasons you love your partner. These can be silly, serious, or somewhere in between. Maybe your partner has a killer sense of humor or does an adorable Donald Duck impersonation to make your kids laugh. Be specific and detailed. Share your lists with each other!

Offer physical affection. Take your partner's hand when you're walking around. Hug. Kiss. Cuddle on the couch. Look deeply into each other's eyes. Create small rituals of PDA-liciousness that will make your kids cringe but that makes your partner feel your affection.

Validate your partner. Nothing makes us feel more connected than feeling understood. Take turns telling each other about what happened in your day. Take the time to really listen (which will mean putting down your phone!) and focus on expressing empathy and support.

Express appreciation for your partner. What's something your partner has done today that you felt grateful for? Washed the dishes? Got up early with the kids? Made you laugh? Thank each other for what you do! Do this daily for the best results.

Do nice things for each other. Make your partner a cup of coffee in the morning, bring home a favorite snack from the grocery store, leave sweet little notes around the house. Not only does it make you each feel cared for, but it may have the bonus of keeping you both committed to your relationship.

Do these exercises sound cheesy to you? Yeah, they do to us, too. As practical people, and just a tad cynical to boot, the idea of actively setting aside time to spout off about why we love and appreciate each other feels super sappy. But we tell ourselves the same thing we're going to tell you . . . get over yourself. Love Guano really works! Gottman and his colleagues have used this handy fertilizer with hundreds of married couples, some of them already on divorce's doorstep, and if the cheese-factor is good enough for them, it's sure as hell good enough for us. Besides, sometimes a bit of extra cheese is delicious (and just like that, now we're craving pizza; our mutual love of dough slathered in tomatoes and cheese is one of the things that we adore about each other . . . *seeeee*, relationship exercise—done!).

Creative compost. While amping up your ongoing feelings of affection for your partner with some Love Guano is all well and good, it sometimes becomes important to give an extra boost of nutrients to your garden with some Creative Compost. This handy fertilizer is designed to help reignite the fiery passion that brought you and your partner together in the first place. To give you an idea of how Creative Compost is made, let's play a quick game of make-believe.

Imagine this: You and your partner show up to a psychological research laboratory to take part in a study on long-term relationships. Instead of being greeted by a stuffy psychologist wearing a lab coat, you find yourself inside a room that looks more like the set of *American Ninja Warrior* than a laboratory. There are foam mats on the floor and bunches of equipment strewn around the room as death traps . . . um, we mean obstacles. You quickly start to wonder if this is worth the ten dollars you are getting paid to do this crazy study. Soon, your right wrist and ankle are bound by the researcher to your partner's left wrist and ankle with Velcro straps as she asks you both to get down on your hands and knees (hey . . . what kind of study is this anyway?). The person running this bizarre setup tells you that you are going to race, while strapped together, across the obstacle course. You soon find yourselves crawling on the floor and climbing over barriers in a quest to beat the times of other couples who previously attempted this course. As you cross the finish line, you feel your heart beating faster and you look over at your partner only to realize they seem to be breathing harder, too . . . and looking sexier than they have in a while. There is little doubt—this novel activity was as weird as it was physiologically arousing.

Now, we're sure you're thinking that this is a completely made-up scenario. No researcher would do something like this, and even if they did, taking part in such a study would have no impact on a romantic relationship. Well, you'd be wrong. This was an actual study done at the State University of New York–Stony Brook by eminent relationship expert Arthur Aron's research team in the late 1990s.[34] Couples who had been together anywhere from two months to fifteen years did exactly what we described above . . . exactly. The researchers found that when couples competed in the weird *American Ninja Course,* they got a boost in how much passionate love they felt for each other.

Other studies have found the same thing—doing new and exciting things together promotes relational satisfaction and feelings of happiness.[35] Notice that it isn't just doing something . . . anything . . . together that is important for fertilizing your garden. The key ingredient in Creative Compost is to do things that are *both* new and exciting together. So, if you want to spice things up with your new partner, try doing something unusual. Play together! Your Creative Compost might be taking dance lessons, going to an escape room, riding a roller coaster, going indoor rock climbing—anything that is new to you (thus combating the boredom of a long-term partnership) and exciting (arousal that you can then apply toward your partner). Creative Compost doesn't have to be extravagant or expensive; it just has to bring you closer to your partner and inject a little passion back into your relationship!

Reaping what you sow.

So, there you have it! In order to cultivate a lasting relationship this time around, you need to tend it. Keep the rotten pests out, give it a lot of positivity and sunshine, build strong support trellises, and rejuvenate your soil with big bags of love fertilizer. All these tasks will put you on the garden path to a "divorce-proofed" new relationship . . . well, at least as close to "divorce-proofed" as it's possible to be. We know it's a lot of work; it's supposed to be. All good things are—and we believe that lasting, fulfilling love is a very, very good thing.

And this, dear reader, is where we leave you: with our gardener's almanac for keeping your new love growing and thriving over time so that you can enjoy its ample harvest for decades to come. We know that the last few months or years of your life have been nothing short of hard. The death of your previous marriage changes everything. It alters your well-being, identity, and future . . . not to mention the well-being, identity, and future of people you love. Like a garden, the old love-plants died, and the ground of your life was fallow. Hopefully, you've gotten (or will soon get) your shit together, you've redefined yourself, and the seeds of a new life have been planted. You've started dating, and fragile green shoots are starting to peek out of the ground. Soon you will have a towering love tree, with ample sun, support, and food . . . not to mention a ruthless pest control regime. We are so proud of you, and you should be, too. Now grow, motherfuckers, grow!

Epilogue

(Or, "We survived this shit, and so can you.")

Anxiety. Tension. Worry. These emotions raced through my mind as I found myself (Patrick) sitting behind a tiny desk waiting for my daughter's elementary school teacher to introduce my child to a room full of parents. The jitters I felt weren't because my legs were slowly falling asleep from sitting too long in a chair designed for only the littlest of humans, but because this was the first school event my daughter's mother and I would attend together with our new spouses. To make matters even more anxiety provoking, our daughter was going to read a poem she wrote about her family titled "Where I'm From." A lot had changed in her life after we told her and her brother that, although we still loved them very much, her mother and I were not going to stay married. Needless to say, I was nervous about where she was going to say she was from. She might say she is from "a broken home," "a fragmented family," or from "two parents who royally fucked up and couldn't get their shit together, so they destroyed her childhood."

Looking across the room, I saw my ex-wife sitting next to her new husband. I could tell she was equally nervous about what our daughter was going to say in front of all these parents. Nothing makes a parent feel more anxious than having their life choices and foibles critiqued by other parents. The divorce was also hard on my ex; and I'm sure, at times, I was just as much of a twat-waffle in her eyes as she was in mine.

It wasn't always easy, but by using many of the strategies discussed in this book, which we've lovingly passed on to you, we were able to work through our bullshit and now have a great co-parenting relationship. We are far from perfect and definitely are still a work in progress, but we've successfully navigated our post-divorce relationship as it slowly transitioned from angry associates, to perfect pals, and finally settling as healthy cooperative colleagues.

Of course, while my ex and I were figuring out our new post-divorce roles, I was busy trying to redefine myself as a midlife single dad/dude and find new love. There were a lot of dates. Lots of coffee. Lots of awkward, end-of-the-night, should-we-shouldn't-we-kiss moments. Lots of . . . stories. Like when I gave new meaning to the term *blind date* after I lost my glasses, and my poor date had to guide me around the city for the rest of the night. Or when I went ice skating, even though I don't know how to ice skate. My lack of skill became painfully obvious to my date when she looked down to discover me flailing on the ice like an overturned turtle in a puffy coat. Then there was the time I ate three Fiber One bars before meeting my date for drinks—I probably don't need to finish that gaseous tale. Oh, dating was definitely an adventure. Although there were many rough ones, I was lucky enough to meet many other divorcees who were also trying to start over and find new love. It taught me as much about myself (and the disconcerting effects of consuming too much fiber) as it did about who I would be happiest with on my second attempt at making a relationship last a lifetime.

Fuck—the teacher just called my daughter's name. I felt my panic start to climb from my numb feet all the way to my rapidly beating heart. She stood in front of the class and, clutching a small piece of paper, smiled at us all watching her in the audience and began to read:

Excerpt from "Where I'm From"
I am from lost hair ties and scrunchies.
From baking and eating lots of munchies.

From my dogs Henry, Ernie and Devilish Tobey.
And learning to always pet them very slowly.

I am from making Erica cry tears of joy
Loving to buy Ernie a new toy

From playing board games and virtual reality.
And never wanting to be away from my family.

But most importantly I am from four amazing and loving parents.

I'm not crying. You're crying.

As I sat in that teensy metal chair, proudly wiping my eyes and hoping no one noticed my tears, I felt a hand come to rest on my shoulder. I looked over at my new wife (Erica) who was standing next to me (she is *way* too smart to sit in one of those tiny chairs). She peered down at me over her very pregnant belly and smiled. A few months later, we would add a new small person to our already wild and weird family, bringing our total insanity count to three children and two old-fart dogs (Ernie and Henry). But in reality, our "family" became even bigger because it also included my ex-wife, her new husband, and their own old-fart dog (Tobey). This was never the family any of us imagined we would have when *we* were children . . . but, here we are. Like every family, there are arguments and grumbling and plenty of stress. But there is also a lot of love, happiness, and support for each other. This is my binuclear family in all its unforeseen, offbeat, and caring glory, and I'm deeply proud of who we are and how far we've come.

Endnotes

Chapter 1

1. Sbarra, D. A., Hasselmo, K., & Bourassa, K. J. (2015). Divorce and health: Beyond individual differences. *Current Directions in Psychological Science, 24,* 109–113.
2. Holmes, T. H., & Rahe, R. H. (1967). The Social Readjustment Rating Scale. *Journal of Psychosomatic Research, 11,* 213–218.
3. Hetherington, E. M., & Kelly, J. (2002). *For better or for worse: Divorce reconsidered.* WW Norton & Company, New York: NY.
4. Bruce, M. L., & Kim, K. M. (1992). Differences in the effects of divorce on major depression in men and women. *The American Journal of Psychiatry, 149,* 914–917.
5. *Mathur MB, Epel E, Kind S, Desai M, Parks CG, Sandler DP, Khazeni N* (May 2016). Perceived stress and telomere length: A systematic review, meta-analysis, and methodologic considerations for advancing the field. *Brain, Behavior, and Immunity. 54,* 158–169.
6. Armanios, M., & Blackburn, E. H. (2012). The telomere syndromes. *Nature Reviews Genetics, 13,* 693–704.
7. Whisman, M. A., Robustelli, B. L., & Sbarra, D. A. (2016). Marital disruption is associated with shorter salivary telomere length in a probability sample of older adults. *Social science & medicine, 157,* 60–67.
8. Alviar, C. L., Rockman, C., Guo, Y., Adelman, M., & Berger, J. (2014). Association of marital status with vascular disease in different arterial territories: a population-based study of over 3.5 million subjects. *Journal of the American College of Cardiology, 63,* A1328.
9. Lorenz, F. O., Wickrama, K. A. S., Conger, R. D., & Elder Jr, G. H. (2006). The short-term and decade-long effects of divorce on women's midlife health. *Journal of Health and Social Behavior, 47,* 111–125.
10. Kiecolt-Glaser, J. K., Fisher, L. D., Ogrocki, P., Stout, J. C., Speicher, C. E., & Glaser, R. (1987). Marital quality, marital disruption, and immune function. *Psychosomatic medicine, 49*(1), 13–34.

11. Hajak, G. O., & SINE Study Group. (2001). Epidemiology of severe insomnia and its consequences in Germany. *European Archives of Psychiatry and Clinical Neuroscience, 251,* 49–56.

12. Donrovich R, Drefahl S, & Koupil I. (2014). Early life conditions, partnership histories, and mortality risk for Swedish men and women born 1915–1929. *Social Science & Medicine,* 108, 60–67.

13. Mancini, A. D., Bonanno, G. A., & Clark, A. E. (2011). Stepping off the hedonic treadmill. *Journal of Individual Differences,* 32, 144–152.

14. Infurna, F. J., & Luthar, S. S. (2016). Resilience to major life stressors is not as common as thought. *Perspectives on Psychological Science, 11,* 175–194.

15. Neff, L. A., & Broady, E. F. (2011). Stress resilience in early marriage: Can practice make perfect? *Journal of Personality and Social Psychology, 101,* 1050–1067.

16. Wang, H., & Amato, P. R. (2000). Predictors of divorce adjustment: Stressors, resources, and definitions. *Journal of Marriage and Family, 62,* 655–668.

17. Slepian, M. L., Ferber, S. N., Gold, J. M., & Rutchick, A. M. (2015). The cognitive consequences of formal clothing. *Social Psychological and Personality Science, 6,* 661–668.

18. Balchin, R., Linde, J., Blackhurst, D., Rauch, H. L., & Schönbächler, G. (2016). Sweating away depression? The impact of intensive exercise on depression. *Journal of affective disorders, 200,* 218–221.

19. Penedo, F. J., & Dahn, J. R. (2005). Exercise and well-being: a review of mental and physical health benefits associated with physical activity. *Current opinion in psychiatry, 18,* 189–193.

20. Christiansen, C. H., & Matuska, K. M. (2006). Lifestyle balance: A review of concepts and research. *Journal of Occupational Science, 13,* 49–61.

21. Bandura, A. (1977). Self-efficacy: Toward a unifying theory of behavioral change. *Psychological Review, 84,* 191–215.

22. Karademas, E. C. (2006). Self-efficacy, social support and well-being: The mediating role of optimism. *Personality and individual differences, 40,* 1281–1290.

23. Pajares, F. (1996). Self-efficacy beliefs in academic settings. *Review of educational research, 66,* 543–578.

24. Gist, M. E., & Mitchell, T. R. (1992). Self-efficacy: A theoretical analysis of its determinants and malleability. *Academy of Management review, 17,* 183–211.

25. Blascovich, J., & Mendes, W. B. (2000). Challenge and threat appraisals: The role of affective cues. In J. P. Forgas (Ed.), *Studies in emotion and social interaction, second series. Feeling and thinking: The role of affect in social cognition* (pp. 59–82). Cambridge University Press, New York, NY.

26. Goldberg, L. R. (1999). A broad-bandwidth, public domain, personality inventory measuring the lower-level facets of several five-factor models.

In I. Mervielde, I. Deary, F. De Fruyt, & F. Ostendorf (Eds.), *Personality Psychology in Europe*, Vol. 7 (pp. 7–28). Tilburg, The Netherlands: Tilburg University Press.

27. Moss, S. (2019). The distinction between challenge and threat appraisals. *Sico Tests*, retrieved from https://www.sicotests.com/psyarticle.asp?id=281.

28. Alter, A. L., Aronson, J., Darley, J. M., Rodriguez, C., & Ruble, D. N. (2010). Rising to the threat: Reducing stereotype threat by reframing the threat as a challenge. *Journal of Experimental Social Psychology*, *46*, 166–171.

29. Jerusalem, M., & Schwarzer, R. (1992). Self-efficacy as a resource factor in stress appraisal processes. In R. Schwarzer (ed) *Self-efficacy: Thought control of action* (195–213), Rutledge, New York, NY.

30. Kross, E., Bruehlman-Senecal, E., Park, J., Burson, A., Dougherty, A., Shablack, H., . . . Ayduk, O. (2014). Self-talk as a regulatory mechanism: How you do it matters. *Journal of Personality and Social Psychology, 106*, 304–324.

31. Neff, K. (2003). Self-compassion: An alternative conceptualization of a healthy attitude toward oneself. *Self and Identity*, *2*, 85–101.

32. Neff, K. D. & Germer, C. (2017). Self-Compassion and Psychological Well-being. In J. Doty (Ed.) *Oxford Handbook of Compassion Science*, Ch. 27. Oxford University Press, New York, NY.

33. Neff, K. D., Long, P., Knox, M., Davidson, O., Kuchar, A., Costigan, A., Williamson, Z., Rohleder, N., Tóth-Király, I., & Breines, J. (2018). The forest and the trees: Examining the association of self-compassion and its positive and negative components with psychological functioning. *Self and Identity, 17*, 627–645.

34. Sbarra, D. A., Smith, H. L., & Mehl, M. R. (2012). When leaving your ex, love yourself: Observational ratings of self-compassion predict the course of emotional recovery following marital separation. *Psychological science, 23*, 261–269.

35. Brown, K. W., & Ryan, R. M. (2003). The benefits of being present: mindfulness and its role in psychological well-being. *Journal of personality and social psychology, 84*, 822–848.

36. McAdams, D. P. (2008). American identity: The redemptive self. *The General Psychologist, 43*, 20–27.

37. McAdams, D. P., & McLean, K. C. (2013). Narrative identity. *Current directions in psychological science, 22*, 233–238.

38. Slotter, E. B., & Walsh, C. M. (2017). All role transitions are not experienced equally: Associations among self-change, emotional reactions, and self-concept clarity. *Self and Identity, 16*, 531–556.

39. McAdams, D. P. (2013). The positive psychology of adult generativity: Caring for the next generation and constructing a redemptive life. In *Positive psychology* (pp. 191–205). Springer, New York, NY.

40. Slotter, E. B., & Ward, D. E. (2015). Finding the silver lining: The relative roles of redemptive narratives and cognitive reappraisal in individuals' emotional distress after the end of a romantic relationship. *Journal of Social and Personal Relationships*, *32*, 737–756.

41. Taylor, S. E. (2011). Social support: A review. In H. S. Friedman (ed.) *The handbook of health psychology*, (pp. 189–214). Oxford University Press, New York, NY.

42. Feeney, B. C., & Collins, N. L. (2015). A new look at social support: A theoretical perspective on thriving through relationships. *Personality and Social Psychology Review*, *19*, 113–147.

43. Uchino, B. N. (2006). Social support and health: a review of physiological processes potentially underlying links to disease outcomes. *Journal of behavioral medicine*, *29*, 377–387.

44. Berkman, L. F., & Syme, S. L. (1979). Social networks, host resistance, and mortality: a nine-year follow-up study of Alameda County residents. *American Journal of Epidemiology*, *109*, 186–204.

45. Cohen, S., & Wills, T. A. (1985). Stress, social support, and the buffering hypothesis. *Psychological bulletin*, *98*, 310–357.

46. Benight, C. C., & Bandura, A. (2004). Social cognitive theory of posttraumatic recovery: The role of perceived self-efficacy. *Behaviour research and therapy*, *42*, 1129–1148.

47. Duffy, M. E. (1993). Social networks and social support of recently divorced women. *Public health nursing*, *10*, 19–24.

48. Aberg, Y. (2009). The contagiousness of divorce. In P. Hedstrom & P. Bearman (eds) *The Oxford handbook of analytical sociology*, (pp. 342–364). Oxford University Press. New York: NY.

49. Greif, G. L., & Deal, K. H. (2012). The impact of divorce on friendships with couples and individuals. *Journal of Divorce & Remarriage*, *53*, 421–435.

50. Brown, E. M. (1982). Divorce and the extended family: A consideration of services. *Journal of Divorce*, *5*, 159–171.

51. Stewart, R. E., & Chambless, D. L. (2009). Cognitive–behavioral therapy for adult anxiety disorders in clinical practice: A meta-analysis of effectiveness studies. *Journal of Consulting and Clinical Psychology*, *77*(4), 595–606.

Chapter 2

1. James, W. (1890). *The principles of psychology*. Cambridge, MA: Harvard University Press.

2. McConnell, A. R. (2011). The Multiple Self-aspects Framework: Self-concept representation and its implications. *Personality and Social Psychology Review*, *15*, 3–27.

3. Markus, H., & Wurf, E. (1987). The dynamic self concept: Social psychological perspective. *Annual Reviews of Psychology, 38,* 299–337.

4. Campbell, J. D., Assanand, S., & Paula, A. D. (2003). The structure of the self-concept and its relations to psychological adjustment. *Journal of Personality, 71,* 115–140.

5. Lewandowski, G. W., Nardone, N., Raines, A. J. (2010). The role of self-concept clarity in relationship quality. *Self and Identity, 9,* 416–433.

6. Lodi-Smith, J., & Roberts, B. W. (2012). Concurrent and prospective relationships between social engagement and personality traits in older adulthood. *Psychology and aging, 27,* 720–727.

7. Mead, G. H. (1934). *Mind, self, and society.* Chicago: University of Chicago Press.

8. Andersen, S. M., & Chen, S. (2002). The relational self: An interpersonal social-cognitive theory. *Psychological Review, 109,* 619–645.

9. Andersen, S. M., Chen, S., & Miranda, R. (2002). Significant others and the self. *Self and Identity, 1,* 159–168.

10. Aron, A., & Aron, E. N. (1997). Self-expansion motivation and including other in the self. In S. Duck (Ed.), *Handbook of personal relationships: Theory, research, and interventions* (2nd ed., pp. 251–270). Hoboken, NJ: John Wiley & Sons.

11. Mikulincer, M., & Shaver, P. R. (2003). The attachment behavioral system in adulthood: Activation, psychodynamics, and interpersonal processes. In M. Zanna (Ed.), *Advances in experimental social psychology* (Vol. 35, pp. 52–153). New York: Academic Press.

12. Slotter, E. B., & Gardner, W. L. (2012). The dangers of dating the "bad boy" (or girl): Romantic desire encourages the adoption of even negative qualities of potential partners. *Journal of Experimental Social Psychology, 48,* 1173–1178.

13. Slotter, E. B., & Gardner, W. L. (2009). Where do "You" end and "I" begin? Pre-emptive self-other inclusion as a motivated process. *Journal of Personality and Social Psychology, 96,* 1137–1151.

14. Slotter, E. B., & Gardner, W. L. (2012). The dangers of dating the "bad boy" (or girl): Romantic desire encourages the adoption of even negative qualities of potential partners. *Journal of Experimental Social Psychology, 48,* 1173–1178.

15. Slotter, E. B. & Emery, L. F. (2017). Social role transitions and self-concept clarity. In Lodi-Smith, J. & DeMarree, K. (Eds). *Self-Concept Clarity: Perspectives on Assessment, Research, and Application* (pp 85–106). Springer International Publishing, Switzerland.

16. Agnew, C. R. (2000). Cognitive interdependence and the experience of relationship loss. In J. H. Harvey & E. D. Miller (Eds.), *Loss and trauma:*

General and close relationship perspectives (pp. 385–398). Philadelphia, PA: Brunner-Routledge.

17. Slotter, E. B., Gardner, W. L., & Finkel, E. J. (2010) Who am "I" without "you"? The influence of romantic breakup on self-concept clarity. *Personality and Social Psychology Bulletin, 36,* 147–160.

18. Lewandowski, G. W., Aron, A., Bassis, S., & Kunak, J. (2006). Losing a self-expanding relationship: Implications for the self-concept. *Personal Relationships, 13,* 317–331.

19. Manvelian, A., Bourassa, K. J., Lawrence, E., Mehl, M. R., & Sbarra, D. A. (2018). With or without you? Loss of self following marital separation. *Journal of Social and Clinical Psychology, 37*(4), 297–324.

20. https://earthquake.usgs.gov/earthquakes/eventpage/official19600522191120_30/executive

21. Weigart, A. J., & Hastings, R. (1977). Identity loss, family, and social change. *American Journal of Sociology, 82,* 1171–1185.

22. Cookston, J. T., & Remy, L. (2015). Who am I if we're not us? Divorce and identity across the lifespan. In K. C. McLean & M. Syed (Eds.), The Oxford handbook of identity development (pp. 454–470). New York, NY: Oxford.

23. Sbarra, D. A., Borelli, J. L. (2013). Heart rate variability moderates the association between attachment avoidance and self-concept reorganization following marital separation. *International Journal of Psychophysiology, 88,* 253–260.

24. Campbell, J. D., Trapnell, P. D., Heine, S. J., Katz, I. M., Lavallee, L. F., & Lehman, D. R. (1996). Self-concept clarity: Measurement, personality correlates, and cultural boundaries. *Journal of Personality and Social Psychology, 70,* 141–156.

25. Emery, L. F., Walsh, C. & Slotter, E. B. (2015) Knowing who you are and adding to it: Reduced self-concept clarity predicts reduced self-expansion. *Social Psychological and Personality Science, 6,* 259–266.

26. Hughes, E., Slotter, E. B., & Lewandowski, G. L. (in press) Preferences for self-expansion: Scale development. *Journal of Personality Assessment.*

27. Mattingly, B. A., Lewandowski, G. W. Jr, Bobrowski, M. E. (2013). *The desire for non-relational self-expansion scale.* Unpublished manuscript, Ursinus College, Collegeville, PA.

28. Markus, H., & Nurius, P. (1986). Possible selves. *American psychologist, 41,* 954–969.

29. Higgins, E. T. (1987). Self-discrepancy: a theory relating self and affect. *Psychological review, 94*(3), 319.

30. Slotter, E. B., Emery, L. F., & Luchies, L. B. (2014). Me after you: Partner influence and perceived effort predict rejecting aspects from the self and self-concept clarity after relationship dissolution. *Personality and Social Psychology Bulletin, 40,* 831–844.

31. Norcross, J. C., Mrykalo, M. S., & Blagys, M. D. (2002). Auld lang Syne: Success predictors, change processes, and self-reported outcomes of New Year's resolvers and nonresolvers. *Journal of Clinical Psychology, 58*, 397–405.

32. Gollwitzer, P. M., & Sheeran, P. (2006). Implementation intentions and goal achievement: A meta-analysis of effects and processes. *Advances in experimental social psychology, 38*, 69–119.

33. Seeley, E. A., & Gardner, W. L. (2006). Succeeding at self-control through a focus on others: The roles of social practice and accountability in self-regulation. In K. D. Vohs, & E. J. Finkel (Eds.), *Self and Relationships: Connecting Intrapersonal and Interpersonal Processes* (pp. 407–424). New York: Guilford Press.

34. Lockwood, P., Jordan, C. H., & Kunda, Z. (2002). Motivation by positive or negative role models: Regulatory focus determines who will best inspire us. *Journal of Personality and Social Psychology, 83*, 854–864.

35. Slotter, E. B., & Gardner, W. L. (2014). Remind me who I am: Social interaction strategies for maintaining the self after a threat. *Personality and Social Psychology Bulletin, 40*, 1148–1161.

36. Cheung, E. O., & Gardner, W. L. (2016). With a little help from my friends: Understanding how social networks influence the pursuit of the ideal self. *Self and Identity, 15*, 662–682.

37. Rands, M. (1988). "Changes in social networks following marital separation and divorce." In *Families and social networks*, Edited by: Milardo, R. M. 127–145. Newbury Park, CA: Sage.

38. Aberg, Y. (2009). The contagiousness of divorce. In P. Hedstrom & P. Bearman (eds) *The Oxford handbook of analytical sociology*, (pp. 342–364). Oxford University Press. New York: NY.

39. Kalmijn, M. and Broese van Groenou, M. 2005. Differential effects of divorce on social integration. *Journal of Social and Personal Relationships, 22*: 455–476.

40. Wicklund, R. A., & Gollwitzer, P. M. (2013). *Symbolic self completion*. New York: NY, Routledge.

41. Fatherly (2017). The 2017 imagination report: What kids want to be when they grow up. Retrieved from https://www.fatherly.com/love-money/work -money/the-2017-imagination-report-what-kids-want-to-be-when-they-grow-up/

42. Slotter, E. B., & Gardner, W. L. (2012). The dangers of dating the "bad boy" (or girl): Romantic desire encourages the adoption of even negative qualities of potential partners. *Journal of Experimental Social Psychology, 48*, 1173–1178.

43. Slotter, E. B., & Walsh, C. (2017). All life events are not experienced equally: The associations between self-change and emotional reactions predicting

self-concept clarity in the wake of role transitions. *Self and Identity, Special Issue on the Self Over Time, 16,* 531–556.

44. Brumbaugh, C. C., & Fraley, R. C. (2007). Transference of attachment patterns: How important relationships influence feelings toward novel people. *Personal Relationships, 14,* 369–386.

Chapter 3

1. Sbarra, D. A., & Emery, R. E. (2005). The emotional sequelae of nonmarital relationship dissolution: Analysis of change and intraindividual variability over time. *Personal Relationships, 12,* 213–232.

2. Kressel, K., Lopez-Morillas, M., Weinglass, J., & Deutsch, M. (1978). Professional intervention in divorce: A summary of the views of lawyers, psychotherapists, and clergy. *Journal of Divorce, 2,* 119–155.

3. Ahrons, C. R. (1994). *The good divorce: Keeping your family together when your marriage comes apart.* New York: HarperCollins.

4. Rubin, K., Fredstrom, B., & Bowker, J. (2008). Future directions in… Friendship in childhood and early adolescence. *Social Development, 17,* 1085–1096.

5. Raboteg-Saric, Z., & Sakic, M. (2014). Relations of parenting styles and friendship quality to self-esteem, life satisfaction and happiness in adolescents. *Applied Research in Quality of Life, 9,* 749–765.

6. Frisby, B. N., Booth-Butterfield, M., Dillow, M. R., Martin, M. M., & Weber, K. D. (2012). Face and resilience in divorce: The impact on emotions, stress, and post-divorce relationships. *Journal of Social and Personal Relationships, 29,* 715–735.

7. Argyle, M., & Henderson, M. (1984). The rules of friendship. *Journal of Social and Personal Relationships, 1,* 211–237.

8. Schneider, C. S., & Kenny, D. A. (2000). Cross-sex friends who were once romantic partners: Are they platonic friends now? *Journal of Social and Personal Relationships, 17,* 451–466.

9. Fein, D. J. (2009). *Spending time together: Time use estimates for economically disadvantaged and nondisadvantaged married couples in the United States.* MDRC.

10. Waldinger, M. D., Quinn, P., Dilleen, M., Mundayat, R., Schweitzer, D. H., & Boolell, M. (2005). A multinational population survey of intravaginal ejaculation latency time. *The Journal of Sexual Medicine, 2,* 492–497.

11. Sharp, T. (2017). *How far is the moon?* Space.com. Retrieved from https://www.space.com/18145-how-far-is-the-moon.html

12. Masheter, C. (1997). Healthy and unhealthy friendship and hostility between ex-spouses. *Journal of Marriage and the Family, 59,* 463–475.

13. Mason, A. E., Sbarra, D. A., Bryan, A. E., & Lee, L. A. (2012). Staying connected when coming apart: The psychological correlates of contact and sex with an ex-partner. *Journal of Social and Clinical Psychology, 31,* 488–507.

14. Ferraro, A. J., Lucier-Greer, M., & Oehme, K. (2018). Psychometric evaluation of the multidimensional co-parenting scale for dissolved relationships. *Journal of Child and Family Studies, 27*, 2780–2796.
15. Galovan, A. M., & Schramm, D. G. (2017). Initial coparenting patterns and postdivorce parent education programming: A latent class analysis. *Journal of Divorce and Remarriage, 58*, 212–226.
16. Gottman, J. M., Coan, J., Carrere, S., & Swanson, C. (1998). Predicting marital happiness and stability from newlywed interactions. *Journal of Marriage and the Family*, 5–22.
17. Mogilski, J. K., & Welling, L. L. (2017). Staying friends with an ex: Sex and dark personality traits predict motivations for post-relationship friendship. *Personality and Individual Differences, 115*, 114–119.
18. Griffith, R. L., Gillath, O., Zhao, X., & Martinez, R. (2017). Staying friends with ex-romantic partners: Predictors, reasons, and outcomes. *Personal Relationships, 24*, 550–584.
19. Mason, A. E., Sbarra, D. A., Bryan, A. E., & Lee, L. A. (2012). Staying connected when coming apart: The psychological correlates of contact and sex with an ex-partner. *Journal of Social and Clinical Psychology, 31*, 488–507.
20. Rodriguez, L. M., Wickham, R. E., Øverup, C. S., & Amspoker, A. B. (2016). Past and present, day by day: communication with former romantic partners, relationship-contingent self-esteem, and current relationship outcomes. *Journal of Research in Personality, 65*, 62–67.
21. Sbarra, D. A., & Emery, R. E. (2005). The emotional sequelae of nonmarital relationship dissolution: Analysis of change and intraindividual variability over time. *Personal Relationships, 12*(2), 213–232.
22. Spielmann, S. S., Joel, S., MacDonald, G., & Kogan, A. (2013). Ex appeal: Current relationship quality and emotional attachment to ex-partners. *Social Psychological and Personality Science, 4*, 175–180.

Chapter 4

1. Amato, P. R., & Irving, S. (2013). Historical trends in divorce in the United States. In *Handbook of divorce and relationship dissolution* (pp. 57–74). Psychology Press.
2. Cohen, P. (2014). Family diversity is the new normal for America's children. *Council on Contemporary Families*. Retrieved from https://familyinequality.files.wordpress.com/2014/09/family-diversity-new-normal.pdf.
3. Ahrons, C. R. (1994). *The good divorce: Keeping your family together when your marriage comes apart*. New York: HarperCollins.
4. West, W. (2012). How divorce ruins children's lives. *Mercatornet*. Retrieved from https://www.mercatornet.com/family_edge/view/how_divorce_ruins_childrens_lives/10241

5. Gumbiner, J. (2011). Divorce hurts children, even grown ones. *Psychology Today*. Retrieved from https://www.psychologytoday.com/us/blog/the-teenage-mind/201110/divorce-hurts-children-even-grown-ones

6. Carlye, R. (2016). Mary Banham-Hall says divorce is worse than death for children. *The Daily Mail*. Retrieved from https://www.dailymail.co.uk/femail/article-3447786/Family-lawyer-says-divorce-worse-death-children.html

7. Amato, P. R., & Keith, B. (1991). Parental divorce and the well-being of children: A meta-analysis. *Psychological Bulletin, 110*, 26–46.

8. Moffitt, T. E. (1993). The neuropsychology of conduct disorder. *Development and Psychopathology, 5*, 135–151.

9. Willoughby, T., Chalmers, H., & Busseri, M. A. (2004). Where is the syndrome? Examining co-occurrence among multiple problem behaviors in adolescence. *Journal of Consulting and Clinical Psychology, 72*, 1022–1037.

10. Nickerson, R. S. (1998). Confirmation bias: A ubiquitous phenomenon in many guises. *Review of general psychology, 2*, 175–220.

11. Hetherington, E. M., & Elmore, A. M. (2003). Risk and resilience in children coping with their parents' divorce and remarriage. In S. S. Luthar (Ed.), *Resilience and vulnerability: Adaption in the context of childhood adversities* (pp. 182–212). New York: Cambridge University.

12. Lamb, M. E. (2012). Mothers, fathers, families, and circumstances: Factors affecting children's adjustment. *Applied Developmental Science, 16*, 98–111.

13. Francis, D. R. (2019). Income declines after divorce. *The National Bureau of Economic Research*. Retrieved from https://www.nber.org/digest/jul02/w8786.html

14. Richardson, T., Elliott, P., & Roberts, R. (2013). The relationship between personal unsecured debt and mental and physical health: a systematic review and meta-analysis. *Clinical Psychology Review, 33*, 1148–1162.

15. McLanahan, S. S. (1999). Father absence and the welfare of children. In E. M. Hetherington (Ed.), Coping with divorce, single parenting, and remarriage: A risk and resiliency perspective (pp. 117–145). Hillsdale, NJ: Erlbaum.

16. García Bacete, F. J., Carrero Planes, V. E., Marande Perrin, G., & Musitu Ochoa, G. (2017). Understanding rejection between first-and-second-grade elementary students through reasons expressed by rejecters. *Frontiers in Psychology, 8*, 462.

17. Hetherington, E. M. (1989). Coping with family transitions: Winners, losers, and survivors. *Child Development, 60,* 1–14.

18. Cohen S. (1992) Stress, social support and disorder. In Veiel H, Baumann U, eds. The meaning and measurement of social support. New York: Hemisphere, pp. 109–124.

19. Wasserstein, S. B., & La Greca, A. M. (1996). Can peer support buffer against behavioral consequences of parental discord? *Journal of Clinical Child Psychology, 25*, 177–182.

20. Ladd G. W., Profilet S. M., Hart C. H. (1992). Parents' management of children's peer relations: Facilitating and supervising children's activities in the peer culture. In: Parke R. D., Ladd G. W., editors. *Family-peer relationships: Modes of linkage.* Hillsdale, NJ: Lawrence Erlbaum. p 215–253.

21. Martin, F., Wang, C., Petty, T., Wang, W., & Wilkins, P. (2018). Middle school students' social media use. *Journal of Educational Technology & Society, 21,* 213–224.

22. Huang, Y., Espelage, D. L., Polanin, J. R., & Hong, J. S. (2019). A Meta-analytic Review of School-Based Anti-bullying Programs with a Parent Component. *International Journal of Bullying Prevention, 1,* 32–44.

23. Young, D. M. (1983). Two studies of children of divorce. In L. A. Kurdek (Ed.), *New Direction for Child Development* (pp. 6169). San Francisco, CA: Jossey-Bass.

24. Healy Jr, J. M., Stewart, A. J., & Copeland, A. P. (1993). The role of self-blame in children's adjustment to parental separation. *Personality and Social Psychology Bulletin, 19,* 279–289.

25. Wallerstein, J. S. and J. B. Kelly. (1980). *Surviving the Breakup: How Children and Parents Cope with Divorce.* New York: Basic Books.

26. Davies, P. T., Sturge-Apple, M. L., Cicchetti, D., & Cummings, E. M. (2008). Adrenocortical underpinnings of children's psychological reactivity to interparental conflict. *Child Development, 79,* 1693–1706.

27. Davies, P. T., & Cummings, E. M. (1994). Marital conflict and child adjustment: An emotional security hypothesis. *Psychological bulletin, 116,* 387.

28. Cummings, E. M., Goeke-Morey, M. C., & Papp, L. M. (2004). Everyday marital conflict and child aggression. *Journal of Abnormal Child Psychology, 32,* 191–202.

29. Amato, P. R., Loomis, L. S., & Booth, A. (1995). Parental divorce, marital conflict, and offspring well-being during early adulthood. *Social Forces, 73,* 895–915.

30. Baumrind, D. (1973). The development of instrumental competence through socialization. In A. D. Pick (Ed.), Minnesota Symposium of Child Psychology (Vol. 7, pp. 3–46). Minneapolis, MN: University of Minnesota Press.

31. Maccoby, E. E., & Martin, J. A. (1983). Socialization in the context of the family: Parent–child interaction. In P. H. Mussen & E. M. Hetherington (Eds.), Handbook of child psychology: Vol. 4. Socialization, personality, and social development. New York: Wiley.

32. Pinquart, M. (2017). Associations of parenting dimensions and styles with externalizing problems of children and adolescents: an updated meta-analysis. *Developmental Psychology, 53,* 873–932.

33. Steinberg, L., Elmen, J. D., & Mounts, N. S. (1989). Authoritative parenting, psychosocial maturity, and academic success among adolescents. *Child Development*, 1424–1436.

34. Long, E. C., Aggen, S. H., Gardner, C., & Kendler, K. S. (2015). Differential parenting and risk for psychopathology: a monozygotic twin difference approach. *Social Psychiatry and Psychiatric Epidemiology*, *50*, 1569–1576.

35. Marguilies, S. Wolper, D.L. (Producers), & Stuart, M. (Director). (1971). *Willy Wonka & the Chocolate Factory* [Motion Picture]. United States: Paramount

36. Weiss, L. H., & Schwarz, J. C. (1996). The relationship between parenting types and older adolescents' personality, academic achievement, adjustment, and substance use. *Child Development*, *67*, 2101–2114.

37. Lamborn, S. D., Mounts, N. S., Steinberg, L., & Dornbusch, S. M. (1991). Patterns of competence and adjustment among adolescents from authoritative, authoritarian, indulgent, and neglectful families. *Child Development*, *62*, 1049–1065.

38. Reimuller, A., Hussong, A., & Ennett, S. T. (2011). The influence of alcohol-specific communication on adolescent alcohol use and alcohol-related consequences. *Prevention Science*, *12*, 389–400.

39. Steinberg, L. (2001). We know some things: Parent–adolescent relationships in retrospect and prospect. *Journal of Research on Adolescence*, *11*, 1–19.

40. Lamborn, S. D., Mounts, N. S., Steinberg, L., & Dornbusch, S. M. (1991). Patterns of competence and adjustment among adolescents from authoritative, authoritarian, indulgent, and neglectful families. *Child Development*, *62*, 1049–1065.

41. Kerr, D. C., Lopez, N. L., Olson, S. L., & Sameroff, A. J. (2004). Parental discipline and externalizing behavior problems in early childhood: The roles of moral regulation and child gender. *Journal of Abnormal Child Psychology*, *32*, 369–383.

42. Nisbett, R. E., & Wilson, T. D. (1977). The halo effect: evidence for unconscious alteration of judgments. *Journal of Personality and Social Psychology*, *35*, 250–256.

43. O'Leary, M., Franzoni, J., Brack, G., & Zirps, F. (1996). Divorcing parents: Factors related to coping and adjustment. *Journal of Divorce and Remarriage*, *25*, 85–104.

44. Campana, K. L., Henderson, S., Stolberg, A. L., & Schum, L. (2008). Paired maternal and paternal parenting styles, child custody and children's emotional adjustment to divorce. *Journal of Divorce and Remarriage*, *48*, 1–20.

45. Donath, C., Graessel, E., Baier, D., Bleich, S., & Hillemacher, T. (2014). Is parenting style a predictor of suicide attempts in a representative sample of adolescents?. *BMC Pediatrics*, *14*, 113.

46. Livingston, G. (2014). Fewer than half of U.S. kids today live in a 'traditional' family. *Pew Research Center*. Retrieved from https://www.pewresearch.org/fact-tank/2014/12/22/less-than-half-of-u-s-kids-today-live-in-a-traditional-family/

Chapter 5

1. Centers for Disease Control and Prevention (2015). National vital statistics system: National marriage and divorce rate trends. Retrieved from https://www.cdc.gov/nchs/nvss/marriage_divorce_tables.htm
2. Slotter, E., & Emery, L. (2018). Timing is everything: Beginning a new relationship post-breakup and self-concept malleability predict self-concept clarity. *Manuscript in preparation*.
3. Hogan, B., & Dutton, W. H. (2011). A global shift in the social relationships of networked individuals: Meeting and dating online comes of age. https://www.oii.ox.ac.uk/archive/downloads/publications/Me-MySpouse_GlobalReport.pdf
4. Yurchisin, J., Watchravesringkan, K., & McCabe, D. B. (2005). An exploration of identity re-creation in the context of internet dating. *Social Behavior and Personality: an international journal, 33*, 735–750.
5. Sautter, J. M., Tippett, R. M., & Morgan, S. P. (2010). The social demography of Internet dating in the United States. *Social Science Quarterly, 91*, 554–575.
6. Barraket, J., & Henry-Waring, M. S. (2008). Getting it on (line) Sociological perspectives on e-dating. *Journal of Sociology, 44*, 149–165.
7. Madden, M., & Lenhart, A. (2006). Online dating. *Pew Internet & American Life Project*, Retrieved from http://www.pewinternet.org/files/old-media/Files/Reports/2006/PIP_Online_Dating.pdf.pdf
8. Rosenfeld, M. J., & Thomas, R. J. (2012). Searching for a mate: The rise of the Internet as a social intermediary. *American Sociological Review, 77*, 523–547.
9. Long, B. L. (2010). *Scripts for online dating: A model and theory of online romantic relationship initiation* (Doctoral dissertation, Bowling Green State University).
10. Finkel, E. J., Eastwick, P. W., Karney, B. R., Reis, H. T., & Sprecher, S. (2012). Online dating: A critical analysis from the perspective of psychological science. *Psychological Science in the Public Interest, 13*, 3–66.
11. Bragdon, J. H., Hortaçsu, A., & Ariely, D. (2010). Matching and sorting in online dating. *The American Economic Review, 100*, 130–163.
12. Toma, C. L., Hancock, J. T., & Ellison, N. B. (2008). Separating fact from fiction: An examination of deceptive self-presentation in online dating profiles. *Personality and Social Psychology Bulletin, 34*, 1023–1036.

13. Hitsch, G. J., Hortaçsu, A., & Ariely, D. (2010). What makes you click?—Mate preferences in online dating. *Quantitative marketing and Economics*, *8*, 393–427.

14. Buss, D. M. (1989). Sex differences in human mate preferences: Evolutionary hypotheses tested in 37 cultures. *Behavioral and brain sciences*, *12*, 1–14.

15. Schwarz, S., & Hassebrauck, M. (2012). Sex and age differences in mate-selection preferences. *Human Nature*, *23*, 447–466.

16. Regan, P. C., Levin, L., Sprecher, S., Christopher, F. S., & Gate, R. (2000). Partner preferences: What characteristics do men and women desire in their short-term sexual and long-term romantic partners?. *Journal of Psychology & Human Sexuality*, *12*, 1–21.

17. Hofstee, W. K., De Raad, B., & Goldberg, L. R. (1992). Integration of the Big Five and circumplex approaches to trait structure. *Journal of personality and social psychology*, *63*, 146.

18. Walster, E., Aronson, V., Abrahams, D., & Rottman, L. (1966). Importance of physical attractiveness in dating behavior. *Journal of Personality and Social Psychology*, *4*, 508–516.

19. Møller, A. P., & Swaddle, J. P. (1997). *Asymmetry, developmental stability and evolution*. Oxford University Press, UK.

20. Karpathy, A. (2015). What a deep neural network thinks about your #selfie. Retrieved from http://karpathy.github.io/2015/10/25/selfie/

21. Little, A. C., Jones, B. C., & DeBruine, L. M. (2011). Facial attractiveness: evolutionary-based research. *Philosophical Transactions of the Royal Society of London B: Biological Sciences*, *366*, 1638–1659.

22. Windhager, S., Schaefer, K., & Fink, B. (2011). Geometric morphometrics of male facial shape in relation to physical strength and perceived attractiveness, dominance, and masculinity. *American Journal of Human Biology*, *23*, 805–814.

23. Kurzban, R., & Weeden, J. (2005). HurryDate: Mate preferences in action. *Evolution and Human Behavior*, *26*, 227–244.

24. Iyengar, S. S., & Lepper, M. R. (2000). When choice is demotivating: Can one desire too much of a good thing?. *Journal of Personality and Social Psychology*, *79*, 995.

25. Lenton, A. P., Fasolo, B., & Todd, P. M. (2008). "Shopping" for a mate: expected versus experienced preferences in online mate choice. *IEEE Transactions on Professional Communication*, *51*, 169–182.

26. Wu, P. L., & Chiou, W. B. (2009). More options lead to more searching and worse choices in finding partners for romantic relationships online: An experimental study. *CyberPsychology & Behavior*, *12*, 315–318.

27. Feingold, A. (1988). Matching for attractiveness in romantic partners and same-sex friends: A meta-analysis and theoretical critique. *Psychological Bulletin*, *104*, 226–235.

28. Priest, R. F., & Sawyer, J. (1967). Proximity and peership: Bases of balance in interpersonal attraction. *American Journal of Sociology, 72*, 633–649.

29. Moreland, R. L., & Beach, S. R. (1992). Exposure effects in the classroom: The development of affinity among students. *Journal of Experimental Social Psychology, 28*, 255–276.

30. Buss, D. M. (1984). Marital assortment for personality dispositions: Assessment with three different data sources. *Behavior genetics, 14*, 111–123.

31. Montoya, R. M., Horton, R. S., & Kirchner, J. (2008). Is actual similarity necessary for attraction? A meta-analysis of actual and perceived similarity. *Journal of Social and Personal Relationships, 25*, 889–922.

32. Ireland, M. E., Slatcher, R. B., Eastwick, P. W., Scissors, L. E., Finkel, E. J., & Pennebaker, J. W. (2011). Language style matching predicts relationship initiation and stability. *Psychological science, 22*(1), 39–44.

33. Sadler, P., Ethier, N., & Woody, E. (2011). Interpersonal complementarity. In L. M. Horowitz & S. Strack (Eds.), *Handbook of interpersonal psychology: Theory, research, assessment, and therapeutic interventions* (pp. 123–142). Hoboken, NJ: John Wiley.

Chapter 6

1. Eastwick, P. W., Luchies, L. B., Finkel, E. J., & Hunt, L. L. (2014). The predictive validity of ideal partner preferences: A review and meta-analysis. *Psychological bulletin, 140*, 623–665.

2. Carels, R. A., Sherwood, A., & Blumenthal, J. A. (1998). Psychosocial influences on blood pressure during daily life. *International Journal of Psychophysiology, 28*, 117–129.

3. Marcenes, W., & Sheiham, S. (1996). The relationship between marital quality and oral health status. *Psychology and Health, 11*, 357–369.

4. Levenstein, S., Kaplan, G. A., & Smith, M. (1995). Sociodemographic characteristics, life stressors, and peptic ulcer: A prospective study. *Journal of Clinical Gastroenterology, 21*, 185–192.

5. Kiecolt-Glaser, J. K., & Newton, T. L. (2001). Marriage and health: His and hers. *Psychological Bulletin, 127*, 472–503.

6. Roelfs, D. J., Shor, E., Kalish, R., & Yogev, T. (2011). The rising relative risk of mortality for singles: meta-analysis and meta-regression. *American Journal of Epidemiology, 174*(4), 379–389.

7. Fiore, A. T., Taylor, L. S., Zhong, X., Mendelsohn, G. A., & Cheshire, C. (2010, January). Who's right and who writes: People, profiles, contacts, and replies in online dating. In *System Sciences (HICSS), 2010 43rd Hawaii International Conference on* (pp. 1–10). IEEE.

8. Lea, M., & Spears, R. (1995). Love at first byte? Building personal relationships over computer networks. In J. T. Wood & S. W. Duck (Eds.),

Understudied relationships: Off the beaten track (pp. 197–233). Newbury Park, CA: SAG.

9. Walther, J. B. (1996). Computer-mediated communication: Impersonal, interpersonal, and hyperpersonal interaction. *Communication Research, 23*, 3–43.

10. Fernando, G. (2016). Zoosk dating survey reveals the biggest online dating turn-off. *News.com.au.* Retrieved from http://www.news.com .au/lifestyle/relationships/dating/zoosk-dating-survey-reveals-the-biggest -online-dating-turnoff/news-story/ab104fb49334e07be8128e5c59b7dd12

11. Toma, C. L., & Hancock, J. T. (2010, February). Reading between the lines: linguistic cues to deception in online dating profiles. In *Proceedings of the 2010 ACM conference on Computer supported cooperative work* (pp. 5–8). ACM.

12. Durante, C. B. (2016). *Adapting nonverbal coding theory to mobile mediated communication: An analysis of emoji and other digital nonverbals.* Liberty University.

13. Arnett, G. (2015). One in four UK smartphone owners does not make phone calls weekly. Retrieved from https://www.theguardian.com/news /datablog/2015/sep/08/one-in-four-uk-smartphone-weekly-phone-calls

14. Ireland, M. E., Slatcher, R. B., Eastwick, P. W., Scissors, L. E., Finkel, E. J., & Pennebaker, J. W. (2011). Language style matching predicts relationship initiation and stability. *Psychological science, 22*(1), 39–44.

15. Anolli, L., & Ciceri, R. (2002). Analysis of the vocal profiles of male seduction: From exhibition to self-disclosure. *The Journal of general psychology, 129*(2), 149–169.

16. Collins, S. A., & Missing, C. (2003). Vocal and visual attractiveness are related in women. *Animal behaviour, 65*(5), 997–1004.

17. Hughes, S. M., Farley, S. D., & Rhodes, B. C. (2010). Vocal and physiological changes in response to the physical attractiveness of conversational partners. *Journal of Nonverbal Behavior, 34*(3), 155–167.

18. McKenna, K. Y. A., Green, A. S., & Gleason, M. E. J. (2002). Relationship formation on the Internet: What's the big attraction? *Journal of Social Issues, 58*, 9–31.

19. Ramirez, A., & Wang, Z. (2008). When online meets offline: An expectancy violations theory perspective on modality switching. *Journal of Communication, 58*, 20–39.

20. Clover (2016). *Top first-date hot spots of 2016.* Retrieved from http://clover.co /blog/top-first-date-hot-spots-of-2016

21. McNearney, A. (2017). Money survey: 78% still think men should pay for first date. Retrieved from http://money.com/money/4668232/valentines -day-men-pay-first-date/

22. Dutton, D. G., & Aron, A. P. (1974). Some evidence for heightened sexual attraction under conditions of high anxiety. *Journal of personality and social psychology, 30*(4), 510–517.

23. Chartrand, T. L., & Lakin, J. L. (2013). The antecedents and consequences of human behavioral mimicry. *Annual review of psychology*, *64*, 285–308.

24. Naumann, L. P., Vazire, S., Rentfrow, P. J., & Gosling, S. D. (2009). Personality judgments based on physical appearance. *Personality and social psychology bulletin*, *35*(12), 1661–1671.

25. Ambady, N. (2010). The perils of pondering: Intuition and thin slice judgments. *Psychological Inquiry*, *21*(4), 271–278.

26. Willoughby, B. J., Carroll, J. S., & Busby, D. M. (2014). Differing relationship outcomes when sex happens before, on, or after first dates. *Journal of sex research*, *51*(1), 52–61.

27. LeFebvre, L. (2017). Ghosting as a relationship dissolution strategy in the technological age. *The impact of social media in modern romantic relationships*, 219–235.

28. Bramlett, M. D., & Mosher, W. D. (2002). Cohabitation, marriage, divorce, and remarriage in the United States. *Vital health statistics*, *23*(22), 1–32.

Chapter 7

1. Smith, Tom W., Davern, Michael, Freese, Jeremy, and Hout, Michael, General Social Surveys, 1972–2016 [machine-readable data file] /Principal Investigator, Smith, Tom W.; Co-Principal Investigators, Peter V. Marsden and Michael Hout; Sponsored by National Science Foundation. —NORC ed.— Chicago: NORC, 2018: NORC at the University of Chicago [producer and distributor]. Data accessed from the GSS Data Explorer website at gssdataexplorer.norc.org.

2. Lindau, S. T., & Gavrilova, N. (2010). Sex, health, and years of sexually active life gained due to good health: evidence from two US population-based cross-sectional surveys of ageing. *BMJ*, *340*, c810.

3. Laumann, E. O., Gagnon, J. H., Michael, R. T., & Michaels, S. (1994). *The Social Organization of Sexuality: Sexual Practices in the United States*. University of Chicago press.

4. Mazur, A., & Michalek, J. (1998). Marriage, divorce, and male testosterone. *Social Forces*, *77*, 315–330.

5. Van Anders, S. M., & Watson, N. V. (2006). Social neuroendocrinology. *Human Nature*, *17*, 212–237.

6. Schmitt, D. P., Shackelford, T. K., Duntley, J., Tooke, W., Buss, D. M., Fisher, M. L., ... & Vasey, P. (2001). Is there an early-30s peak in female sexual desire? Cross-sectional evidence from the United States and Canada. *Canadian Journal of Human Sexuality*, *11*, 1–18.

7. Brody, S. (2010). The relative health benefits of different sexual activities. *The Journal of Sexual Medicine*, *7*, 1336–1361.

8. Kinsey, B. V. A. (1998). The Kinsey Report: Historical overview and lasting contribution. *The Journal of Sex Research*, *35*, 127–31.

9. Drucker, D. J. (September, 2007). " A Noble Experiment": The Marriage Course at Indiana University, 1938–1940. *Indiana Magazine of History*.

10. Herbenick, D., Bowling, J., Fu, T. C. J., Dodge, B., Guerra-Reyes, L., & Sanders, S. (2017). Sexual diversity in the United States: Results from a nationally representative probability sample of adult women and men. *PloS one*, *12*, e0181198.

11. Fletcher C. (June 7, 2012). 50 Shades Under the Tree Means Surge for Sex Toy Sales: Retail. *Bloomberg*. Retrieved from https://www.bloomberg.com/news/articles/2012-12-12/50-shades-under-the-tree-means-surge-for-sex-toy-sales-retail

12. Bost C. (December 11, 2012). Hardware Stores Are Experiencing A Boom In Rope Sales Thanks To A Certain Erotic Novel. *Business Insider*. Retrieved from https://www.businessinsider.com/fifty-shades-of-grey-has-increased-rope-sales-at-hardware-stores-2012-6

13. Ingraham C. (February 11, 2015). Sex toy injuries surged after 'Fifty Shades of Grey' was published. *Washington Post*. Retrieved from https://www.washingtonpost.com/news/wonk/wp/2015/02/10/sex-toy-injuries-surged-after-fifty-shades-of-grey-was-published/?utm_term=.d0887521306d

14. Rehor, J. E. (2015). Sensual, erotic, and sexual behaviors of women from the "kink" community. *Archives of Sexual Behavior*, *44*, 825–836.

15. Montoya, R. M., Horton, R. S., & Kirchner, J. (2008). Is actual similarity necessary for attraction? A meta-analysis of actual and perceived similarity. *Journal of Social and Personal Relationships*, *25*, 889–922.

16. Ireland, M. E., Slatcher, R. B., Eastwick, P. W., Scissors, L. E., Finkel, E. J., & Pennebaker, J. W. (2011). Language style matching predicts relationship initiation and stability. *Psychological science*, *22*, 39–44.

17. Swann, W. B., Jr., Chang-Schneider, C., & Angulo, S. (2007). Self-verification in relationships as an adaptive process. In J. Wood, A. Tesser, & J. Holmes (Eds.), *Self and Relationships*. New York: Psychology Press.

18. Purnine, D. M., & Carey, M. P. (1997). Interpersonal communication and sexual adjustment: the roles of understanding and agreement. *Journal of Consulting and Clinical Psychology*, *65*, 1017–1025.

19. Reis, H. T., & Aron, A. (2008). Love: What is it, why does it matter, and how does it operate?. *Perspectives on Psychological Science*, *3*(1), 80–86.

20. Armstrong, J. (February, 2018). Philly fans threw an Eagles-themed wedding on Super Bowl Sunday. *The Inquirer*. Retrieved from https://www.philly.com/philly/super-bowl-lii/eagles-wedding-super-bowl-2018-patriots-20180204.html

21. Smith, M. (2017). How many dates should you wait before having sex with someone? *YouGov*. Retrieved from https://yougov.co.uk/topics

/relationships/articles-reports/2017/03/30/how-many-dates-should
-you-wait-having-sex-someone

22. Janus, S. S., & Janus, C. L. (1993). *The Janus Report on Sexual Behavior.* John Wiley & Sons.

23. Cohen, S. (January, 2009). Romance and STDs's: Inside Florida's wild retiree getaway. *New York Post.* Retrieved from https://nypost.com/2009/01/25 /retire-to-the-bedroom/

24. Witheridge, A. (June, 2014). Ten women to every man, a black market in Viagra, and a thriving swingers scene. *The Daily Mail.* Retrieved from https://www.dailymail.co.uk/news/article-2657325/Ten-women-man-black-market-Viagra-thriving-swingers-scene-Welcome-The-Villages-Florida-elderly-residents-Sex-Square-cocktail-honor-woman-68-arrested-public-sex-toyboy.html

25. Centers for Disease Control (2013). Incidence, Prevalence, and Cost of Sexually Transmitted Infections in the United States. Retrieved from https://www.cdc.gov/std/stats/sti-estimates-fact-sheet-feb-2013.pdf

26. Pereto, A. (2018). Patients over 60? Screen for STIs. *Athena Insight.* Retrieved from https://www.athenahealth.com/insight/over-60-stis-may -not-be-done-you

27. Yu, M. (2019). How to talk sex (and consent): 4 lessons from the kink community. *National Public Radio.* Retrieved from https://www.npr.org /sections/health-shots/2019/06/01/728398532/how-to-talk-about-sex -and-consent-4-lessons-from-the-kink-community

28. Caso, K. (2017). Why sleeping with your ex-husband will only hurt you. *Singlemom.com.* Retrieved from http://www.singlemom.com/why-sleeping -with-your-ex-husband-will-only-hurt-you/

29. Mason, A. E., Sbarra, D. A., Bryan, A. E., & Lee, L. A. (2012). Staying connected when coming apart: The psychological correlates of contact and sex with an ex-partner. *Journal of Social and Clinical Psychology, 31,* 488–507.

30. Spielmann, S. S., Joel, S., & Impett, E. A. (2019). Pursuing Sex with an Ex: Does It Hinder Breakup Recovery? *Archives of Sexual Behavior, 48,* 691–702.

31. Meston, C. M., & Buss, D. M. (2007). Why humans have sex. *Archives of Sexual Behavior, 36,* 477–507.

32. Cooper, M. L., Shapiro, C. M., & Powers, A. M. (1998). Motivations for sex and risky sexual behavior among adolescents and young adults: A functional perspective. *Journal of Personality and Social Psychology, 75,* 1528.

33. Sanchez, D. T., Moss-Racusin, C. A., Phelan, J. E., & Crocker, J. (2011). Relationship contingency and sexual motivation in women: Implications for sexual satisfaction. *Archives of Sexual Behavior, 40,* 99–110.

34. Patrick, M. E., Maggs, J. L., Cooper, M. L., & Lee, C. M. (2011). Measurement of motivations for and against sexual behavior. *Assessment, 18,* 502–516.

35. Muise, A., Impett, E. A., & Desmarais, S. (2013). Getting it on versus getting it over with: Sexual motivation, desire, and satisfaction in intimate bonds. *Personality and Social Psychology Bulletin, 39,* 1320–1332.

36. Cooper, M. L., Barber, L. L., Zhaoyang, R., & Talley, A. E. (2011). Motivational pursuits in the context of human sexual relationships. *Journal of Personality, 79,* 1333–1368.

37. Carter, C. S. (1992). Oxytocin and sexual behavior. *Neuroscience & Biobehavioral Reviews, 16,* 131–144.

Chapter 8

1. Mongeau, P. A., & Henningsen, M. (2008). Stage theories of relationship development. *Engaging theories in interpersonal communication: Multiple perspectives,* 363–375.

2. Fisher, H. (2000). Lust, attraction, attachment: Biology and evolution of the three primary emotion systems for mating, reproduction, and parenting. *Journal of Sex Education and Therapy, 25,* 96–104.

3. Tennov, D. (1998). *Love and limerence: The experience of being in love.* New York. Scarborough House.

4. Aron, A., Fisher, H., Mashek, D. J., Strong, G., Li, H., & Brown, L. L. (2005). Reward, motivation, and emotion systems associated with early-stage intense romantic love. *Journal of neurophysiology, 94,* 327–337.

5. Christie, G. L (1969) Falling in Love and Infatuation, *Australian and New Zealand Journal of Psychiatry, 3,* 17–21.

6. Eastwick, P. W., & Finkel, E. J. (2008). The attachment system in fledgling relationships: An activating role for attachment anxiety. *Journal of personality and social psychology, 95,* 628–647.

7. Acevedo, B. P., Aron, A., Fisher, H. E., & Brown, L. L. (2012). Neural correlates of long-term intense romantic love. *Social cognitive and affective neuroscience, 7,* 145–159.

8. Marazziti, D., Akiskal, H. S., Rossi, A., & Cassano, G. B. (1999). Alteration of the platelet serotonin transporter in romantic love. *Psychological medicine, 29,* 741–745.

9. Takahashi, K., Mizuno, K., Sasaki, A. T., Wada, Y., Tanaka, M., Ishii, A., ... & Watanabe, Y. (2015). Imaging the passionate stage of romantic love by dopamine dynamics. *Frontiers in Human Neuroscience, 9,* 191.

10. Reynaud, M., Karila, L., Blecha, L., & Benyamina, A. (2010). Is love passion an addictive disorder?. *The American Journal of Drug and Alcohol Abuse, 36,* 261–267.

11. Fisher, H. E., Xu, X., Aron, A., & Brown, L. L. (2016). Intense, passionate, romantic love: a natural addiction? How the fields that investigate romance and substance abuse can inform each other. *Frontiers in psychology, 7,* 687.

12. Aron, A., Dutton, D. G., Aron, E. N., & Iverson, A. (1989). Experiences of falling in love. *Journal of Social and Personal Relationships, 6,* 243–257.
13. Shaver, P. R., & Hazan, C. (1988). A biased overview of the study of love. *Journal of Social and Personal Relationships, 5,* 473–501.
14. Reis, H. T., & Shaver, P. (1988). Intimacy as an interpersonal process. In S. Duck (ed) *Handbook of personal relationships.* New York. John Wiley, Inc.
15. Diamond, L. M. (2004). Emerging perspectives on distinctions between romantic love and sexual desire. *Current directions in psychological science, 13,* 116–119.
16. Campbell, A. (2010). Oxytocin and human social behavior. *Personality and Social Psychology Review, 14,* 281–295.
17. Rusbult, C. E., & Buunk, B. P. (1993). Commitment processes in close relationships: An interdependence analysis. *Journal of Social and Personal Relationships, 10,* 175–204.
18. Eastwick, P. W., Finkel, E. J., & Simpson, J. A. (2019). Relationship Trajectories: A Meta-Theoretical Framework and Theoretical Applications. *Psychological Inquiry, 30,* 1–28.
19. Harrison, M. A., & Shortall, J. C. (2011). Women and men in love: Who really feels it and says it first?. *The Journal of Social Psychology, 151,* 727–736.
20. Sternberg, R. J. (2006). A duplex theory of love. In R.J Sternberg (ed) *The new psychology of love,* (pp. 184–199), New York. Yale University Press.
21. Sternberg, R. J. (1987). Liking versus loving: A comparative evaluation of theories. *Psychological Bulletin, 102,* 331–345.
22. Hatfield, E. C., Pillemer, J. T., O'Brien, M., & Le, Y. C. L. (2008). The endurance of love: Passionate and companionate love in newlywed and long-term marriages. *Interpersona: An International Journal on Personal Relationships, 2,* 35–64.
23. Sprecher, S., & Regan, P. C. (1998). Passionate and companionate love in courting and young married couples. *Sociological Inquiry, 68,* 163–185.
24. Mark, K. P., & Lasslo, J. A. (2018). Maintaining sexual desire in long-term relationships: A systematic review and conceptual model. *The Journal of Sex Research, 55,* 563–581.
25. Finkel, E. J., Cheung, E. O., Emery, L. F., Carswell, K. L., & Larson, G. M. (2015). The suffocation model: Why marriage in America is becoming an all-or-nothing institution. *Current Directions in Psychological Science, 24,* 238–244.
26. Rusbult, C. E., & Arriaga, X. B. (1997). Interdependence theory. In S. Duck (Ed.), Handbook of personal relationships: Theory, research and intervention (2nd ed., pp. 221–250). Chichester, England: Wiley.
27. Simpson, J. A., Fletcher, G. J., & Campbell, L. (2001). The structure and function of ideal standards in close relationships. *Blackwell handbook of social psychology: Interpersonal processes,* 86–106.

28. Fletcher, G. J., & Simpson, J. A. (2000). Ideal standards in close relationships: Their structure and functions. *Current Directions in Psychological Science, 9*, 102–105.

29. Morry, M. M., & Sucharyna, T. A. (2016). Relationship social comparison interpretations and dating relationship quality, behaviors, and mood. *Personal Relationships, 23*, 554–576.

30. Clayton, R. B., Nagurney, A., & Smith, J. R. (2013). Cheating, breakup, and divorce: Is Facebook use to blame?. *Cyberpsychology, Behavior, and Social Networking, 16*, 717–720.

31. Campbell, L., Simpson, J. A., Kashy, D. A., & Fletcher, G. J. (2001). Ideal standards, the self, and flexibility of ideals in close relationships. *Personality and Social Psychology Bulletin, 27*, 447–462.

32. Sprecher, S. (1986). The relation between inequity and emotions in close relationships. *Social Psychology Quarterly*, 309–321.

33. Utne, M. K., Hatfield, E., Traupmann, J., & Greenberger, D. (1984). Equity, marital satisfaction, and stability. *Journal of Social and Personal Relationships, 1*, 323–332.

34. Hatfield, E., & Traupmann, J. (1981). Intimate relationships: A perspective from equity theory. *Personal relationships, 1*, 165–178.

35. Lachance-Grzela, M., & Bouchard, G. (2010). Why do women do the lion's share of housework? A decade of research. *Sex roles, 63*, 767–780.

36. Charbonneau, A., Lachance-Grzela, M., & Bouchard, G. (2019). Housework Allocation, Negotiation Strategies, and Relationship Satisfaction in Cohabiting Emerging Adult Heterosexual Couples. *Sex Roles*, 1–16.

37. McMunn, A., Bird, L., Webb, E., & Sacker, A. (2019). Gender divisions of paid and unpaid work in contemporary UK couples. *Work, Employment and Society*, 1–19.

38. Guerrero, L. K., La Valley, A. G., & Farinelli, L. (2008). The experience and expression of anger, guilt, and sadness in marriage: An equity theory explanation. *Journal of Social and Personal Relationships, 25*, 699–724.

39. Clark, M. S., Mills, J., & Powell, M. C. (1986). Keeping track of needs in communal and exchange relationships. *Journal of Personality and Social Psychology, 51*, 333–338.

40. Morton, L. C., & Markey, P. M. (2009). Goal agreement and relationship quality among college students and their parents. *Personality and Individual Differences, 47*, 912–916.

41. Fitzsimons, G. M., & Finkel, E. J. (2018). Transactive-Goal-Dynamics Theory: A Discipline-Wide Perspective. *Current Directions in Psychological Science, 27*, 332–338.

42. Shah, J. (2003). The motivational looking glass: how significant others implicitly affect goal appraisals. *Journal of Personality and Social Psychology, 85*, 424–439.

43. Michaels, M. L. (2006). Factors that contribute to stepfamily success: A qualitative analysis. *Journal of Divorce & Remarriage, 44,* 53–66.

44. Golish, T. D. (2003). Stepfamily communication strengths: Understanding the ties that bind. *Human Communication Research, 29,* 41–80.

45. Ahrons, C. R. (2009). *We're still family: What grown children have to say about their parents' divorce.* New York: Harper Collins.

46. Ganong, L., Coleman, M., Fine, M., & Martin, P. (1999). Stepparents' affinity-seeking and affinity-maintaining strategies with stepchildren. *Journal of Family Issues, 20,* 299–327.

47. Ahrons, C. R. (1994). *The good divorce: Keeping your family together when your marriage comes apart.* New York: HarperCollins.

48. Svare, G. M., Jay, S., & Mason, M. A. (2004). Stepparents on stepparenting: An exploratory study of stepparenting approaches. *Journal of Divorce & Remarriage, 41,* 81–97.

49. Ferraro, A. J. (2016). Binuclear families. *Encyclopedia of Family Studies,* 1–4.

50. Roberts, T. W., & Price, S. J. (1989). Adjustment in remarriage: Communication, cohesion, marital and parental roles. *Journal of Divorce, 13,* 17–43.

51. Emery, R. E., & Dillon, P. (1994). Conceptualizing the divorce process: Renegotiating boundaries of intimacy and power in the divorced family system. *Family Relations,* 374–379.

52. Cartwright, C., & Gibson, K. (2013). The effects of co-parenting relationships with ex-spouses on couples in step-families. *Family Matters, 91,* 18–28.

53. Olson, L. N. (2002). Exploring "common couple violence" in heterosexual romantic relationships. *Western Journal of Communication, 66,* 104–128.

54. Wade, T. J., Salerno, K., & Moran, J. (2017). Unreciprocated Love or Sexual Attraction: Which is Most Upsetting?. *EvoS Journal: The Journal of the Evolutionary Studies Consortium,* 70–77.

Chapter 9

1. Tejada-Vera, B., & Sutton, P. D. (2010). Births, marriages, divorces, and deaths: Provisional data for 2009. *National Vital Statistics Reports, 58,* 1–6.

2. Cohn, D. (2010). At long last, divorce. *Pew Research Center.*

3. Amato, P. R. (2010). Research on divorce: Continuing trends and new developments. *Journal of marriage and family, 72,* 650–666.

4. Goldberg-Meehan, S. (Writer), & Mancuso, G. (Director). (September 30, 1999). The one where Ross hugs Rachel. In D. Crane & M. Kauffman (Creators), *Friends.* New York: NBC.

5. Clark, W., & Crompton, S. (2006). Till death do us part? The risk of first and second marriage dissolution. *Canadian Social Trends, 81,* 23–33.

6. Gottman, J. M. (2014). *What predicts divorce?: The relationship between marital processes and marital outcomes.* Psychology Press. New York, NY.

7. Gottman, J. M., & Silver, N. (2015). *The seven principles for making marriage work: A practical guide from the country's foremost relationship expert.* Harmony. New York, NY.

8. Solomon, B. C., & Jackson, J. J. (2014). Why do personality traits predict divorce? Multiple pathways through satisfaction. *Journal of Personality and Social Psychology, 106,* 978–996.

9. Drigotas, S. M., Safstrom, C. A., & Gentilia, T. (1999). An investment model prediction of dating infidelity. *Journal of Personality and Social Psychology, 77,* 509–524.

10. Reis, H. T. (2007). Steps toward the ripening of relationship science. *Personal Relationships, 14,* 1–23.

11. Williamson, H. C., Hanna, M. A., Lavner, J. A., Bradbury, T. N., & Karney, B. R. (2013). Discussion topic and observed behavior in couples' problem-solving conversations: Do problem severity and topic choice matter? *Journal of Family Psychology, 27,* 330–335.

12. Carrere, S., and Gottman, J. M., (1999). Predicting Divorce among Newlyweds from the First Three Minutes of a Marital Conflict Discussion, *Family Process,* Vol. 38, 293–301.

13. Gottman, J. M., & Levenson, R. W. (2000). The timing of divorce: Predicting when a couple will divorce over a 14-year period. *Journal of Marriage and Family, 62,* 737–745.

14. Gottman, J. M., Coan, J., Carrere, S., & Swanson, C. (1998). Predicting marital happiness and stability from newlywed interactions. *Journal of Marriage and the Family,* 5–22.

15. Gottman, J. M., Driver, J., & Tabares, A. (2015). Repair during marital conflict in newlyweds: How couples move from attack–defend to collaboration. *Journal of Family Psychotherapy, 26,* 85–108.

16. Finkel, E. J., Slotter, E. B., Luchies, L. B., Walton, G. M., & Gross, J. J. (2013). A brief intervention to promote conflict reappraisal preserves marital quality over time. *Psychological Science, 24,* 1595–1601.

17. Murray, S. L., Holmes, J. G., & Griffin, D. W. (1996). The self-fulfilling nature of positive illusions in romantic relationships: Love is not blind, but prescient. *Journal of Personality and Social Psychology, 71,* 1155–1180.

18. Luchies, L. B., Wieselquist, J., Rusbult, C. E., Kumashiro, M., Eastwick, P. W., Coolsen, M. K., & Finkel, E. J. (2013). Trust and biased memory of transgressions in romantic relationships. *Journal of Personality and Social Psychology, 104,* 673–694.

19. Murray, S. L., & Holmes, J. G. (1993). Seeing virtues in faults: Negativity and the transformation of interpersonal narratives in close relationships. *Journal of Personality and Social Psychology, 65,* 707–722.

20. Sprecher, S. & Hendrick, S. S. (2004). Self-Disclosure in Intimate Relationships: Associations with Individual and Relationship Characteristics Over Time. *Journal of Social and Clinical Psychology*: Vol. 23, No. 6, pp. 857–877.

21. Duck, S. (1994). Steady as (s)he goes: Relational maintenance as a shared meaning system. In D. J. Canary & L. Stafford (Eds.), *Communication and relational maintenance* (pp. 45–60). San Diego, CA, US: Academic Press.

22. Ryan, R. M., & Deci, E. L. (2001). On happiness and human potentials: A review of research on hedonic and eudaimonic well-being. *Annual review of psychology, 52*, 141–166.

23. Bauer, J. J., McAdams, D. P., & Pals, J. L. (2008). Narrative identity and eudaimonic well-being. *Journal of happiness studies, 9*, 81–104.

24. Taylor, S. E. (2011). Social support: A review. In H. S. Friedman (ed.) *The handbook of health psychology*, (pp. 189–214). Oxford University Press, New York, NY.

25. Feeney, B. C., & Collins, N. L. (2015). A new look at social support: A theoretical perspective on thriving through relationships. *Personality and Social Psychology Review, 19*, 113–147.

26. Sullivan, K. T., Pasch, L. A., Johnson, M. D., & Bradbury, T. N. (2010). Social support, problem solving, and the longitudinal course of newlywed marriage. *Journal of Personality and Social Psychology, 98*, 631–644.

27. Taylor, S. E. (2011). Social support: A review. In H.S. Friedman (ed.) *The handbook of health psychology*, (pp. 189–214). Oxford University Press, New York, NY.

28. Feeney, B. C., & Thrush, R. L. (2010). Relationship influences on exploration in adulthood: The characteristics and function of a secure base. *Journal of Personality and Social Psychology, 98*, 57–76.

29. Rusbult, C. E., Kumashiro, M., Stocker, S. L., Kirchner, J. L., Finkel, E. J., & Coolsen, M. K. (2005). Self processes in interdependent relationships: Partner affirmation and the Michelangelo phenomenon. *Interaction Studies, 6*, 375–391.

30. Selcuk, E., Stanton, S. C., Slatcher, R. B., & Ong, A. D. (2017). Perceived partner responsiveness predicts better sleep quality through lower anxiety. *Social Psychological and Personality Science, 8*, 83–92.

31. Welker, K. M., Baker, L., Padilla, A., Holmes, H., Aron, A., & Slatcher, R. B. (2014). Effects of self-disclosure and responsiveness between couples on passionate love within couples. *Personal Relationships, 21*, 692–708.

32. Selcuk, E., Gunaydin, G., Ong, A. D., & Almeida, D. M. (2016). Does partner responsiveness predict hedonic and eudaimonic well-being? A 10-year longitudinal study. *Journal of Marriage and Family, 78*, 311–325.

33. VanLandingham, J., Johnson, D. R., & Amato, P (2001). Marital happiness, marital duration, and the U-shaped curve: Evidence from a five-wave panel study. *Social Forces, 79*, 1313–1341.

34. Aron, A., Norman, C. C., Aron, E. N., McKenna, C., & Heyman, R. E. (2000). Couples' shared participation in novel and arousing activities and experienced relationship quality. *Journal of Personality and Social Psychology*, *78*, 273–284.

35. Aron, A., Norman, C. C., & Aron, E. N. (2001). Shared self-expanding activities as a means of maintaining and enhancing close romantic relationships. In *Close romantic relationships* (pp. 55–74). Psychology Press.

Index